Transporting the Deceased to Eternity: The Ancient Egyptian Term *ḥ3i*

Kelly-Anne Diamond

BAR International Series 2179
2010

Published in 2017 by
BAR Publishing, Oxford

BAR International Series 2179

Transporting the Deceased to Eternity: The Ancient Egyptian Term 'ḥꜣi͗'

ISBN 978 1 4073 0729 9

BAR Publishing is the trading name of British Archaeological Reports (Oxford) Ltd. British Archaeological Reports was first incorporated in 1974 to publish the BAR Series, International and British. In 1992 Hadrian Books Ltd became part of the BAR group. This volume was originally published by Archaeopress in conjunction with British Archaeological Reports (Oxford) Ltd / Hadrian Books Ltd, the Series principal publisher, in 2010. This present volume is published by BAR Publishing, 2017.

Printed in England

BAR
PUBLISHING

BAR titles are available from:

BAR Publishing
122 Banbury Rd, Oxford, OX2 7BP, UK
EMAIL info@barpublishing.com
PHONE +44 (0)1865 310431
FAX +44 (0)1865 316916
www.barpublishing.com

Table of Contents

Preface and Acknowledgments

This work is an updated version of my doctoral dissertation for the Department of Egyptology at Brown University, entitled Ancient Egyptian Funerary Ritual: The Term *ḥ3i*.

First of all, I would like to dedicate this work to Dr. Lanny Bell who gave me his constant support and assistance in the writing of my doctoral dissertation. I also greatly appreciate his cooperation in the long-distance communication that was necessary. His Egyptological insight and editorial assistance have been invaluable. Additionally, I am indebted to Dr. Susan Tower Hollis who read the final draft of my work and offered constructive suggestions and guidance. I would also like to thank Professor Leo Depuydt for his continued help and encouragement throughout the seven years I spent as his student at Brown University.

None of this would have been possible were it not for the Department of Egyptology at Brown and the Brown Graduate School for the financial support given to me during my years at the University. This support allowed me to concentrate fully on my dissertation research.

Once I had moved to Pennsylvania I was in need of an Egyptological library and the Department of Near Eastern Archaeology and Languages at the University of Pennsylvania graciously provided me with access to their extensive library collection, for which I am very grateful.

I would also like to thank Gloria Rosati for sending me a hand-drawn copy of fragment Nr. 1594 from the Florence Museum, and Dr. Maria Christina Guidotti, Director of the Egyptian Museum in Florence, for additional correspondence. I would like to thank Danielle Nyce for technical support, and Dr. Caroline Rocheleau for help in a variety of areas.

Finally, I would like to thank my family for their patience, cooperation, and encouragement, through not only graduate school but the continued time spent on preparing this manuscript for publication. I would especially like to thank my mother for her assistance in editing both my dissertation and my current manuscript and the many hours she spent with my children while I was hard at work.

List of Figures

List of Tables

Introduction

Funerary ritual in ancient Egypt consisted of elaborate series of rites and practices which evolved over time. These rituals reach the modern historian through the complex mortuary remains, appearing in architectural form, textual form, and representational form. The farther in time one goes back the more imprecise the record becomes. With the emergence of the Pyramid Texts in the Fifth Dynasty one has for the very first time access to a narrated version of the funeral rituals, albeit for a king or queen. Prior to this time the scholar must rely on tomb inscriptions – an invaluable source. It is apparent that what is being conveyed in these texts is a conglomeration of many rites and rituals that spanned a long period of time and may have originated in a variety of geographical contexts. It does not seem to have concerned the ancient Egyptians that their "theology" or "dogma" might be contradictory – if one can even speak of these concepts existing at that time. Most would agree that at this stage the two former terms are not appropriate; in fact, the narration, or script for ritual is usually called myth. This is one of the significant aspects of the Pyramid Texts – they reveal allusions to ancient Egypt's mythology.

Ritual action can be considered a process that revives a memory and links the present to the past.[1] The ritual actions and the mythological words that are part of the funerary rituals are only two parts of a larger compendium of knowledge:[2]

> [The] construction of the funerary ritual itself is based on the creation of a symbolic language that is built upon different forms of communication by the group to which the individual dead belongs, and in which the elements of the material culture – the objects composing the funerary set, the dead body, the mythological stories, the religious beliefs, the songs and lamentations of the living – can express the need to transform a negative event, such as death, into a positive one.[3]

Laneri points out in his chapter on the archaeology of funerary ritual in the Second Annual University of Chicago Oriental Institute Seminar "Performing Death" that the power of the elite is a major component of the practice of funerary rituals in that the rituals serve to reinforce said power. Furthermore, he addresses the very relevant issue of changing political patterns, noting that when the social structure of a given community encounters dramatic social, economic, and cultural transformations, the importance of the political dimension becomes even stronger.[4]

The research conducted for this work revolves around the Egyptian word *ḥꜣi*. The context described above is of prime importance for discussing the term *ḥꜣi* and its function. *ḥꜣi* has the connotation of "ritually transport" with the express purpose of revivifying or rejuvenating the deceased.

This subject emerged from a more general study of "mourning words," in that while collecting the citations for words meaning "to mourn" (a deceased individual) the word *ḥꜣi* emerged. Because it is accompanied by the A 28 determinative the word appears to have strong ties with the act of rejoicing. The same determinative (Gardiner's A 28) is used in writing both *ḥꜣi* and *ḥꜥi* ("rejoice"), which renders the two words similar, both visually and aurally.[5] According to Faulkner, the ancient Egyptians believed that there was no such thing as coincidence in their language, and that if one word resembled another, then there was an innate relationship.[6] In fact, different modern translations of the same ancient text employ either "rejoice" or "mourn" as the English translation of *ḥꜣi*. The fact that these are two contrasting emotions is intriguing. Even the earliest attested example of *ḥꜣi* is initially puzzling, in that it is included in a caption accompanying a funeral scene where women are dancing. This confusion has made its way into the most modern dictionaries. It is for this reason that more research should be focused on the word *ḥꜣi*.

The results of this research are arranged under the following headings: genre of sources, participants (divided chronologically into three chapters), the avian motif that is connected to many references, location and time, the significance of the A 28 gesture, and a catalogue of sources. Generally, each chapter follows in chronological sequence. On a few occasions, for ease of discussion, similar sources have been grouped together within a particular period.

In order to understand the meaning of the word *ḥꜣi*, or the nature of the ritual, one needs to consider the phenomenon of the creation of myth and early funerary patterns in ancient Egypt, because the rite occurs in both ordinary contexts and mythologized contexts. This work does not focus on, nor debate, any theory about early Egyptian religion. However, it is useful to give a summary of the myth-ritual theories and highlight some of the significant ideas. Likewise, a synopsis as such contributes to a description of the general situation in which the ritual of *ḥꜣi* may have originated. It would be quite useful to apply a myth-ritual theory to the *ḥꜣi* phenomenon but this work does not provide an adequate platform.

---

[1] Laneri 2007, 2.
[2] Laneri 2007, 5.
[3] Quote from Laneri 2007, 5; Goody 1962, 28-52.
[4] Laneri 2007, 6.

[5] The word *ḥꜣi resembles* both *ḥꜥi* and *ḳꜣi*; all three words use the A 28 sign as a determinative. For *ḳꜣi*, see Chapter Seven below.
[6] Faulkner 1994, 146.

The earliest known private source containing the word *ḥ3i* is the tomb of Debehni at Giza, which dates to the late Fourth Dynasty.[7] Shortly thereafter, at the end of the Fifth Dynasty, the Pyramid Texts present various examples of this word. It is commonly held that these utterances would have been transmitted orally prior to being carved in stone.[8] Thus we can assume that the word *ḥ3i* was being used in a royal context much earlier. The Pyramid Texts are a major source of information for the religious environment before and during their emergence. Anthes points out that the mythological conceptions presented in this conglomeration of utterances change, based on the date of origin of the particular utterance.[9] It is for this reason that these texts do not elucidate the beginnings of Egyptian theology. These early circumstances can best be described by a quote from Breasted: "We have before us the complicated results of a commingling of originally distinct beliefs which have long since interpenetrated each other and have for many centuries circulated thus a tangled mass of threads which it is now very difficult or impossible to disentangle."[10] Therefore, by using the available textual sources one cannot confirm exactly when the *ḥ3i* ritual began to be practiced. Its emergence, however, may date to as early as the Naqada period if images on pots and figurines are any indication.

Myth-Ritual Theory

One of the original scholars to make a significant contribution to the myth-ritual theory was William Robertson Smith[11] who held that practice (or ritual) was fixed but the meaning behind such action fluctuated and that different explanations for the same rite were satisfactory. These rituals were then explained by stories, or myths, in that these actions had been decreed by a god or were done by a god. In the early stages of civilizations this mythology took the place of what was later termed dogma. Therefore, myth was derived from ritual and it arose once the reason for the ritual had been forgotten. Likewise, Smith believed that myth was superfluous as long as the reason for the ritual was clear.

However, earlier Edward Tylor attempted to demonstrate that myth actually explains the environment, or the world.[12] He believed that myth cannot explain ritual and the world simultaneously and that the ritual is the application of myth, not the subject.

After Smith and Tylor, Frazer made a significant contribution to myth-ritualism with his *Golden Bough*.[13] Frazer suggested that ritual may presuppose myth but was created independently. Frazer had two versions of his theory which were not necessarily consistent.[14] In the first theory, he maintained that myth describes the life of the god of vegetation and ritual enacts this myth. Imitation of the act makes it happen. The god who controls the vegetation can be equated with religion; while the king controlling the vegetation can be equated with magic. Therefore, myth and ritual equal religion and magic. In Frazer's second theory the divine king is central. The king is a god who is involved in a reciprocal relationship with nature. In this case the king is killed in the prime of his life to make way for his successor, thus securing the life force and sustenance of his kingdom.

For Frazer myth arises later than ritual and thus gives ritual its meaning. His theory opposed that of Smith who maintained that myth was secondary to ritual. Frazer and Tylor alike, claim that myth explains the world. Frazer furthered this assumption by remarking that the purpose of myth is to control the environment and should be considered the ancient counterpart to science.

Jane Harrison was another major contributor to myth-ritualism; she applied Frazer's theory to Greek religion in *Themis*.[15] In her work Harrison places ritual prior to myth but also acknowledges that the two may also arise simultaneously: "They arise 'pari passu'."[16] In the latter case she postulated that the rite is performed because of myth, and provides the following example — a myth recounts the birth of Zeus while a ritual enacts the birth. She further explained that ritual is an utterance of an emotion, a thing felt, in action; and myth is words or thoughts.[17] Harrison did not claim that the myth is at first aetiological, as it does not arise to give a reason. It is representative, another form of utterance or expression. Like Smith, Harrison asserted that "when the emotion that started the ritual has died down and the ritual, though hallowed by tradition, seems unmeaning, a reason is sought in the myth and it is regarded as aetiological."[18] She furthered her point by noting that the social agents (or worshippers) exist prior to god, insinuating that the ritual act is prior to divinity.[19]

Along with Harrison, S. H. Hooke[20] applied the myth-ritual pattern to the ancient world. Both scholars maintained that people had customary actions that would ensure that the sun would rise every day, that the

[7] S. Hassan 1943. There is some controversy about the date. Kloth suggests a mid Fifth Dynasty date and indicates that it may have been constructed posthumously by his son (2002, 38-39). Strudwick notes this but is not sure if the text should be dated later or should be considered a very early example of a biography (2005, 43, 271).
[8] Van Dijk 1995, 1697. It can be assumed that the texts would have originally been written on papyrus.
[9] Anthes 1959, 170.
[10] Breasted 1912, 51.
[11] Smith 1889.
[12] Tylor 1871, vol. 1, chapters 8-10.
[13] Frazer 1890.
[14] Segal 1998, 4.
[15] Harrison 1912.
[16] Harrison 1912, 16.
[17] Harrison 1912, 16.
[18] Harrison 1912, 16.
[19] Harrison 1912, 29.
[20] Hooke 1933.

moon would appear, and that the rivers would flood annually. Certain rituals were used to control these and other aspects of nature and thus myth-ritualism was the earliest stage of religion. Neither Harrison nor Hooke believed that myth explains ritual or the world.[21] Harrison asserted that myth flourishes along-side ritual to provide its script instead of it arising after the meaning of the ritual is forgotten. But she also maintained that when the emotion has died down myth eventually explains ritual. Segal suggests that one can still say that myth explains the "living" ritual, in that myth is the spoken correlative.[22]

It was S. H. Hooke who first attempted to establish a myth-ritual pattern in the Near East.[23] His work is derived from Frazer's myth-ritual theory. The core of Hooke's premise is the enactment of the myth about the death and rebirth of the god of vegetation. The ritual is magical and through it the myth becomes effective. The difference between the theory of Frazer and that of Hooke is the source of the pattern. Hooke asserted that it comes from Mesopotamia while Frazer posited an independent origin:

> When we exam these early modes of behavior we find that their originators were not occupied with general questions concerning the world but with certain practical and pressing problems of daily life. These were the main problems of securing the means of subsistence, to keep the sun and moon doing their duty, to ensure the regular flooding of the Nile, to maintain the bodily vigor of the king who was the embodiment of the prosperity of the community.[24]

Hooke maintained that the original myth, which he saw as inseparable in the first instance from its ritual, embodies in a symbolic fashion, the original situation which is seasonally re-enacted in ritual.[25] Accordingly, Hooke suggested the origin of these actions/rituals is related to attempts to deal with or control the unpredictable elements in the human experience.[26]

In summation, Harrison and Hooke claimed that myth and ritual arise simultaneously and are complimentary, while Frazer placed myth before ritual and Smith placed ritual before myth.

Other scholars who have made significant contribution to the myth-ritual theory are Malinowski[27] and Eliade.[28] Eliade, for example, saw the ritualistic reenactment of myth as ritual. Therefore, the function is to carry one back to the time of myth and bring one closer to the gods.

Such revisionists as Theodore Gaster[29] and Clyde Kluckhohn[30] made additional contributions to the theory. Kluckhohn asserted that myth and ritual are inseparable and that they have a psychological function in that they alleviate anxiety. Myth is the proscribed way of understanding and ritual the proscribed way of behaving. He also followed Harrison and Hooke in maintaining that myth explains what ritual enacts.

Hocart, in *The Life-Giving Myth*, follows Frazer, Harrison, and Hooke.[31] He postulated that myth provides the script for ritual and that ritual is the enactment of myth. And therefore, myth is for the provision of food and other necessities. For Hocart, Harrison, and Hooke a ritual works like magic, "the myth itself confers, or helps to confer, the object of men's desire — life."[32] Hocart pointed out that myth is necessary in that it gives the ritual its intention. Knowledge is essential; one must know what he's doing and why he's doing it. Myth makes the intention plain.[33]

And the debate on myth-ritualism continues until today. In one way or another all forms of the myth-ritual theory have been rejected and there has been much criticism.[34]

Myth-Ritual Pattern in Ancient Egypt

In addition to the aforementioned remarks on the work of Harrison and Hooke, in *The Golden Bough* Frazer discusses the myth of Osiris with regard to his myth-ritual pattern.[35] It is useful to see how the myth-ritual theory has been applied to a particular area of ancient Egyptian culture. Frazer saw Osiris as the personification of corn who dies and comes back to life each year mimicking the agricultural cycle. Frazer used the timing of the Osirian festivals as evidence for his agricultural origin. He further suggested that the king played the role of Osiris.[36] Blackman agreed with this supposition by remarking that the Osiris-Horus myth is surely not the origin of the fertility of crops, cattle, and tribe being bound with the person of the king, but that the latter is the origin of certain elements in the myth.[37]

---

[21] Segal 1998, 7.
[22] Segal 1998, 7.
[23] Hooke 1933. For commentary see Segal 1998, 7-8, 83-92.
[24] Segal 1998, 85.
[25] Segal 1998, 85.
[26] Segal 1998, 85.
[27] Malinowski 1926.
[28] Eliade 1963.
[29] Gaster 1954.
[30] Kluckhohn 1942.
[31] Hocart 1952.
[32] Hocart 1952, 16.
[33] Hocart 1952, 16.
[34] Segal 1998, 13, note 19.
[35] Frazer 1922, Chapter 38-40.
[36] Frazer 1922, Chapters 38-40; see also Segal 1998, 53-57.
[37] Blackman 1933, 37.

Griffiths describes the mythologization of ritual as the superimposition of mythological beings on ritual.[38] He further states that when a text includes a mythological interpretation it can be considered as more recent than one that does not.[39] Accordingly, myth is implemented to explain ritual.

Faulkner provides a good example of the mythologization process: "Since the funerary arts are attested in Egypt long before the appearance of Osiris, the ritual [Opening-of-the-Mouth] most likely had its origin among the artisans who carved out the burial equipment. The mythological reference given for the carving tools was undoubtedly a later priestly interpretation. Through the association of myth and object, an action in the earthly realm could be effective in recreating the mythical event which led to the revitalization of Osiris."[40] Anthes suggests that the concept of Horus the living king, and Osiris the dead king, originated in the performance of royal rites, and "was not arbitrarily invented."[41] According to Griffiths, the pre-Osirian texts indicate that the son summoned the father from the grave to eat his food offerings.[42] This may account for Horus' performing the same act for his deceased father, Osiris, in the myth. Likewise, the predynastic custom of dismembering the corpse may account for Osiris' body parts being spread at random.[43] Frazer asserts that the dismembering of the corpse may be linked to Osiris as a corn god who ensured crop growth by being buried in pieces for next year's harvest.[44] According to Anthes, the concept of Isis and Nephthys as kites also stems from the burial customs, which will be discussed below.[45] Therefore, it seems that the myth of Osiris can be traced back to the rites performed for the deceased in the early periods, and possibly earlier to the agricultural rituals.[46] Unfortunately, the early texts do not offer long passages of coherent myth, but instead present allusions to it that relate to ritual.[47]

[38] Griffiths 1980, 34. See also van Dijk 1995 and Blackman 1933. For more extensive information on the myth-ritual theory see: Tylor 1871; Smith 1889; Harrison 1912; Frazer 1922; Malinowshi 1926; Hocart 1933; Hooke 1933; Frankfort and Frankfort 1946; Raglan 1949; Culshaw 1949; Harrison 1951; Hocart 1952; Gaster 1954; Raglan 1955; Eliade 1963; Weisinger 1965; Tobin 1988; Tobin 1991; Segal 1998; Laneri 2007.

[39] Griffiths 1980, 35.

[40] Faulkner 1994, 146-7.

[41] Anthes 1959, 180.

[42] Griffiths 1980, 17.

[43] Anthes 1959, 206; Griffiths 1980, 24; Frazer 1922, Chapters 28-30. Wengrow 2006,116-119; Assmann 2008, 23-38.

[44] Frazer 1922, Chapters 38-40.

[45] Anthes 1959, 207. See Chapter Three. According to Griffiths, it is difficult to locate a spot in the funeral program where the seeking and finding of Osiris could be mimicked (1980, 26). The appellation *dmḏ(y)t*, which occurs in the Funerary Liturgy, TT 82, and TT 100, denotes the woman who is responsible for ritually collecting the limbs/bones of the deceased in the funerary ceremony. See Diamond 2008a.

[46] Anthes 1959, 208.

[47] Griffiths 1980, 1.

Restricted Knowledge

The "mythologization of ritual"[48] is a central notion for understanding the significance of the word *ḥ3i*. The evidence for this study is difficult to interpret because, as Baines points out, the earliest periods in ancient Egypt present sparse and problematic evidence for myth.[49] Frankfort and Frankfort remark in the opening passage of their work on myth and reality that there is very little in the documents of the ancients that resembles "thought."[50] The Pyramid Texts do offer small excerpts of myth but with little commentary. It has been supposed by Assmann that there were no myths at that time,[51] while Brunner-Traut suggests that they did exist, but may not have survived.[52] Likewise, Baines maintains that the explanation of myth may have been restricted to oral tradition.[53] Van Dijk believes that the absence of myth in early documents stems from the fact that mythical knowledge was reserved for the elite and priestly classes: "myths were sacred knowledge that was kept secret."[54] He strengthens his argument by noting that when there are official recordings of myth, they are found in areas of restricted use, like the innermost parts of temples or royal tombs.[55] Baines furthers this supposition by noting that such knowledge could not normally be displayed so only fragmentary evidence of it would exist and only in special contexts.[56] Baines continues this line by remarking that knowledge is an instrument of power and that it should be expected that there existed restricted religious knowledge because access to religious practice was restricted.[57] Until writing became widespread restricted knowledge would have been passed through oral communication. With that, Baines maintains that the means of restriction was through the social hierarchy.[58]

The most feasible solution seems to lie in this idea of restricted or sacred knowledge (requiring initiation). In the early periods there is no evidence for the democratization of religion; certain elite or priestly personages would have been entitled to the use of sanctified knowledge, while others from the lower classes would not have been privy to this information. Baines suggests that this democratization of religion from the king to the elite probably took place earlier than the First Intermediate Period, as is usually suggested. He references the inscription in the tomb of Pepiankh at Meir and the Old Kingdom Coffin Texts from

[48] A term used by Faulkner 1994, 146.

[49] Baines 1991, 82.

[50] Frankfort and Frankfort 1946, 3, 8. On page 9 they define speculative thought as "mythopoeic speculative thought."

[51] "*Verborgenheit*"; cited in Baines 1991, 83.

[52] Brunner-Traut, "Mythos" *LÄ*, vol. 4, 277-86; cited in Baines 1991, 84.

[53] Baines 1991, 84.

[54] van Dijk 1995, 1698.

[55] van Dijk 1995, 1698.

[56] Baines 1990, 5.

[57] Baines 1990, 6.

[58] Baines 1990, 7.

Balat.[59] This suggestion is significant because *ḥ3i* appears in Old Kingdom private contexts without mythological allusions, and in Old Kingdom royal contexts with mythological allusions. These allusions are what is visible of this mythic truth[60] that was at first accessible only to the king —the sacred knowledge.

The original myth-ritual pattern of the ancient Near East centered on a divine king.[61] Therefore it is not surprising that the earliest myths are associated with royalty and the symbolic rebirth or resurrection of the king.[62] It was only after some time that the elite had access to this mythopoeic speculative thought[63] which turned their mundane ritual activity into something more powerful and authoritative. The ritual they were already performing had a functional purpose — the passage from death to life. The ritual was the actual means of the changeover.[64]

The Term ḥ3i

The connection between the Osiris myth and royalty can also be seen in the names Isis, "the throne," and Nephthys, "Mistress of the *ḥwt*."[65] This connection, together with the idea of sacred knowledge and the mythologization of ritual, may account for the fact that the Fourth Dynasty tomb of Debehni appears to be devoid of Osirian allusions, and that some of the Pyramid Texts that contain the word *ḥ3i* include Osirian references.[66]

Many scholars have studied the different beliefs that existed prior to the Fifth Dynasty, when the Pyramid Texts were first written down. Prominent at this time was the Solar religion, where the Hereafter is located in the eastern part of the sky.[67] According to Breasted there were many ancient folk tales about how the sun god reached the sky from earth, and the Egyptians prayed that their king would ascend in the same fashion.[68] When the ancient Egyptians contemplated this very question, the idea of a bird lifting the deceased king to the sky would have been appealing. After all, birds were the only creatures able to reach the sky. One can clearly see this idea in the Pyramid Texts. To name only a few, Pyramid Text Utterance 245 describes the deceased king as turning into a falcon in order to ascend to the goddess Nut. Utterance 267 talks about the deceased king flying up as a bird. Utterance 417 describes the goddess Tait lifting the king up to the sky in her form of a bird. Utterance 467 speaks of the deceased king soaring to the sky as a heron and kissing it as a falcon. Utterance 470 tells of a goddess telling the king he will ascend to the sky like the falcons, his feathers being those of a duck. Utterance 519 states that the deceased flew as a bird to the sky above his foes. And finally, Utterance 573 speaks of the king flying up to the sky using various avian similes: a duck, a falcon, and a kite. The Pyramid Texts chronicle the deceased kings' ascent to heaven, in some instances flying on, or as, a bird.[69] This notion is more archaic than the concept of the deceased king becoming Osiris.[70] One can also see later examples of this avian notion in the Twelfth Dynasty Story of Sinuhe where King Amenemhet I dies and rises to heaven, "the god ascended to his horizon...flew to heaven and united with the sun-disk, the divine body merging with its maker."[71] These are only a few of the numerous examples that can be found in the ancient Egyptian sources and the ritual of *ḥ3i* is intimately connected with this avian ascension.

This ascension could be visualized in various ways. One could ride on a bird to the sky to reach the Hereafter. One could transform into any type of bird and ascend alone. This may have been an acceptable allegory to the real life situation observed by the ancient Egyptians – that is, birds feeding on corpses and lifting the old life to heaven or sustaining themselves through the dead corpse.[72] Essentially they were turning old life into new through its ascension to the sky.

If one gives credence to the abovementioned theory of the mythologization of ritual, the tomb of Debehni may display the more archaic funerary ritual, devoid of mythological allusion, which functioned as a means of revitalization to secure eternal life for the deceased. In the royal funerary tradition, at the point in time that sources become available, this same ritual was interpreted from a mythological perspective.

An early version of the mythologized ritual can be found in excerpts from various Pyramid Texts — whether or not they employ the term *ḥ3i* — which describe the ceremony accompanying the mythical transportation and resurrection of the deceased king. In effect, there is a summoning of the deceased normally performed by two female deities. Typically it is Isis and Nephthys, the Mooring Post, or the *smntyt* who summon the deceased; and at times Isis or Nephthys call the deceased in the form of one of the two latter deities. Sometimes the Souls of Pe come to greet the deceased at the calling.

[59] Baines, 1990, 8, note 44.
[60] Frankfort and Frankfort 1946, 8.
[61] Weisinger 1965, 121.
[62] Hooke 1933, 1-14; Frazer 1922, chapters 38-40.
[63] Term used by Frankfort and Frankfort 1946.
[64] Weisinger 1965, 122.
[65] Levai 2007, 19; see Chapter Two for a detailed discussion on the name "Nephthys."
[66] It is assumed that the oral tradition of the Pyramid Texts predates the Fifth Dynasty, and that the funerary rites appearing in the tomb of Debehni also appeared earlier. See Griffiths (1980) for the origin of the cult of Osiris.
[67] Breasted 1912, 100-101.
[68] Breasted 1912, 10.
[69] See brief discussion in Mercer 1952, 4:5-6; Griffiths 1980, 65-66.
[70] Breasted 1912, 101-102; Griffiths 1980, 65-66.
[71] Lichtheim 1973, 1:223. For two Saite examples of a similar motif see Leahy 1996, 151, note s.
[72] These ideas are explained in Chapter Five.

Either simultaneously or immediately after the calling, a dance is performed to ritually transport the deceased to the celestial realm. With the completion of the dance, the deceased has ascended to the Hereafter.

The ceremony described above, in light of the mythologization of ritual, provides a basis for understanding the rite of *ḥ3i*. Originally the ceremony did not contain Osirian allusions; this is what is portrayed in the Old Kingdom private tomb scenes. It is during the Old Kingdom that the circumstances under which the rite appears are the most homogeneous. As time goes on, the rite exists in more varied contexts. This homogeneity indicates an early origin for the rite.

The ceremony is not originally Osirian but was adapted by the royal cult at some point during the first five dynasties. In the early Old Kingdom, only royalty had access to the cult of Osiris. Private people participated in other funerary traditions, namely those that existed prior to the advent of the cult of Osiris. Griffiths attributes this transformation of tradition to a change in regime, "It is not hard to understand why this ceremonial (Butic tradition) would not always be given prominence in the royal funerary cult of the early dynastic period. This regime reflected an Upper Egyptian supremacy which would not be anxious to follow Lower Egyptian traditions. Their funerary cult had its origin in Abydos."[73] The rite of *ḥ3i* may have belonged to the Butic ceremonies in that it developed from a Lower Egyptian tradition and had spread among private persons. The cult of Osiris eventually absorbed the Butic traditions and reinterpreted them. Hence, the result is a new understanding of the old ceremonies.

On the other hand, there is some evidence to support the idea that the *ḥ3i* ritual originated in the Naqada culture. The earliest confirmed examples of the A 28 pose date to the Naqada II/Gerzean Period, where it is illustrated on pottery and exhibited in female figurines.[74] It is not coincidental that these female figurines with upraised arms have been compared to birds.[75]

Beginning at least as early as the Fourth Dynasty, the rite of *ḥ3i* is an important element in the resurrection process which magically enabled the deceased to reach the Hereafter. According to Breasted it was necessary to help the deceased in becoming a spirit; it did not happen automatically.[76] In the mid to late Old Kingdom, in the royal sphere, the ritual of *ḥ3i* was part of the procedure to transform Horus into Osiris. Griffiths notes that the Osirian resurrection was very potent, because if Osiris could be revived so could anyone.[77] After the Old Kingdom, the rite of *ḥ3i* occurs only with reference to the mythological realm.[78] The nature of this rite reveals its jubilant character, as the arrival of the deceased in the Afterlife was a time to celebrate and rejoice.

To conclude, one reads in the opening line of Chapter Seven of E. O. James' *The Beginnings of Religion*:

> At all times and everywhere man's intense desire and determination to destroy death and 'put on immortality' has found expression not only in his ritual behavior but also in his mythology.

The ritual of *ḥ3i s*hould be understood in this light. In conjunction with the preservation of the corpse, the deposition of grave goods with the body, and the ceremonial act of burial, the ancient Egyptians devised a symbolic journey for the dead in order for them to pass on to a new life – this is the ritual of *ḥ3i*.

[73] Griffiths 1980, 60.
[74] Needler 1984, 206, 336-337.
[75] Graff 2008.
[76] Breasted 1912, 59.
[77] Griffiths 1980, 3.

[78] The exception is Gardiner's Funerary Liturgy that was found in a Middle Kingdom context but may date back to the Third Dynasty.

Chapter One

Introduction

The purpose of this chapter is to present an argument for the reconsideration of the meaning of *ḥ3i*, and to introduce the criteria for the first stage of analysis. The traditional definitions of *ḥ3i* as "mourn" and "dance and sing at a funeral" are not satisfactory. There is a better explanation for this apparent dichotomy in meaning. This chapter will present the existing definitions and discuss the anomalous features in the sources.

Before the material is introduced it will be necessary to give an overview of the modern sources and what they say about the definition of *ḥ3i* in order to understand the apparent complexity in the interpretation of the word. The main sources are as follows: *Wörterbuch der ägyptischen Sprache* edited by A. Erman and H. Grapow, *A Concise Dictionary of Middle Egyptian* by Raymond O. Faulkner, *Die Sprache der Pharaonen: Großes Handwörterbuch* by Rainer Hannig, and *The Inflection of the Verb in the Pyramid Texts* by James P. Allen.

The entries for *ḥ3i* occur in *Wb* III 6, 10-11 and 7, 1-8 with three supplementary entries appearing in *Wb* III 7, 10-12. The first entry refers to the third-weak verb, *von tanzenden und singenden Frauen beim Leichenbegängnis*. This source is the only one to distinguish two separate verbs, "dance and sing" and "mourn," *ḥ3i* and *ḥ3*, respectively. Other scholars tend to think these verbs are one and the same,[1] and I agree. There is only one root, and it is *ḥ3i*. This source defines *ḥ3* as *klagen (um den Toten, bes. um Osiris)*. The next entry, *ḥ3* with a crying woman as the determinative, is defined as *die Klage*(?). The subsequent entry, *ḥ3i.t*, is defined as the name of a goddess: *die Klagende*. The following entry is *ḥ3i.ti*, referring to *die beiden Klagenden, als Bez. der Isis und Nephthys*. The next entry is *ḥ3(i)t*, referring to *ein Vogel, der klagenden Isis*. Further down is another entry for *ḥ3t*, *Kummer, Leid*. These examples are taken into account during the analysis of *ḥ3i* to see if there is a connection between this variant and the third-weak verb. They are presented chronologically below. Lastly, there is a separate entry for *ḥ3* written with a different determinative. The editors suggest the definition of *suchen*(?). This entry is noteworthy because there is an example of this word in the Pyramid Texts which traditionally has been translated as "mourn." This example will be discussed below.

Raymond Faulkner, in *A Concise Dictionary of Middle Egyptian*, includes three entries for *ḥ3i* and its derivatives *ḥ3yt* and *ḥ3w*.[2] Under his first entry he categorizes the word as a third-weak verb and defines *ḥ3i* as 1. "mourn," 2. "wail," 3. "screech" (of falcon or kite), and 4. "dance" (at funeral). Under his second entry, *ḥ3yt*, he lists "mourning" for the definition, and under his third entry, *ḥ3w*, he lists "mourners." The lexicographer recognizes the predominant meaning to be one of mourning or lamenting; however, he is aware that certain examples do not fit into this framework. Hence, he includes a fourth definition under his first entry to satisfy these other circumstances which tend to give support to the sense of dancing and singing as the meaning of *ḥ3i*.

Rainer Hannig, in *Die Sprache der Pharaonen, Großes Handwörterbuch* I: *Ägyptisch-Deutsch*, includes the following four entries: *ḥ3i* [3 inf] 1. *klagen (um), beklagen, beweinen* 2. *klagen* (*ḥr um*) 3. *schreien (von Weihe oder Falke)* 4. *tanzen (beim Begräbnis)*; *ḥ3yt f. Trauer*; *ḥ3ytiw* [pl] *die Trauernden*; *ḥ3t* f. *die Trauernde*; and *ḥ3w der Trauernde (viell a. beruflich)*.[3] In volume II: *Wortschatz der Pharaonen in Sachgruppen*, under section 91. *Trauer, Klage*, Hannig lists *ḥ3i* [3inf] *klagen (um), beklagen, beweinen, klagen*, and *ḥ3yt Trauer*.[4] Under section 269. *Personen*, b) *Trauernde, Klagende*, Hannig lists *ḥ3ytiw* [pl] *die Trauernden*; *ḥ3t die Trauernde*; *ḥ3w Trauernder (viell a. beruflich)*. *Die Sprache der Pharaonen, Großes Handwörterbuch* III: *Deutsch-Ägyptisch* reiterates the abovementioned definitions.[5] As is evident, Hannig generally agrees that *ḥ3i* has a mourning connotation, although he also recognizes the fact that certain circumstances where *ḥ3i* appears require the meaning to be altered to indicate the action of dance.

Allen has one entry for *ḥ3i*, which he translates as "mourn, bewail," quoting *Wb* III 6, 10; 6-7, 4 as additional references.[6] He also notes that *ḥ3t* is the infinitive in Old Egyptian and cites the tomb of Hetepherakhti as evidence (see below).

Alan Gardiner discusses the meaning of *ḥ3i* in his article on the funerary liturgy from the Ramesseum Papyri.[7] His work will be examined below.

Observations on the Traditional Definitions of ḥ3i

Scholars have been fairly consistent in their analyses of *ḥ3i*, and tend to agree that in most situations *ḥ3i* connotes "mourn," and elsewhere signifies "dance and sing (at a funeral)." It is troublesome the idea that one word could fundamentally signify two such dissimilar actions, and it is more likely that the true meaning of *ḥ3i*

---

[1] Gardiner 1955, 10, n. 6; Allen 1984, 571.

[2] Faulkner 1991, 160.

[3] Hannig 1995, 501.

[4] Hannig 1999, 342.

[5] Hannig 1999, 612. There are further references to *ḥ3i* in *Handwörterbuch* III: *Deutsch-Ägyptisch* (2000) pages 169, 202, 713, 792, 1275, 1309, 1310.

[6] J. Allen 1984, 571.

[7] Gardiner 1955.

may contain aspects of both ideas. So a new survey of the material containing this word is in order.

The first item to examine is the determinative of the man with upraised arms (A 28)[8] that appears regularly in the writing of the word *ḥ3i*. Also, this gesture itself can appear in a scene accompanying a caption, acting as a substitute for the determinative. This would seem to be a curious complement to a word signifying "mourn," because on the one hand, there are other more appropriate determinatives like D 3 (hair), D 9 (eye with flowing tears), or Hannig's B 28 (woman in mourning gesture)[9] that would be more suitable for conveying a sense of mourning. On the other hand, this gesture (A 28) can symbolize rejoicing (see Chapter Six), which would seem to communicate an emotion in conflict with mourning. The A 28 sign is also used as a determinative in the word *ḥꜥi*, to rejoice.[10] It is noteworthy that in the Coffin Texts, for example, Gardiner's D 36 sign (forearm) can replace the A 28 sign in the word *ḥ3i*. This may signify that *ḥ3i* denotes an action, possibly involving movement of the arms, thus emphasizing the importance of the upraised arms in the A 28 sign.

It is also intriguing to note that the A 28 determinative does not occur in the more common words meaning "to mourn/mourning."[11] In fact, this determinative does not appear in the general corpus of mourning words, except for three examples.

The first example is from Pyramid Texts §1973 where an abbreviated version of the determinative appears in the word *iww* (Figure 1).[12] The only part of the A 28 hieroglyph employed is the upper portion containing the head and upraised arms (Hannig's D 115). Utterance 670 (PT §1973) is described by Faulkner as a variant of Utterance 482 (PT §§1004-1005) and reads as follows:

> [The doors of the sky are opened, the doors of the celestial expanses are thrown open; the gods who are in Pe are full of sorrow, and they come to Osiris the King at the sound of the weeping[13] of Isis, at the cry[14] of Nephthys,] at the wailing of these two spirits...[15]

The second example comes from the Ptolemaic Stundenwachen at Edfu (14, 105) and appears in the second hour of the night in the word *hh* (Figure 2).[16] The relevant section reads as follows:[17]

hh[*.i*] *kw n mt isk r.k*

Ich beweine dich [?], du sollst nicht sterben...

The third example comes from a demotic writing of *nhp* in the Catalogue of the Demotic Papyri in the John Rylands Library (IX 19/16) (Figure 3).[18] The word appears in a papyrus from el-Hiba entitled "The Petition of Peteêsi." The passage reads as follows:

Ich habe gehört, daß er nach Buto gegangen ist, um ḥr, den Vater des ḥr-ḫnsw, der zu seinen Vätern gegangen ist, zu betrauern.[19]

When taking into account the other mourning words in the Egyptian language, there appears to be a stock number of determinatives applied to these words, some of them listed above. The fact that sign A 28, the man with upraised arms, is not one of them, indicates that there is something out of the ordinary about the usage of this hieroglyph in relationship to mourning. Therefore, since *ḥ3i* is frequently written with this very determinative, the traditional definitions given for *ḥ3i* are at the very least dubious.

Additionally, the A 28 sign is used with words that have a rejoicing connotation (*ḥꜥi*, for example), and this gesture is common in Old Kingdom tomb scenes of singing and/or dancing. The joyous context displaying this pose indicates the true meaning of the word *ḥ3i*. Noting the occurrence of this pose, observing its employment over time and documenting the placement of this gesture in its various scenarios will provide the information necessary to comprehend the nature of this ritual action further. It will be through an analysis of these sources, in conjunction with the textual evidence, that patterns and themes in the ritual activities associated with this gesture will be determined (see Chapter Four).

The action of *ḥ3i* occurs in diverse contexts particularly notable in the repertoire of funerary scenes.[20] For example, in the Old Kingdom tomb of Qar at Giza, in the scene where four performing women are accompanied by the legend "*ḥ3(i)t* in *šnḏt(y)t*," these women are also complemented by individual legends stating the particular action being performed by each one of them: *ib3*, *ib3*, *ib3* and *m3ḥ*, respectively.[21] It therefore seems

[8] Gardiner 1994, 445.
[9] In Buurman et al. (1988, 71) determinative B 28 includes the additional variant of a woman with tears pouring forth from her eyes. This form does not appear in Hannig.
[10] Faulkner 1991, 164; Gardiner 1994, 445.
[11] For example *i3kb*, *imw*, *nhwt*, *sbḥ*, *sgb*, *kni*, or *g3s*.
[12] Sethe 1908, 476; Faulkner 1998, 285-286. See also Junker (1910, 30) where the word *iwḥ* appears with an upside down A 28 determinative.
[13] *ḫrw rmm*.
[14] *šbḥ*.
[15] Faulkner 1998, 285.
[16] *Wb* II 502, 9.
[17] Junker 1910, 86.
[18] Griffith 1909, 362; Gardiner 1967, 163; Redford 2001, 3:24.
[19] Vittmann 1998, 1:183. Griffith (1909, 3:104, 362) supplies the following translation, "...I have heard that he went to Puto to mourn for Hôr the father of Khelkhons, who hath gone to his fathers."
[20] See descriptions of funerary scenes in Chapter Five.
[21] Simpson 1976, fig. 24.

doubtful that *ḥ3(i)t* has exactly the same connotation as either *ib3* or *m3ḥ*.[22] The definition of *ḥ3i* more likely includes the notions of the actions expressed by *ib3* and *m3ḥ*.

A second example that appears to suggest the performance of a separate action can be seen in the tomb of Pepiankh at Meir, where a man with the title *ḥ3(i)w* stands beside an offering table filled with food.[23]

Another incongruity appears in the New Kingdom tomb of Amenemhet (TT 82), where two men are riding in a skiff carrying a naos, with a caption reading "*ḥ3it* in faring upstream."[24] In this example there are no gestures of mourning, although the men are participating in funerary activity; likewise, there is no dancing or singing. Gardiner has chosen to translate the passage using the traditional definition of the verb *ḥʿi*, instead of *ḥ3i*.[25]

These are just some of the examples that demonstrate the assorted contexts in which *ḥ3i* can appear.[26] I have not yet found any instances where the word *ḥ3i* appears in the caption of a scene depicting the traditionally recognizable mourners. Similarly, the people who do appear in the scenes featuring captions containing the word *ḥ3i* regularly perform the gesture of upraised arms (A 28).

The relationship between *ḥ3i* and mourning needs to be reexamined. Those sources where additional words for mourning or lamenting appear in close proximity to *ḥ3i* may enable us to elaborate on this connection. When examining the sources it becomes evident that *ḥ3i* is not synonymous with mourning, but is instead a related activity. Listed in Table 1 are the Pharaonic sources that mention the word *ḥ3i* and also contain additional words that have a recognized mourning connotation.

The most common mourning word occurring in close proximity to *ḥ3i* is *rmi*. *ḏryt* is also a common counterpart for *ḥ3iw*/*ḥ3it*. It is my belief that on numerous occasions the modern translator has tailored the definition of *ḥ3i* to fit the meaning of the nearby mourning word. For example, when *ḏryt* and *ḥ3(i)w*/*ḥ3(i)t* appear together the latter word is translated as either "mourner" or "screecher" depending on the definition given to *ḏryt* (either "mourner" or "Kite"). Likewise, when *ḥ3i* occurs in connection with *rmi* and/or *i3kb* it is assigned a synonymous meaning. I also believe that there is nothing substantial in any one of these sources to clearly indicate that *ḥ3i* means "to mourn." I do, however, agree that the action of *ḥ3i* is related to mourning, even if through context alone.

Genre of Sources

All references to the word *ḥ3i* occur in ritualistic material, namely, captions in tomb scenes, a tomb inscription, religious texts (Pyramid Texts, Coffin Texts, Book of the Dead, Amduat, and Book of Gates), a funerary liturgy, and a hymn to Osiris (See Table 2). The word *ḥ3i* is ritualistic in nature and refers to an action performed in a ceremonial setting.

Contextual Setting

The contexts in which *ḥ3i* appears can be classified into two groups: the real world and the mythological world (Table 3). In every circumstance the word *ḥ3i* occurs in the event of a death, and assumedly prior to the termination of the spiritualization, or rebirth, of the deceased into the Afterlife.

The examples occurring in the tomb scenes of Debehni, Hetepherakhti, Qar, Pepiankh, and Amenemhet,[27] in the inscription of Sabni, and in the Funerary Liturgy, appear in relation to a real funeral. The remaining sources can be categorized as funerary literature, where *ḥ3i* takes place in a mythological setting.

The Pyramid Texts are innately funerary, in that they are a collection of utterances that were first carved on the walls of the pyramids of nine kings and queens of the late Old Kingdom, beginning with King Unas, the last king of Dynasty Five. They represent the oldest body of Egyptian religious and funerary literature now extant.[28] This corpus is comprised of both very ancient texts and others that are contemporary with the pyramids. The purpose of the Pyramid Texts was to help the deceased king in the Afterlife. They were inscribed on the walls of the corridors and burial chambers; however, their sequence is still a matter of debate. Some of the texts deal with various rituals that would have been performed at the royal funeral where the deceased is addressed as Osiris. Scenes do not accompany the texts because it was thought that a picture could come alive and harm the king.[29] There are many spells related to the revivification of the deceased and the protection of his body. These texts were intended only for the benefit of the king and the royal family.

[22] Gardiner 1955, 10-11.

[23] This figure appears twice in two separate scenes (Blackman 1953, pls. 42, 43).

[24] Gardiner 1915, 52.

[25] Gardiner 1915, 52.

[26] See Chapter Five for a description of each source where *ḥ3i* is found.

[27] By the New Kingdom the ordinary funeral practice has been inundated by mythological allusion.

[28] Faulkner 1998, v; J. Allen 1988, 38-39.

[29] Hieroglyphs were treated like pictures and were thus ritually mutilated to prevent them from harming the deceased king. This is particularly true for those hieroglyphs appearing in the burial chamber (See R. Wilkinson 1994, 7 and G. Pinch 1994, 69).

The Coffin Texts are also funerary in nature, and were first inscribed on the walls of burial chambers, and later on the inside of wooden coffins of private persons, as well as on a few papyri beginning in the First Intermediate Period and during the Middle Kingdom. These texts are related to the aforementioned Pyramid Texts, and also provided an assurance of survival in the Afterlife. At this time private individuals were appropriating the king's funerary privileges and were increasingly being identified with Osiris without having any connection to the royal cult.[30]

The Book of the Dead is directly related to both of these groups of spells, as each new group of mortuary texts exhibits some degree of overlap with the older literature.[31] The earliest chapters of the Book of the Dead appeared in the Seventeenth Dynasty and eventually became one of the most important pieces of burial equipment.[32] Usually private people used the Chapters of the Book of the Dead, while a number of examples are also found in royal contexts. Normally the Book of the Dead was written on a papyrus roll, and it was placed in the coffin of the deceased, in the deceased's hand, in a hollowed out Osiris figurine, or in a box.

The Book of Gates, officially untitled, first appears in the royal tomb of Horemheb just after the Amarna Period. Some suspect that the book may date as far back as the Middle Kingdom; however, due to the cosmopolitan nature of some of the accompanying scenes, Hornung believes that this date is too early.[33] Seti I is the first king to display a complete version of the Book of Gates on his alabaster sarcophagus. With Ramesses IX the book disappears from the royal tomb. Excerpts from the Book of Gates appear infrequently after the New Kingdom.[34] Like the Amduat, the Book of Gates also displays the twelve hours of the night in three registers.[35]

The Amduat, actually entitled the Book of the Hidden Chamber,[36] is another funerary book that first appears in the early Eighteenth Dynasty, and is inscribed on the walls of some royal tombs.[37] The earliest copies of the book come from the tomb of Thutmosis III and his vizier Useramun.[38] The text contains a detailed description of the Netherworld, describing the journey of the sun god through the twelve hours of the night, beginning with his setting and ending with his rising.[39] This is the first completely illustrated book that has matching text and pictures.[40] This book appears in part, or in whole, in most of the royal tombs of the Eighteenth, Nineteenth and Twentieth Dynasties, and also in private Theban papyri of the Twenty-First Dynasty.[41] In the latter part of the Twenty-First Dynasty excerpts begin to appear on a variety of funerary equipment.

The next source in which *ḥꜣi* appears is the fragmentary Funerary Liturgy discovered by Quibell beneath the Ramesseum.[42] Originally this text was termed a processional papyrus, but was subsequently renamed by Gardiner because of the funerary references. The purpose of this text was to present a normal funerary program.[43] This source is badly preserved, but there are a number of clues regarding the nature of this text. First, the phrase "circulating around the mastaba four times" appears regularly. Second, the *imy-ḫnt* priest and the lector-priest are mentioned. And third, the person for whom the rites are performed is "*Wsir mn pn*," "the Osiris this So-and-So."[44] Additionally, the word *ḥꜣi* appears on at least four separate occasions; however, the context is not always clear enough to indicate exactly what is taking place.

The context is strictly mythological in the Pyramid Texts, Coffin Texts, Book of the Dead (including Louvre C 286), Book of Gates, and Amduat. The participants in these cases are divine. This can be contrasted with the contexts in which *ḥꜣi* appears in the private tombs and the funerary liturgy. In these latter examples the ritual occurs at an authentic funeral for an individual.

The hymn to Osiris on Louvre C 286 functions in a way similar to that of the literature above, namely, it is employed in a funerary context. In fact, T. G. Allen classifies this hymn as Chapter 185A of the Book of the Dead.[45] This hymn reflects the myth of Osiris; therefore, the content is mythological and the participants are divine. The stela is dedicated by Amenmose and his wife, Nefertari.[46] On the upper portion of the stela there is a double offering scene. On the left, the official Amenmose and his wife are seated before an offering table, and on the right the lady Baket is seated. One son stands behind the couple, while another son stands in front of the offering table raising one arm in an offering gesture. A priest is performing offering rites before the lady Baket. More sons and daughters are seated below.[47] According to Moret, Amenmose, Nefertari and their children are alive and well and are participating in a

[30] Bard 2008, 174.
[31] Goelet 1994, 139.
[32] Parkinson and Quirke 1992.
[33] Hornung 1999, 55.
[34] Hornung 1999, 56.
[35] Hornung 1999, 57.
[36] Hornung 1999, 32.
[37] Hornung 1999, 27-28.
[38] Hornung 1999, 28.
[39] Hornung 1999, 27.
[40] Hornung 1999, 32.
[41] Hornung 1999, 30, 33. The 21st Dynasty version is called the shorter, or abridged version of the Amduat.
[42] Gardiner 1955.
[43] Gardiner 1955, 17.
[44] J. Allen (1988, 39) shows that mn could be substituted for the deceased's name, even for royalty.
[45] T. G. Allen 1974, 203ff.
[46] Moret 1931.
[47] Moret 1931, 727, pl. III.

funerary meal dedicated to their ancestor Baket.[48] It is on this occasion that Amenmose chants the hymn to Osiris.[49] In general, a funerary stela was the focus of a cult place, the point of transition between this world and the next.[50] Although the provenance of this particular stela is unknown, such stelae were usually associated with the funerary complex. In this case, it may come from Abydos, the cult place of Osiris.

The funerary motif is present in all citations, and there is a relationship between the use of the word *ḥ3i* and the Osirian myth. Table 4 illustrates this link.

The Cult of Osiris

The word *ḥ3i* functions primarily in contexts alluding to Osiris. There is a stark contrast between the Old Kingdom private sources and the others. There are no Old Kingdom private sources where *ḥ3i* appears in connection with clear allusions to the myth of Osiris. On the other hand, the royal sources of the Old and Middle Kingdoms show that the performance of *ḥ3i* almost always took place in a context including these allusions. The New Kingdom sources are not as straightforward. Aside from the Louvre stela whose content is purely Osirian, the funerary books involve numerous characters and demonstrate an amalgamation of many religious ideas. Osiris is included in these funerary books, but the texts themselves are not overtly Osirian.

Conclusion

By way of summation, the word *ḥ3i* can no longer be classified as a mourning word. It appears only in ritual sources, and more precisely, in contexts of a strictly funerary character.

In the private sources, the ritual of *ḥ3i* is depicted as occurring on earth amongst the living. In the sources that stem from a royal context, the ritual is depicted as occurring in a mythological setting. Often these contexts are laden with Osirian overtones; however, the early private sources do not exhibit an Osirian influence.

---

[48] Alternatively, the parents may also be deceased and are sharing in the funerary meal of Baket.

[49] Moret 1931, 728.

[50] Taylor 2001, 136.

TABLE 1: SOURCES CONTAINING ADDITIONAL MOURNING WORDS

	Source	Additional Mourning Word	Definition of Additional Mourning Word	Form of *ḥ3i*	Definition Given to *ḥ3i* by Previous Translator
1	Pepiankh's Rock Tomb at Meir	*ḏryt*	Kite or Mourner[51]	*ḥ3(i)w*	Mourner[52]
2	PT §550	*rmi; i3kb*	Weep or Beweep;[53] Mourning or Wailings[54]	T - *ḥ3(i)* P - *ḥ3y*[55]	Mourn[56]
3	PT §744	*wršiw*	Watchers, Sentries, Klagefrauen[57]	T - *ḥ3i* P - *ḥ3(i)*[58]	Wail[59]
4	PT §1255	*ḏryt*	Kite or Mourner	*ḥ3(i)t*[60]	'screecher'[61]
5	PT §1280	*ḏryt; rmi* (weeping eye only)	Kite/Mourner; Weep	*ḥ3(i)t*[62]	'screecher'[63]
6	PT §1585	*rmi*	Weep	*ḥ3(i)*[64]	Mourn[65]
7	PT §§2117-2118	*rmi*	Weep	*ḥ3(i)*[66]	Mourn[67]
8	CT I 303	*ḏryt*	Kite or Mourner	*ḥ3(i)t*[68]	screecher[69]
9	CT IV 373	*rmi*	Weep	*ḥ3, ḥ3y, ḥ3(i)w*[70]	Mourn[71]
10	CT VI 385o	*rmi*	Weep	*ḥ3(i)*[72]	Lament[73]
11	Funerary Liturgy	*dmḏ(y)t*	Group of Women[74]	*ḥ3(i)*[75]	Wail[76]
12	Tomb of Amenemhet	*mnknw; dmḏ(y)t*[77]	Isis; Nephthys[78]	*ḥ3(i)*[79]	Rejoicing[80]
13	BD 1	*i3kbywt*	The women who mourned	*ḥ3yw*[81]	The men who lamented[82]
14	BD 172	*rmi* (1st stanza)	Weep	*ḥ3(i)*[83]	Mourn[84]

[51] Faulkner 1991, 323; *Wb* V 596, 6-13.
[52] Blackman 1953, 53, 55.
[53] Faulkner 1991, 149; *Wb* II 417, 10.
[54] Faulkner 1991, 9; *Wb* I 34, 9.
[55] Sethe 1908, 281.
[56] Faulkner 1998, 109.
[57] Faulkner 1991, 65; *Wb* I 336, 12.
[58] Sethe 1908, 407.
[59] Faulkner 1998, 138.
[60] Sethe 1908, 210.
[61] Faulkner 1998, 200.
[62] Sethe 1908, 219.
[63] Faulkner 1998, 203.
[64] Sethe 1908, 343.
[65] Faulkner 1998, 238.
[66] Sethe 1908, 515.
[67] Faulkner 1998, 299.
[68] De Buck 1935, 303.
[69] Faulkner 2004, 1:68.
[70] De Buck 1951, 373.
[71] Faulkner 2004, 1:280.
[72] De Buck 1961, 385.
[73] Faulkner 2004, 2:289.
[74] Faulkner 1991, 313; *Wb* V 461, 12.
[75] Gardiner 1955, 12.
[76] Gardiner 1955, 12.
[77] I am not able to locate a published definition for *mnknw*. See Chapter Two for a discussion of the titles *mnknw* and *dmḏ(y)t*.
[78] Plate X shows two women kneeling and presenting bowls of water before four tanks. Some sources suggest the women represent Isis and Nephthys. According to Gardiner, these women are called *mnknw* and *ḏmdyt*, respectively. Gardiner notes that the former reference may have something to do with the word for "garden," and quotes a similar example in the tomb of Rekhmire (Gardiner 1915, 52). See Chapter Two below.
[79] Gardiner 1915, pl. XI.
[80] Gardiner 1915, 52.
[81] Faulkner 1994, pl. 5.
[82] Faulkner 1994, pl. 5.

TABLE 2: GENRE OF SOURCES[85]

	Source	Captio Tomb Scene	Tomb Inscription	Book of the Afterlife[86]	Funerary Liturgy	Religious Hymn
1	Tomb of Debehni	X				
2	Tomb of Hetepherakhti	X				
3	Tomb of Qar	X				
4	Inscription of Sabni		X			
5	Tomb of Pepiankh	X				
6	PT §550			X		
7	PT §744			X		
8	PT §1255			X		
9	PT §1280			X		
10	PT §1585			X		
11	PT §1791			X		
12	PT §2112			X		
13	PT §2117			X		
14	CT I 73d			X		
15	CT I 74			X		
16	CT I 303g			X		
17	CT II 177h			X		
18	CT II 238b			X		
19	CT II 239a			X		
20	CT III 22a			X		
21	CT III 297i			X		
22	CT III 307a			X		
23	CT III 307b			X		
24	CT III 308d			X		
25	CT III 308d			X		
26	CT III 311h			X		
27	CT III 317e			X		
28	CT III 317e			X		
29	CT III 317l			X		
30	CT IV 331g			X		
31	CT IV 373a)			X		
32	CT IV 373a)			X		
33	CT V 332c			X		
34	CT VI 360j			X		
35	CT VI 385o			X		
36	CT VII 28o			X		
37	CT VII 51s			X		
38	Funerary Liturgy col. 16				X	
39	F.L. col. 44-45				X	
40	F.L. col. 64				X	
41	F.L. col. 84				X	
42	Tomb of Amenemhet	X				
43	BD 1			X		
44	BD 172			X		
45	Book of Gates			X		
46	Louvre Stela C 286					X
47	Amduat IV 34			X		

[83] Naville 1971, pl. CXCIII.
[84] Faulkner 1994, 129.
[85] In Table 1:2, I have chosen to omit the examples appearing in the Sun Temple of Niuserre, P. Sallier IV verso, P. Chester Beatty III, the Onomasticon fragment and the Tombos Stela. Since these citations refer to *ḥ3yt-* or *ḥ3yw*-birds, are strictly avian in nature, appear in parallelism with various other birds, and have no apparent funerary connection, I consider these sources irrelevant for the rest of this section of the study.
[86] This title is derived from Hornung's designation for this literature (1999).

TABLE 3: SOCIAL CONTEXT PRESENTED IN SOURCES

Source	Human Funeral	Divine World
Tomb of Debehni	X	
Tomb of Hetepherakhti	X	
Tomb of Qar	X	
Inscription of Sabni	X	
Tomb of Pepiankh	X	
All Pyramid Texts		X
All Coffin Texts		X
Funerary Liturgy col. 16	X	
F.L. col. 44-45	X	
F.L. col. 64	X	
F.L. col. 84	X	
Tomb of Amenemhet	X	
BD 1		X
BD 172		X
Book of Gates		X
Louvre Stela C 286		X
Amduat IV 34		X

TABLE 4: ALLUSIONS TO THE CULT OF OSIRIS

Source	Evidence for Osirian Allusions	No Osirian Allusions
Tomb of Debehni		X
Tomb of Hetepherakhti		X
Tomb of Qar		X
Inscription of Sabni		X
Tomb of Pepiankh		X
PT §550	X	
PT §744	X	
PT §1255	X	
PT §1280	X	
PT §1585		X
PT §1791		X[87]
PT §2112	X	
PT §2117	X	
CT I 73d	X	
CT I 74e	X	
CT I 303g	X	
CT II 177h	X[88]	
CT II 238b	X	
CT II 239a	X	
CT III 22a		X
CT III 297i	X	
CT III 307a	X	
CT III 307b	X	
CT III 308d	X	
CT III 308d	X	
CT III 311h	X	
CT III 317e	X	
CT III 317e	X	
CT III 317l	X	
CT IV 331g	X	
CT IV 373a	X	
CT IV 373a	X	

[87] Faulkner (1998, 262) suggests that the feminine pronoun in this spell is referring to Isis.

[88] Osiris is mentioned only once at the beginning of the spell. However, this spell does not have allusions to rejuvenation and life in the Hereafter like other Osirian spells. It speaks of assembling the deceased's family in the realm of the dead.

CT V 332c	X	
CT VI 360j	X	
CT VI 385o	X	
CT VII 28o	X	
CT VII 51s	X	
Funerary Liturgy col. 16		X
F.L. col. 44-45		X
F.L. col. 64		X
F.L. col. 84		X
Tomb of Amenemhet	X	
BD 1	X	
BD 172		X
Book of Gates XI	X	
Louvre Stela C 286 (BD 185A)	X	
Amduat IV 34	X[89]	

[89] In his book *The Ancient Egyptian Books of the Afterlife*, Hornung (1999, 34) states that Osiris is mentioned over and over again in the Amduat; however, he remains passive and does not speak even once.

Chapter Two

Introduction

One way to clarify the nature of the *ḥ3i* ritual is to look at its participants. As certain people are given particular responsibilities at a funeral and different functionaries are allotted duties with more or less religious prestige, it may be possible to determine the nature of the *ḥ3i* ritual through an analysis of its performers. To do this, it is useful to separate the private sources from the royal sources in the Old Kingdom, and to discuss the sources from the Old, Middle and New Kingdoms separately, in order to focus on the patterns in each class at each specific time. The Funerary Liturgy will still be considered a Middle Kingdom source (see below).

Chapter Two will deal with the Old Kingdom Sources, Chapter Three will deal with the Middle Kingdom Sources, and Chapter Four will deal with the New Kingdom Sources. However, there are participants that are common to more than one period; when this occurs the participant will be discussed in the earliest category and reference will be made to later examples. Likewise, concluding remarks pertaining to the evolution of the participants can be found at the end of Chapter Four.

The Egyptian Funeral

To begin, it is necessary to make a few remarks regarding the circumstances surrounding the Old Kingdom funeral scene, which is one type of source used in this study. The selection of scenes is not the same in each tomb. In fact, no tomb contains all of the episodes of a complete funeral; however, an entire funeral may be reconstructed through the selected scenes in the various tombs. Funeral scenes begin to appear in tombs in the Fourth Dynasty during the reign of Khafre, first at Giza and then at other Memphite sites (Saqqara and Abusir). In the provinces they begin between the Fifth and Sixth Dynasties.[1] The earliest large-scale funeral scene is in Room Two of the rock-cut chapel of Debehni at Giza.[2] The most fully developed scenes are in the late Sixth Dynasty chapel of Pepiankh: Heny the Black at Meir.[3] Andrey Bolshakov has studied the scene content in some of the Old Kingdom tombs and notes that only the last stages of the funeral are shown in the earliest tombs.[4] These rites include the transferring of the body toward the tomb, the mastaba itself and the rites performed on the roof. All of these rituals took place on the last day of the funeral, after the body had been embalmed. In later tombs, transfer scenes and scenes of rites at the mastaba are absent. In the Sixth Dynasty, funeral scenes are more abundant, and the earlier events of the procession are illustrated.[5]

To summarize, the funeral procession begins at the home of the deceased where the ritual of mourning takes place. Then the corpse is taken to the water for transport. At this point the coffin is ferried in a boat, which is either towed by barges or dragged by men on the shore. This voyage is thought by some to be of a purely ritualistic nature.[6] In most cases, there was no need to cross the river because both the home of the deceased and the cemetery would have been located in the Memphite region, or on the west bank at Meir, for example.[7] The first stop in the procession was the *ibw*, the purification tent. The next stop was the embalming workshop where the body was left for possibly seventy days.[8] When the corpse was retrieved, it was taken to the tomb on the day of burial.[9] Then the ritual ferrying to Sais occurred, when men on the shore usually dragged the boat.[10] After this the statue within the naos, or the coffin, was dragged to the tomb by a team of oxen. When the procession had reached the tomb there were certain rituals that took place on the roof of the mastaba or in the courtyard.[11]

Old Kingdom Private Sources

Debehni and Qar: The šnḏt

The first two sources under discussion are the Old Kingdom tombs of Debehni (Figure 4) and Qar[12] at Giza. In the tomb of Debehni there are seven women participating in a ritual dance. The women have their hair cut short and wear transparent dresses with one strap over each shoulder. Four of these women exhibit the A 28 pose, and three appear to be clapping and singing. The captions above the women read: *ḥ3(i)t i(w)f.f tmi* "*ḥ3(i)t*: His flesh is complete," and *ḥs(i)t n(yt) ḥ3(i)t* in [*šnḏt(y)t*];[13] "The singing of the *ḥ3(i)*t by the women of the Acacia House." The same people are referred to in the tomb of Qar, where there are three women each with her right arm raised and a fourth woman clapping behind them. The first three women appear to be topless, with their dress straps hanging down in front of them. The clapper still has her dress tied up. Their dresses are not transparent like those that the women wear in the tomb of Debehni. These women

---

[1] Harpur 1987, 254.
[2] S. Hassan 1943, 176.
[3] Harpur 1987, 113.
[4] Bolshakov 1991, 43.

[5] See both Harpur (1987) and Bolshakov (1991) for general descriptions and patterns in Old Kingdom funerary scenes.
[6] Contrast Taylor 2001, 187 with Assmann 2005, 305.
[7] Bolshakov 1991, 38.
[8] See Dawson (1927) and Smith and Dawson (2002) for more information on mummification. The seventy days is first encountered in the New Kingdom.
[9] Most scholars believe the *wʿbt* was a collapsible structure located near the tomb (see Chapter Three).
[10] As per it being a symbolic journey, the same applies to the Sais pilgrimage as does to the Abydos pilgrimage.
[11] J. Wilson 1944; Settgast 1963; Harpur 1987; Bolshakov 1991.
[12] See Simpson 1976, figure 24.
[13] See Hannig 2003, 1314. For the designation for *šnḏt* as *Acacia nilotica,* see Baum 1988.

also have their hair cut short. The caption in the tomb of Qar reads: *ḥ3(i)t* in *šnḏt(y)t*, "*ḥ3(i)t* by those belonging to the Acacia House."[14] It is clear that both groups of signs refer to the same entity — the women of the Acacia House — despite their variant spellings.[15] These captions clearly state who these women are: women associated with the *šnḏt*.

There has been some debate over how to read this group of signs. In his 1944 article, J. Wilson refers to this group of signs as X, as he is unable to translate them. He concludes that this designation points to a place, most likely the women's quarters, and notes that these people played a special role in the ritual at the door of the tomb. He thinks the group of signs should be read *im3t* but also considers *nht* (the sycamore-house) and attempts to link the location with the goddess Hathor. He further notes that in the Middle Kingdom and the New Kingdom it is the *mww* who replace these performers at the tomb door.[16] Until recently, *im3t* has been translated as maiden's tent, based on Grdseloff's 1937 study that determined the word was derived from *im3w*, "tent."[17] Fischer, in his 1960 article entitled, "The Butcher PH-r-nfr," continues to transliterate the group of signs as *im3t*, and follows Grdseloff's[18] supposition that *im3t* refers to something like "gynaeceum."[19] However, this transliteration and translation have both now been discarded. In 1970 Edel published his short book, entitled *Das Akazienhaus und seine Rolle in den Begräbnisriten des alten Ägyptens*. In it he determines that this group of signs should be read *šnḏt* and that they refer to the Acacia House.[20] He also determines that this designation has a direct relationship with the cult of Sakhmet.[21] He examines four instances of the Acacia House from the Old Kingdom, appearing in the tombs of Debehni (Figure 4), Qar, the Vizier Ptahhotep (Figure 5), and the Vizier Mereruka.[22] Edel also notes two additional references to the Friends of the Acacia House in the tombs of Qar[23] and Debehni.[24] In both cases two men bearing the title *ḫnmsw šnḏt*, "Friends of the Acacia House," accompany the dancers. The inscription in the tomb of Debehni has recently been reconstructed by Edel, and one can see these men standing each with his left hand on his right shoulder and each carrying a staff in his right hand. In the tomb of Qar the men are bowing slightly; each has his left hand on his right shoulder and carries something that resembles a whip in his right hand. All of the men have cropped hair and wear triangular kilts.

Both Fischer[25] and Edel,[26] in their respective works, list the titles that contain the word *šnḏt*. To summarize, Fischer points out that the title *sšmty šnḏt*, "butcher of the *šnḏt*," (although he transliterates *šnḏt* as *im3t*) occurs as a designation for butchers in at least four Old Kingdom tomb reliefs that depict the slaughter of cattle.[27] These reliefs range in date from the early Fourth Dynasty to the end of the Sixth Dynasty. Likewise, the title *ḫrp sšmty(w) šnḏt*, "Controller of the Butchers of the *šnḏt*," appears in the titularies of five queens from the Fourth and Fifth Dynasties: Hetepheres I, Meritites, Hetepheres II, Khamerernebty and Meresankh IV.[28] In these cases, *šnḏt* is always written with the feminine ending, and the three later examples are all written with the house determinative.[29] Fischer continues his list with two more entries: *sr šnḏt*, "sr-official of the *šnḏt*" (Cairo Cat. 1373), and *(i)r(y) mḏ3t šnḏt*, "document keeper of the *šnḏt*" (Berlin 7721).[30]

In addition to these examples there is also a pair of ostraca that contain the word *šnḏt*.[31] The ostraca were found by Zaki Saad at Helwan.[32] This particular title on the two ostraca reads: *imyt-r šnḏt*, "Overseer of the *šnḏt*".[33] The relevant sections can be translated as follows: "In the forecourt of the *Pr-wr* temple: *mni(wt) wrt*; overseer of the *šnḏt*." The woman who bears the title *mni(wt) wrt* is also the overseer of the *šnḏt*.[34] This passage reveals a link between the *Pr-wr* (temple of Nekhbet at Elkab), the *mni(w)t wrt* (great Mooring-post) and the *šnḏt* (Acacia House). Saad also found more ostraca that connected three other women with the *Pr-wr*; however, these women are called *mni(w)t*, not *mni(w)t wrt*.[35] Edel believes that the Two Acacias refer to

[14] Edel 1970,12-13, 23-24.

[15] Edel 1970, 23. The same phenomenon appears in spellings of the sycamore and its affiliation with Hathor. Fischer notes the variance in spelling as a problem (1960, 187). He states that the designation for the butchers does not include the house determinative nor do some of the Fourth Dynasty titles for Queens Heterpheres I and Meritites, or the inscription in the tomb of Debehni. However, Fischer supposes that the group of signs without the house determinative must have constituted a clear unit that did not need further clarification.

[16] J. Wilson 1944, 212. See below for a discussion on the *mww*.

[17] Nord 1981, 141; Grdseloff 1937.

[18] Grdseloff 1942.

[19] Fischer 1960.

[20] Edel 1970.

[21] Edel 1970, 17.

[22] See J. Wilson 1944, plate XV; Edel 1970, 9-18.

[23] See Simpson 1976, figure 24.

[24] Edel 1970, 16.

[25] Fischer 1960.

[26] Edel 1970.

[27] Fischer 1960, 180-183. In addition to the statue of PH-r-nfr, Louvre A 107, and the basin discussed in the article, this designation appears in the tomb of *Mṯn*, dating to the reign of Sneferu; on a relief fragment that may date to the end of the Old Kingdom and derives from a non-royal funerary chapel possibly located at Giza (BM 865); on a fragment from the sun temple of Niuserre; and on fragments from the pyramid temple of Pepy II.

[28] Fischer 1960, 184-185.

[29] It seems that the house determinative did not appear in the earliest writings of *šnḏt* (see Fischer 1960, 187).

[30] Fischer 1960, 186-187.

[31] Fischer 1960, 187-188.

[32] Saad 1947, pls. 42, 43; Cairo J. d'E. 86853 A and B.

[33] See Fischer 1960, 188, figure 7; from SASAE 3, plate 42 B.

[34] Edel (1970, 35-36) discusses these titles with reference to the *sḥ n(y) ḫnwt* being the continuation of the *šnḏt* in the New Kingdom.

[35] Fischer 1960, 189.

a shrine in the north (Heliopolis) and a shrine in the south (Elkab). Fischer assumes that the *šnḏt* is the place where the bearer of this title and her subordinates assembled. He expands on this theory by noting that the word *šnḏt* appears in captions attached to funerary scenes where women (he calls them the *ḫnr*) perform. As the *ḫnr* is associated with temple cults and funerary rites, he predicts that this same group of women performed services for the gods and the dead.[36] This theory differs from that of Edel in that this latter scholar suspects the *šnḏt* to be associated with the goddess Sakhmet. I will revisit this issue below.

As I mentioned above, there has been some debate over the reading of this group of signs, specifically in the tomb of Debehni (see above). In addition to the reading *im3t, ḫnr* is another alternative. Nord mentions that "most authors had restored the group as *ḫnrt*";[37] among them are Fischer[38] and Settgast.[39] The *ḫnr*[40] has traditionally been thought to refer to a "harem"; however, more recently it has been translated as "musical troop."[41] Such musical troupes can be attached to religious institutions, funerary estates, and royal and private households. They were involved in religious ritual and were included in the temple personnel.[42] Gay Robins suggests that musical troupes were associated with goddess cults, for example Bat, Isis, Nekhbet, Bastet and Hathor.[43] This would fall in line with the connection that Edel makes between the women in the tombs of Debehni and Qar, and the cult of Sakhmet; likewise, it would confirm Fischer's assertion that the women of the *šnḏt* perform services for the gods and the dead. In some instances, however — for example, in the tomb of Ptahhotep — the word *ḫnr* is found in conjunction with the *šnḏt*. There may not be any difference between the performers in the tombs of Debehni and Qar, and those labeled as belonging to a *ḫnr* in the tomb of Ptahhotep. The women depicted in the two former tombs belong to a designated group (the Acacia House) and are dancing and singing, which can essentially be linked to the concepts of music and performance; hence, they also can constitute a musical troupe. It has been thought that the tomb of Ptahhotep features the earliest *ḫnr* associated with a temple.[44] If Edel and Fischer are correct, then we have an earlier group of women who dance and sing at the tomb and have an association with the Acacia House (possibly in the cult of Sakhmet or another such goddess) in the tomb of Debehni.

It is now clear that the women who are depicted in the tombs of Debehni and Qar are not mourners — neither professionals nor members of the deceased's family. Additionally, the reference in the tomb of Debehni is to the *šnḏt* and not the *ḫnr*, as has been suggested previously.

There are three additional points that need to be addressed now. First of all, it is no coincidence that the women depicted in the aforementioned tomb scenes are scantily dressed or bare-breasted. Unclothed women are intimately connected with fecundity, fruitfulness and regeneration. The bare breasts may have been meant to stimulate, or symbolize the process of the rebirth of the deceased into the Afterlife.[45] Even though Robin's 1996 chapter pertains to New Kingdom art, her work is useful when looking at earlier examples. Robins notes that in the New Kingdom funerary scenes the unclothed adolescent girls are linked with fertility, birth, and rebirth.[46] There are further examples mentioned below. Interestingly enough, the earliest appearance of the word to be naked is *ḥ3y*.[47] In his 1993 article, Goelet points out that nudity was associated with rebirth. Osiris is called the "naked one" (*ḥ3y*).[48]

Secondly, the style of the hair of the performers of the ritual of *ḥ3i* is repeatedly alluded to in the sources. In the cases of Debehni and Qar the women's hair is cut short, or cropped. This is rather enigmatic since we know that hair and sexuality were connected.[49] I will return to this subject below.

Lastly, the mention of the *mnit wrt* (or just *mnit*) reinforces the meaning of the word *ḥ3i* as meaning to ritually transport the deceased to the Afterlife. The *mnit wrt* personified the Mooring Post to which the deceased was docked once he reached the next world - and was reborn. Now we have a connection between the personification of rebirth and the members of the Acacia House who perform the ritual for transporting the deceased for the express purpose of rebirth.

Sakhmet

To the best of my knowledge, the notion of the Acacia House being synonymous with the cult of Sakhmet in the Old Kingdom is an idea not generally promoted by

[36] Fischer 1960, 189.
[37] Nord 1981, 140, n. 29.
[38] Fischer 1960.
[39] Settgast 1963.
[40] Hannig 2003, 953; Faulkner 1991, 193.
[41] Nord 1981.
[42] Robins 1993, 120, 146.
[43] Robins 1993, 148-149.
[44] Nord 1981, 141.

[45] See Robins 1993, 183-185 for the connection between costume and female sexuality.
[46] Robins 1996, 30-31, 33.
[47] Goelet 1993, 20.
[48] Goelet 1993, 22.
[49] Robins 1996, 30, 33; Manniche 1987, 42.

the scholarly community.[50] Sakhmet is a lioness goddess, the consort of Ptah and mother of Nefertem, the three of whom make up the Memphite triad. Sakhmet can be linked to Lower Egypt by her epithet "mistress of red linen,"[51] and her name means "the powerful one." She is seen as both destructive and beneficial at the same time, and is one of the many forms of the Eye of Re; she features in one version of the "Eye" myth. She is closely associated with the goddess Hathor as the Eye of Re. The Middle Kingdom tomb of the Hathor priestess Senet (TT 60) equates Hathor with Sakhmet.[52] A wall painting illustrates a ritual involving song and dance that was performed to welcome the funeral procession as it approached the tomb. The chorus sang this hymn to Hathor: "Hail to thee, Lady of fragrance, Great Sekhmet, Sovereign Lady...."[53] Likewise, in the later New Kingdom, Hathor is sometimes paired with Sakhmet.[54] Sakhmet's connection with Hathor is significant primarily because many Old Kingdom tombs located in the Memphite necropolis exhibit Hathoric rites. This topic will be discussed below. Furthermore, Sakhmet is recognized as having conceived the king in the Pyramid Texts.[55]

At this point it would be constructive to go through the evidence provided by Edel to establish the relationship between the goddess Sakhmet and the *šndt*. First of all, Edel begins by quoting PT §436, "I am Horus who came forth from the acacia, who came forth from the acacia...."[56] He then comments that the dead king was to be equated with Horus. According to Koemoth, the spell is offering the protection of the acacia tree in order to ensure the life of the deceased in the Hereafter.[57] Edel then mentions a passage from a Ptolemaic mythological text that connects the concept of life and death with the goddess Yusas[58] and the acacia tree (Figure 6):[59]

tkn.f r ꜥt twy šps(yt) n(y)t Ἰw.s-ꜥ3(i).s
m šndt m(w)t pw ꜥnḫ im.s[60]

Er ist genaht jenem herrlichen Raum der Iws-aAs. Mit der Akazie, in der Tod und Leben (beschlossen) ist.[61]

Following this, Edel quotes from CT VI 283, "'I know the name of the mortar in which it was pounded; it is the acacia of Yusas-town north of Souls-of-On.'"[62] Edel continues with CT VI 284, "'I know the name of the bowl in which it is cooked; it is the base (?) of the acacia north of Yus(as)-town and south of Souls-of-On.'" These spells equate the acacia with the town of Yusas. Edel points out that the connection between the holy acacia and Yusas goes back to the Pyramid Texts, where the birth of the king takes place "under the tresses of the goddess of Yusas town, north of On, who ascended from the vertex of Geb" (PT §1210). Here we are presented with another reference to hair being symbolic of rebirth. Edel then notes, *"Die Locken des personifiziert gedachten Baumes (= der Baumgöttin) entsprechen den Zweigen des Baumes."* At this point Edel introduces the goddess Sakhmet as *"Herrin der beiden Akazien"* (*nbt šndty*) and deems these two acacia trees as the same acacia trees near Heliopolis referred to in the two citations quoted above. His source is an epithet of Sakhmet that appears on one of her Eighteenth Dynasty statues in the British Museum (Figure 7).[63] This equation is then strengthened by the fact that the neighboring city of Memphis is considered to be the main cult place of the goddess Sakhmet.[64]

To recapitulate, according to Edel, Sakhmet and the acacia are one and the same, as evidenced by PT §262 where the king is conceived by Sakhmet, and PT §436 where Horus — and thus the king — comes forth from the acacia. Likewise, the idea presented in PT §436 is reiterated in PT §1210 where the king is born under the tresses of the goddess of Yusas-town, which is an allusion to the acacia tree. This theory is then supported by the idea presented in *Urkunden* VI 20-21 where the acacia signifies the life and death force. The acacia tree symbolizes the second birth of the king initiating his life in the Hereafter. This is the extent of Edel's evidence

[50] The reason I say that the concept is not generally promoted by the scholarly community is that in the process of researching this connection I rarely found this point reiterated in the sources. Moreover, I came across an association between the acacia tree and Horus (Wilkinson 1999:91; 2003:168; PT §436). Many scholars have also noted a connection between this tree and various female deities in the Ptolemaic Period (see below).

[51] Wilkinson 2003, 182. The papyrus scepter she is often depicted holding may be another indication of her origin; however, by the time of the New Kingdom most goddesses carry this scepter.

[52] See Parkinson (1991, 81, 85, 87) for information on the correct identity of the owner of the tomb.

[53] Davies 1920, 10-11, 22-25, pls. 3, 23, 23a, b.

[54] Wilkinson 2003, 181.

[55] Wilkinson 2003, 181.

[56] This and all other translations of the Pyramid Texts will be taken from Faulkner 1998.

[57] Koemoth 1994, 175. This furthers my supposition as to the meaning of *ḥ3i*.

[58] Yusas was a Heliopolitan goddess whose name means "she comes who is great"; she acted as a feminine counterpart of the male solar-creator (Atum). Yusas is depicted as anthropomorphic and with a scarab beetle for a head. She was not important in terms of cultic activity or worship (Wilkinson 2003:150).

[59] This passage occurs in a ritual for the temple of Osiris at Abydos, which appears in Papyrus Louvre 3129 (columns B, 39 – E, 42) and British Museum 10252 (columns 13, 1 – 18, 27).

[60] In Schott's note 2 he reconstructs the latter part of the sentence *ꜥs ꜥnḫ pw im.s* and he translates accordingly. Edel follows his translation. I think the translation should end with "it is the dead who live (again) through/in it."

[61] *Urk.* VI 20-21, 15-16.

[62] This and all other translations of the Coffin Texts will be taken from Faulkner 2004.

[63] Budge 1909, 114; Gauthier 1919, 189. The statue is made of black granite and is a colossal figure (6 ft. 8 in.) of a seated Sakhmet. She wears the solar disk and holds the symbol of life in her left hand. Amenhotep III dedicated the statue to the goddess in her character of "Lady of the Two Acacias." It is from Karnak.

[64] Bonnet 1952, 643-644.

supporting his theory that the *šnḏt* is the sanctuary of the goddess Sakhmet. Furthermore, he notes that the Acacia Shrine played a role in the royal funerary ritual and was eventually taken over by the private realm, just as the Butic funeral ceremony was. Edel concludes his argument by stating that the women who appear in the funerary rituals illustrated in the tomb scenes are the women of the harem of Sakhmet and that the Acacia House is the cult place for the shrine of the acacia. Later in the book, when he is explaining the connection between the butchers and the *šnḏt*, he cites evidence from the temple of Edfu that mentions bringing antelope and butchers to pacify Sakhmet.[65] This source provides a connection between the butchering practices and the goddess Sakhmet in the Ptolemaic period. Edel's arguments are largely restricted to the earlier period; however, incorporating later evidence can further clarify the situation. The fact that Sakhmet is associated with funerary butchers (albeit through a later text) and that there are funerary butchers who belong to the *šnḏt* in the Old Kingdom, may tie Sakhmet more closely to the Acacia House in the earlier period. Finally, I came across a Ptolemaic epithet of Sakhmet linking her again to the acacia tree: *"O, Sekhmet, Uraeus qui ouvre l'acacia, souveraine, la Grand."*[66] Edel makes a convincing argument.

Hathor

Another point I would like to discuss is J. Wilson's attempt to link the group of signs in the tomb of Debehni to *nht* (sycamore), and thus to the cult place of Hathor.[67] Wilson immediately notes that this reading is incorrect; however, he was tempted to make the connection for the same reason I mentioned above — Hathoric rites sometimes appear in funerary scenes depicted in Old Kingdom tombs and regularly in Middle Kingdom tombs. Fischer remarks on Wilson's observation and agrees that this transliteration can be excluded for the word in question.[68]

The goddess Hathor may have originated in predynastic or early dynastic times.[69] She appears infrequently in the Pyramid Texts but is attested frequently in later periods. She was popular, and appears in many different contexts. From early times she was a supplier of food and drink for the deceased in the Memphite region. One of her many titles was "Mistress of the West," and she welcomed the deceased to the Afterlife. Likewise, Hathor was the goddess of fertility, song and dance, and joy and happiness. At some point she merged with the cow goddess Mehet-Weret, and her bovine form

protected the king and acted as royal nurse.[70] Indicative of Hathoric ceremonies are dancers or priests who wear or carry *menat*-necklaces,[71] scarves,[72] and who shake sistra.[73] The cult of Hathor was extremely popular by the end of the Old Kingdom.[74] Sometimes the aforementioned emblems make it possible to distinguish a Hathoric rite represented in a tomb scene; also musical performances often invoke Hathor by name or by her epithet "The Golden One."[75] According to Marianne Galvin, Nebtynubkhet, the wife of Kagemni, is recognized as wearing the menat-necklace in an Old Kingdom context.[76] Likewise, Imi, a Priestess of Hathor, also wears a menat-necklace in the Sixth Dynasty tomb of Ihy at Thebes (TT 186).[77] In the Fifth Dynasty tomb of Iy-Mery at Giza there are two registers of dancers and singers performing before a seated statue of the deceased.[78] The inscription between the first pair of male dancers reads: *mk ṯrf it(ỉ)t nbw*, "Behold the *ṯrf*-dance bringing the Golden One."[79] Another example of a Hathoric dance occurs in chamber B3 of the Sixth Dynasty mastaba of Mereruka at Sakkara. The dance scene belongs to Wa'tetkhethor, the wife of Mereruka, and features the caption: *mk it(ỉ)t nbw*. Nord translates this passage as "behold (the dance?): 'bringing the Golden One'";[80] however, Van Lepp prefers "look, the movement is gold."[81] I tend to agree with the former translation because in the Middle Kingdom tomb of Senet one sees a similar scene with a similar caption that specifically refers to a goddess. This tomb makes the meaning very clear in that the captions read: *wn ʽȝwy pt pr(ỉ) nṯr, mk nbw iỉ.t(ỉ)*, "The doors of heaven open and the god comes forth; The gold goddess has come."[82] Likewise, the women in the tomb of Senet wear the heavy disks in their hair, which are indicative of Hathoric dancers.[83] Additionally, the tomb of Idu features a celebration that involves dancers of Hathor.[84]

---

[65] Edel 1970, 38; Edfu IV, 342.

[66] Germond 1981, 81 (*Edfu* VI, 269, 3; *Edfu* I, 548, 12; *Dendera* VII, 107, 3; *Kom Ombo* II, no. 985). Koemoth 1994, 78.

[67] J. Wilson 1944, 212.

[68] Fischer 1960, n. 2.

[69] According to Susan Tower Hollis the earliest reference to the goddess Hathor dates to the Second Dynasty (Brooklyn).

[70] Wilkinson 2003, 140-141.

[71] The *menat* is a heavy necklace that hangs low on the chest, a ritual object that makes its first appearance toward the end of the Old Kingdom. The main part of the necklace consists of numerous strands of tiny beads that are bunched together and suspended from a chain of larger beads at the other end of which there are two counterweights (Galvin 1981, 205-206).

[72] Galvin 1981, 228-231.

[73] Blackman 1915, 24 and plates XXXII, 3; XXXV, 2. See also Blackman 1914, 23, pl. II.

[74] Galvin 1981, 72.

[75] Nord lists six Old Kingdom examples (1981, 141, n. 39): Iymery, Nebkauhor, Idu, Kagemni, Mereruka, Pepiankh-Heryib.

[76] Galvin 1981, 212.

[77] Galvin 1981, 213.

[78] *LD* II, 52. Weeks 1994, 44 and folding plate 35.

[79] Nord 1981, 141-142, n. 41.

[80] Nord 1981, 142.

[81] Van Lepp 1987, 29.

[82] Davies and Gardiner 1920, 22.

[83] Davies and Gardiner 1920, plate XXIII.

[84] Simpson 1976, 25. There is no parallel scene in the tomb of Qar. Also, the nature of this scene is different from the ones with which I am concerned. This scene does not occur as part of the funeral procession near the tomb.

The *ḫnr* associated with the cult of Hathor was involved in the funerary rites in the cemetery or in the funeral procession. Gay Robins suggests that the women who appear in tomb scenes bare-breasted, or scantily clad may have been symbolic of fertility, birth and rebirth.[85] For example, in the Twelfth Dynasty tomb chapel of Senbi's son Ukhhotep at Meir one can see that the funerary dance was performed in the name of Hathor in order to resurrect the deceased and prolong life in the Hereafter.[86] In addition, the Middle Kingdom tomb of Senet, mentioned above, contains a wall painting illustrating a ritual with song and dance performed to welcome the funeral cortege to the cemetery. The chorus sings a hymn to the goddess Hathor. There are numerous other allusions to the cult of Hathor dating to the Middle and New Kingdoms.[87]

Hathor can also be linked to the Acacia, as she bears the epithet "Lady of the Acacia."[88] In his 1965 article, Richard Parker writes about two Demotic papyri from Deir el-Ballas, where several references to Hathor with the epithet *nbt šn* appear. He concludes that this title should be read as *nbt šnt* and translated "Lady of the Acacia." Parker cites the statue of Hornefer from the Museum of Fine Arts in Lausanne (no. Eg. 7), which bears the title, *"le prophète de Hathor, dame de l'Acacia,"*[89] and the bronze situla which bears the title, *"prophète de Hathor, dame du domaine de l'Acacia, prophète de Harsomtous, seigneur (du domaine) de l'Acacia,"*[90] as examples of hieroglyphic texts where similar epithets occur.[91] Parker also states that *šnt* is located in the region from Dendera on the north to Qus on the south.[92]

As is apparent, a good case can be made for associating the goddess Hathor with the Acacia House. However, the scenes we are concerned with are strictly devoid of all Hathoric regalia and accoutrements.

Neith

There is also an argument to be made for the acacia tree's connection to the goddess Neith. Neith is associated with weaponry (hunting and warfare) through her names of "mistress of the bow" and "ruler of arrows." She is also a mother goddess, namely the mother of the god Sobek, and is sometimes shown in a nursing motif. Neith can also be a funerary goddess, as she watches over the deceased Osiris, along with Isis, Nephthys and Selket.[93] Additionally, Neith was the inventor of weaving and was further associated with the funeral procedure by providing the bandages and shrouds for the mummy.[94] Nathalie Baum points out that in one of Taharka's reliefs at Karnak, the goddess Neith bends her bow near the burial mound of Osiris on which an acacia tree grows at Djeme (the small temple at Medinet Habu).[95] As well, there is a hieratic papyrus from Tebtunis that mentions the Acacia Temple of Neith in the Fayum region. This temple was located in the Crocodilopolite nome on the edge of the lake *bddw-kꜣ*, close to the sanctuary of Sobek.[96] This area had Tamarisk groves that apparently were used to make bows and arrows for this goddess. The cult of Neith at the Acacia shrine included rites aimed at protecting the king and guaranteeing his perpetual power.[97] The association between Neith and the acacia was first made in the Saite period.[98]

There are also some texts at Edfu which are of interest.[99] Here the acacia nilotica stands at the *st-wnp* "the place of stabbing,"[100] the toponym designating Edfu as the site where Horus stabs his enemy, Seth. The scenes in the Chapel of the Throne Room of Re at Edfu show that the acacia nilotica is tied to the extermination of harmful elements in Egypt, namely the massacre of the king's and Osiris' adversaries.[101] The acacia in the royal funerary rites constitutes a hiding place for the young god pursued by Seth. This tree was closely tied to Horus in his taking revenge for the death of his father, and his inheriting the throne. The texts at Edfu invoke the myth of Horus exclusively; here Horus is armed with his harpoon in pursuit of Seth and his acolytes who infest Egypt in the form of crocodiles and hippos. His aim is to establish his absolute mastery over Egypt. Baum suggests a play on words, in that *šnḏt* sounded like *šnṯyw* "enemies."[102]

Baum associates the acacia nilotica with maternal goddesses who are equipped with a savagery used to destroy their enemies; she notes that documents testify to the existence of a link between the acacia and divinities known for spreading terror.[103] This corresponds to the connection between the acacia and

[85] Robins 1996, 31.
[86] Blackman 1915, 24.
[87] Galvin 1981.
[88] Parker 1965, 151.
[89] Wild 1954, 197-198.
[90] De Meulenaere 1959, 247-248.
[91] Parker 1965, 151. See also Parker 1963, 114-115; 1964, 92.
[92] In her book *Arbres et arbustes de l'Égypte ancienne* Nathalie Baum states that the twentieth nome (Heracleopolis) in Upper Egypt has the *šnḏt* for its sacred tree, as noted in the texts at Edfu. However, the *šnḏt* is listed as a sacred tree for almost every Egyptian nome (Baum 1988, 187; 305-6; P. Wilson 1997, 1024-1025; Brugsch 1879, 788-89).
[93] PT §606.
[94] Wilkinson 2003, 156-159.
[95] Parker, Leclant and Goyon 1979, pl. 25, 10.
[96] Baum 1988, 319, 331.
[97] Baum 1988, 331.
[98] El-Sayed 1975, 28-29.
[99] See also Yoyotte 1961, 100.
[100] *wnp* appears only in Greek sources (P. Wilson 1997, 234).
[101] Baum 1988, 318.
[102] P. Wilson 1997, 1025.
[103] Baum 1988, 331.

Neith as a war goddess.[104] On the other hand, she suggests that the relationship between the acacia and Isis and Nephthys may be one of a maternal nature and have to do with Isis aiding her son Horus against Seth.[105]

As noted above, the connection between the goddess Neith and the acacia tree was not established until the Saite Period.[106] Since the Saite era is known to have had archaizing tendencies, it is possible that the religious trends of that time were harking back to developments of the Old Kingdom. In any case, a strong connection between Neith and the *šnḏt* in the Old Kingdom cannot be confirmed from the available sources.

To conclude this line of research, there are a number of gods and goddesses who have had some connection to the acacia tree during the Pharaonic period. Serious arguments can be made to support a connection between the Acacia House and three separate goddesses: Sakhmet, Hathor and Neith. There are many similarities between Sakhmet and Hathor in that both goddesses bear the title "Mistress of Red Linen," both are the Eye of Re, and both have a connection to the lioness. There is no doubt that Hathoric rites took place during the Old Kingdom, as evidenced by the numerous sources cited above. However, these sources show clear indications that the cult of Hathor is involved, namely, through the presence of the *menat*-necklace, the sistrum, or the scarf. Moreover, the majority of these scenes show Hathoric rituals taking place in front of the statue of the deceased, and not in front of the tomb or the embalming workshop. These scenes also often contain representations of acrobats, musicians and people playing games. None of these Hathoric emblems is present in the relevant scenes in the tombs of Debehni and Qar. Therefore, I believe these facts rule out the possibility that the *šnḏt* is necessarily connected with Hathor, at least in these Old Kingdom contexts.
Through Edel's discussion on Sakhmet and the Acacia House he demonstrates the rejuvenating qualities of the acacia tree and its association with life and death. Accordingly, the Pyramid Texts (§§436, 1210) recount that Horus is born from the acacia tree. Coffin Text Spell 755 indicates that the one who comes from the acacia tree of the double lion prevents the putrefaction of Horus, who is in the midst of his corruption. Horus embodies the new life of Osiris, in that the life cycle is continuous.[107] The fact is, it is not the goddess herself who is important, but the symbolism of the acacia tree which is related to the concept of rebirth, and thus the ritual of *ḥ3i*.

[104] Baum 1988, 331. This could also be true for the goddess Sakhmet, especially in her role in the *Deliverance of Mankind from Destruction* (Pritchard 1958, 3-5)
[105] Baum 1988, 318. Nephthys is the traditional companion of Isis.
[106] El-Sayed 1982, 28-29.
[107] Koemoth 1994, 177.

The Ptolemaic sources are much clearer about the associations of the acacia tree. In fact, numerous scholars have been able to demonstrate the religious ideas of the time, Baum, el-Sayed, and Koemoth being but a few. It is apparent in the Ptolemaic Period that the acacia tree is related to the myth of Osiris.[108] It is very likely that this conforms to an association that existed much earlier in the Pharaonic Period, perhaps as early as the Old Kingdom. As Baum points out, there is an acacia tree on the burial mound of Osiris in one of Taharka's reliefs at Karnak. Additionally, the cult of Neith at the Acacia focused on the protection of the king and his everlasting power, which corresponds to the acacia's significance at Edfu where it represents the annihilation of Osiris' enemies. Likewise, in the first Osirian Chapel at Dendera, Sokar-Osiris is depicted as lying in a tree within his coffin.[109] Koemoth interprets this scene to mean that the mummy symbolically lies at the heart of the tree. An acacia tree was regularly depicted on top of the burial mound of Osiris, and was protected by a lioness. A feline, lioness, cheetah, or cat was capable of discouraging the fiercest of rebels.[110] These were the defenders of Osiris and the killers of Apophis, and thus guardians of his tomb.[111] This explains the apparent connection between the acacia tree and the goddess Sakhmet, among others.

There are three sources from the Roman period that testify to the connection between Osiris and the acacia tree.[112] Here Osiris is *"Unique-dans-l'acacia."*[113] Koemoth suggests that the tree is Osiris' earthly icon, *"Sans doute Osiris est-il 'Unique-dans-l'acacia' en ce sens que le dieu 'Unique' est present à la fois dans la sphere céleste par son ba, sur terre par l'icône de l'arbre, et enfin dans la Douat, où repose son cadaver...l'arbre y constitue une icône terrestre d'Osiris."*[114] The new growth of the acacia would symbolize prosperity for the new king and thus for the entire country.[115] One of the more interesting illustrations that pertain to this study occurs among the reliefs of the Temple of Hibis in Kharga Oasis where a man stands on the funerary mound of Osiris with his arms in the A 28 pose.[116] This scene is clearly an illustration of Osiris' revivification. This depiction confirms the connection between the A 28 gesture and the concept of rebirth (see Chapter Seven).

As has been noted above, the *šnḏt* appears to refer to the name of an institution, or to the title of an

[108] Koemoth 1994, 67-74; 78-79; 82-86; 168-183; 292-296.
[109] Koemoth 1994, fig. 22.
[110] Koemoth 1994, 294.
[111] Koemoth 1994, 85.
[112] Koemoth 1994, 171. pLeiden T 32, V°, V, 17; Mariette, Dend., IV, pl. 75, col. 38; Goyon, *Dieux-gardiens*, I, 291).
[113] Koemoth 1994, 171.
[114] Koemoth 1994, 173.
[115] Koemoth 1994, 174.
[116] See Pinch 2002, figure 33.

organization that resides at the institution referred to by this designation. The symbolism of the acacia tree was inherent in the term, and thus emblematically revealed the purpose of the group that functioned under the auspices of the acacia. Throughout the section dedicated to the Acacia House the significance of the acacia tree has been discussed — the life and death force that renews and resurrects.[117]

Axis Mundi

An intriguing concept was developed by Mircea Eliade early last century that focused on the idea of a sacred mountain, tree, or monumental building that stood at the "center of the world" in early civilizations.[118] Eliade maintains that early people imagined that this was a representation of that which was sacred,[119] and was considered to be the meeting point of heaven, earth, and hell. In this case, I am primarily concerned with the concept of the tree acting in this capacity, namely, the acacia tree. We can find parallels for this in ancient Egypt. Every temple was regarded as a meeting point between this world and the world of the gods, as divine temples were in fact considered to be the home of a particular deity. We may find another similar phenomenon in one of the functions of the pyramids. We know from their names that they were places of transformation.[120] Lehner calls these monuments, "the union of heaven and earth"[121] and speaks of them as functioning as "cosmic engines."[122] The acacia tree may therefore function as the axis point where passage from one cosmic region to another could occur. This was a popular idea in both Mesopotamia[123] and Syro-Palestine,[124] and therefore it is not surprising to find the same concept prevalent in ancient Egypt. Once the acacia tree is connected with the cult of Osiris we can include a third realm of existence, that of the underworld, or the realm where Osiris resides. The acacia would then have acted as the common center where communication between the world of the gods, the world of the living, and the underworld took place.[125] The branches reached upward, the trunk stood on the ground, and the roots penetrated the earth. Although Trigger does not believe that this notion existed in ancient Egypt;[126] however, one can make an argument supporting its existence.

Hetepherakhti

The next Old Kingdom private source is the tomb of Hetepherakhti.[127] In this example there are four women performing the rite of *ḥ3i* in front of two oxen who pull a statue of the deceased toward the tomb (Figure 8). The caption above the women reads: *ḥ3(i)t*. Unfortunately, there are no other inscriptions to indicate what is taking place; however, there are scenes in other tombs (in addition to Debehni and Qar) that can provide some parallels. The three women who hold the A 28 pose are topless and wear short kilts with a tie around the waist. The fourth woman who is behind them is fully clothed and wears a long dress with two straps. All four women have short hair, similar to the women in the tombs of Debehni and Qar.

Scenes featuring the dragging of the statue of the deceased first appear at Giza at the end of the Fourth Dynasty in the tomb of Meresankh III.[128] According to Harpur, "most examples are depicted in various Fifth Dynasty chapel types at Sakkara, while rather similar scenes of men hauling shrines on sledges are attested in later Sixth Dynasty provincial tombs in Middle Egypt."[129] It was after the *Saisfahrt* that the dragging to the tomb of the statue and naos, or the coffin, took place (*Sargschlittenzug*).[130] This is the most common scene depicted in the Old Kingdom funeral representations,[131] and it is the scene I am concerned with here. It has been suggested that the Egyptians thought the mummy to be impure and preferred to represent a statue of the deceased In its place.[132] Bolshakov is apprehensive about this theory and proposes an alternative interpretation. He notes that the general theme of tomb decoration is joyful, and includes events that were to be repeated in the Afterlife. He does acknowledge that funeral scenes are different in that no one wishes to repeat death; however, the purpose of this type of scene is to establish that the deceased has indeed passed away and was taken care of properly. He further suggests that inaccurately depicting an event was not an Egyptian custom, and that an actual statue of the deceased was buried with the corpse, as evidenced by an inscription found in the tomb of Debehni: [...] *ir.w n.f m wˁb.t r is [šm]s [twt in] is.t n.t pr-[mr]ḥ[.t]*, "[Bringing the statue] which was made for him in the *wˁbt* to the tomb. [Esc]orting [the statue by] the crew of the house

[117] Widengren discusses the connections between the king and the tree of life in his 1951 article. He notes that the king is the custodian of the tree of life (15) in that it was planted in a temple grove and the king would have had to take care of it. The revivification of the tree meant the revivification of the dying god. The acacia tree in Egypt is the place of purification which is synonymous with rejuvenation. Widengren also points to the Epic of Gilgamesh for a reference to a piece of the tree being used to call the dead to life (21).
[118] Eliade 1954, 12 ff.
[119] Trigger 2003, 445-446.
[120] Lehner 1997, 17.
[121] Lehner 1997, 9.
[122] Lehner, 1997, 20.
[123] Trigger 2003. 445.
[124] Eliade 1954, 13.
[125] See Trigger 2003, 447 for concept.
[126] Trigger 2003, 445.
[127] Mohr 1943, 39; Eaton-Krauss 1984, 65, n. 319.
[128] Harpur 1987, 84.
[129] Harpur 1987, 84; See also Bolshakov (1991, 45).
[130] Bolshakov 1991, 40.
[131] Bolshakov 1991, 40.
[132] Bolshakov 1991, 42; Settgast 1963, 18, 20, 23.

of *mrḥ.t*."[133] Bolshakov states that some of the statues were put into the tomb while the owner was still alive and others were made to be a part of the procession.[134] He concludes: "In representations of funerals statues were not stipulated substitutes of corpses, they made part of the funeral procession in fact, so that the reproduction of a statue and not of a mummy did not run contrary to reality, the emphasis was just made on the aspect of reality that best conformed to the system of tomb decoration."[135]

In some Old Kingdom funerary scenes women or men walk with upraised arms in the A 28 gesture and accompany the dragging of the statue or coffin. Dragging scenes without people in the A 28 pose are far more common than dragging scenes with people in the A 28 pose. Women hold this pose in the earlier examples; and beginning in the Middle Kingdom men assume this posture, although women still participate in the ritual as well. Table 5 lists some of the parallels for the scene depicted in the tomb of Hetepherakhti.[136]

The closest contemporary parallels appear in the Fifth Dynasty tomb of the vizier Ptahhotep at Sakkara (Figures 5 and 9) and in a tomb at Barnûgi (Figure 10). With regard to the former example, the singing and dancing by the *ḫnr* of the *šnḏt* occur in the same register as the oxen drawing the coffin. These women precede the oxen just as in the tomb of Hetepherakhti. There are four women who have their arms in the A 28 pose, and two clapping women with a priest of Sokar following them. Trailing the priest is another woman, and one can see the head of an ox jutting out from a break in the scene. This scene in the tomb of Ptahhotep links the tombs of Debehni and Qar and the tomb of Hetepherakhti, in that the *šnḏt*-women who perform the ritual in the tombs of Debehni and Qar also function in the procession that leads the coffin or statue in the tomb scene of Ptahhotep. In fact, the tomb of Ptahhotep may indicate that the tomb of Hetepherakhti also depicts the *šnḏt*-women, but without a label.

The Barnûgi tomb scene is similar (Figure 10). The main contrast is with the behavior of the women in the A 28 pose; unlike the aforementioned scenes, these women in the Barnûgi tomb appear more sedate and there are no clappers in this scene. The procession consists of the following participants: a person holding an object,[137] two women with their arms in the A 28 pose, a man carrying a staff/standard, two oxen and four men dragging the coffin, a woman with her arms in the A 28 pose, and the sledge carrying the bier which is flanked by a man at the foot and a woman with her arms in the A 28 pose at the head.

There are similar scenes that date to the Middle and New Kingdoms that deserve some attention. Among the preserved scenes are the following eight examples: In the Twelfth Dynasty tomb of Senet there are six people, three men and three women, who walk with their arms in the A 28 pose in her funeral procession. These people precede the dragging of the bier on the sledge on the west bank after the ceremonial rites on the water (Figure 11).[138] The main difference between this and the scene in the tomb of Hetepherakhti is that it is the coffin that is being hauled instead of the statue. This reflects a change that occurred in the latter part of the Old Kingdom.[139] While the women in the tomb of Hetepherakhti are not labeled, the six individuals walking in the A 28 pose in the tomb of Senet represent the populations of five centers of worship: Sais,[140] Dep, Pe, Unu (Hermopolis Parva)[141] and Hutweru.[142] Four of these people appear again once the cortege has reached the cemetery, where they hold the rope that the oxen are using to drag the coffin. In this latter scene the men do not hold their arms in the A 28 pose. The caption reads: "To the west, to the west, the place where thy hope lies. [Thou art drawn to the place which] thou hast chosen (?) by young oxen. The inhabitants of Pe, of Dep, of Busiris, of Unu and of Hutweru say, 'Come in peace to the west...For thou hast not come dead. Thou hast come

---

133 Bolshakov 1991, 45-46; Eaton-Krauss 1984, 143, pl. IX; Hassan 1943, fig. 122. This section is not reproduced by Lepsius in *LD*.

134 Bolshakov 1991, 46.

135 Bolshakov (1991, 48) lists ten Old Kingdom examples of the *Sargschlittenzug*, which represents the transport of the statue to the tomb. He lists eleven examples of the *Sargschlittenzug*; however, on page 40 he lists only ten examples. The first table includes the additional tomb of Debehni. Likewise, the author specifically states that the naos with statue or coffin is hauled by oxen; however, in the tombs of Aba and Djau there are no oxen, and the scene in the tomb of Debehni is so fragmentary that I cannot see any oxen associated with the hauling of a statue there either (1991, 36).

136 There are oxen and men dragging something in the tomb of Ptahhotep II, but the scene is broken (Junker 1940, 4, Abb. 3). For this reason it is not included in the chart.

137 It is difficult to tell whether this person is a man or a woman from the drawing I have available (Eaton-Krauss 1984, plate ix).

138 Davies and Gardiner 1920, plate XIX. Davies suggests that the front group of six provides for a change of teams (1920, 20). I am suspicious of this conclusion primarily because I do not think that the women would be pulling the sledge in dresses, or at all for that matter. Supposedly the cortege is sailing downstream to Abydos. Davies does say that there is no sequence of acts depicted in these scenes (1920, 21). Likewise, he states that the group shouts, "The god comes. Prostrate (yourselves)." This phrase does not appear in the figure.

139 Bolshakov 1991, 45.

140 Gardiner translates this group of signs as "Siut," but it seems to be "Sais" (see Faulkner 1991, 209).

141 Hannig 1997, 1325.

142 Davies notes that participation of the laity in the cult ritual is rare. However, the people, or Souls, of Pe and/or Dep regularly appear as participants in the funerary procession. Furthermore, there are many contrasting opinions as to who these people were (see below). Men with similar captions also occur in the Eighteenth Dynasty tomb of Ramose. They represent the localities of Pe and Dep, Hermopolis Parva, Sais, and Hutweru (Hannig 1997, 1364). The latter place is still unidentified (Hodel-Hoenes 2000, 54). This designation seems to refer to a town in the Western Delta according to Griffiths, and he notes its appearance after Dep in PT 189a, in a series of cultic allusions (Griffiths 1958, 119). Similar designations occur in TT 17 and 24 (Griffiths 1958, 118).

alive. Seat thyself on the throne of the living and control the charges which thou hast laid on the living.'"[143] This latter scene is comparable to the selection of scenes listed in the chart below. The participants in both scenes appear to belong to the same group. The inscription claims that the deceased has now been rejuvenated and is arriving alive, ready to reside in the Hereafter. The people who hold their arms in the A 28 pose are performing, or symbolizing, the revivification rite of *ḥꜣi* (see below for Souls of Pe).

Another Middle Kingdom tomb that labels the people who drag the coffin on the bier as the inhabitants of these sacred localities is tomb no. 1 from el-Bersha, belonging to Djehutynakht (Figure 12).[144] Fragment no. 8 (from original publication) depicts a sledge drawn by at least six men. One man following them carries an animal haunch and another carries a scroll. There is a caption above the six that reads: "The people of Pe, the people of Dep, the people of Hermopolis [Parva], the people of Sais,[145] the people of [Hutweru] ..., the children of the king, the household of the king, the..., the royal friends."[146] These men do not have their arms in the A 28 gesture.

A similar dragging scene also occurs in the Eighteenth Dynasty tomb of Amenemhet (TT 82).[147] Here two men hold the A 28 pose while they follow the man who drives two red oxen that draw the bier and coffin (Figures 13 and 14). There are six men who walk behind them in two groups of three with their hands on the rope. The caption between the two groups of the men pulling reads: "All the patricians and all the common folk are dragging."[148] It is clear from the inscriptions that the procession is on its way to the tomb. Gardiner classifies all eight of these men as mourners who belong to the public.[149] It may be that the inscription is referring only to the men who actually drag the coffin. These men are not labeled as coming from the sacred Delta cities mentioned above. In the register above the aforementioned scene, the men representing the various Delta cities appear: the people of Pe, Dep, Hermopolis Parva, Tell el-Balamun,[150] Sais and Hutweru.[151] They appear to be pulling the canopic chest. All of the men in these two scenes look alike. Upon the arrival at the tomb the *mww* dancers perform, accompanied by the caption: "Dancing to him by the people of Pe,"[152] and below that "the dance of the *mww*"[153] (Figure 15).

In the New Kingdom tomb of Paheri at Elkab, on the north end of the west wall, the owner's funeral rites are depicted (Figure 16).[154] In the top register there are two oxen dragging the coffin on a bier. In between the coffin and the oxen there are nine men walking. The first man drives the oxen, the next three men have their arms upraised in the A 28 pose (Tylor and Griffith suggest they are chanting[?]),[155] and five men follow. Four of these men have their hands on the rope, and one is burning incense. Between these men and the *ḏryt* directly preceding the bier (not represented in Figure 16), there is a patch indicating an erasure. The erased figure is undoubtedly the priest of Sokar who is represented in other examples of the dragging scene. The caption over the entire scene reads: "Making a good burial for the prince Paheri, conveying the Prince Paheri justified to his chamber of the necropolis, in peace, in peace before the great god. Proceeding in peace to the horizon, to the Field of Reeds, to the [Duat in order to lead (the procession) to the] place where [this] prince Paheri [is]."[156] The individual players are not labeled.

A comparable scene appears in the tomb of Rekhmire (TT 100).[157] In the passage, on the western half of the south wall, in the bottom register, oxen lead a procession toward the goddess of the West. The oxen driver has one arm in the A 28 pose, which is common,[158] followed by nine men in three groups of three who have both arms raised in the A 28 gesture.[159] Six more men follow with their hands on the rope, then comes a man burning incense and sprinkling milk.[160] He is followed by another man, a priest of Sokar, a *ḏryt*, and then finally the bier carrying the coffin of the deceased. The placement of the men who have their arms upraised is the same as in all of the previously cited examples (except for the tomb of Senet, TT 60). The caption over the first man with one hand in the air who is driving the oxen reads, *rmṯw ḏt* "the people of the funerary estate."[161] The captions over the men in the A 28 pose read: *pꜥt nbt, rḫyt nbt*, "all the patricians, all the

[143] Davies and Gardiner 1920, 21. Cf. PT §§134 and 833.
[144] Griffith and Newberry 1890, 20, pl. IX.
[145] For the hieratic form of this sign see Goedicke 1988, 16 (G 39/ 216: Heqanachte, Reisner).
[146] Griffith and Newberry 1890, 20, n. 1. The text is written retrograde.
[147] Davies and Gardiner 1915, pl. XI.
[148] Davies and Gardiner 1915, 49, pl. XII.
[149] Davies and Gardiner 1915, 49.
[150] Hannig 1997, 1332.
[151] Davies and Gardiner 1915, 50, pl. XI.
[152] Davies and Gardiner 1915, 51, pl. XI.
[153] Davies and Gardiner 1915, 51, pl. XI. In this tomb the people of Pe do the *mww* dance.
[154] Tylor and Griffith 1894, 19-22, pl. V.
[155] Tylor and Griffith 1894, 19.
[156] Tylor and Griffith 1894, 20.
[157] Davies 1943, pl. XCII.
[158] According to R. Wilkinson, sometimes one hand may be used to perform this gesture if the other is engaged in holding an object (1999, 206).
[159] The *psḏw smrw* or "nine companions" (Hodel-Hoenes 2000, 164). In *PM* I.I there is a list of all the scenes in the Theban Necropolis that include the nine friends (*PM* I.I, 472).
[160] See below for more information on the importance of milk.
[161] Settgast 1963, 35; *"Leute seiner Totenstiftung."*

common folk."[162] This is reminiscent of the caption presented in the tomb of Amenemhet (TT 82) above.

The New Kingdom tomb of Neferhotep (TT 49) offers another example of this scene.[163] On the south side of the east wall, in the top register, the transport of the corpse to the tomb is depicted. Following the tekenu, the lector reads from a papyrus while the man who precedes the oxen sprinkles milk. Next, the representatives of the holy cities draw the oxen.[164] These four men have long hair and wear fillets around their foreheads, and look different from the illustrations of draggers in the other scenes. These same men are identified as four of the Nine Friends in Porter and Moss.[165] They have their hands on the rope; however, the man who drives the oxen has his left arm raised in the A 28 gesture and the right hand holds the whip.[166] A parallel gesture has already been noted in the tomb of Rekhmire. The priest of Sokar is also present. Davies does not mention any captions for these scenes, and the published plates provide no legends.

An analogous scene also occurs on the west side of the south wall in the tomb of Amenmose (TT 112).[167] Since the scene is fragmentary it is impossible to see what exactly is being dragged. However, one can see that three oxen are pulling something, probably the coffin, and between this item and the oxen there is the driver, six men walking with their arms in the A 28 pose, six other men with their hands on the rope, a man burning incense and sprinkling water, and another man — whose image barely survives — who may be the priest of Sokar. There is no inscription presented in the publication.[168]

Yet another example of the dragging scene is to be found in TT 54, the tomb of Hui and Kel.[169] Four men, identified as *rmṯw P*, are dragging a statue of Anubis. In front of them is a group of female mourners, three of whom hold the A 28 pose. This is analogous to the Old Kingdom examples from the tombs of Hetepherakhti, Ptahhotep, and the tomb at Barnûgi only in the sense that the women execute the A 28 pose.[170]

[162] See below for discussion of the two designations.
[163] Davies 1973, 42 and pl. XX.
[164] Davies 1973, 42. There are no captions available to confirm this designation.
[165] *PM* I.I, 472.
[166] See also the tomb of Horemheb (TT 78).
[167] Davies and Davies 1933, pl. XXXVIII.
[168] There may have been painted inscriptions originally but at the time of entry by this author there was no trace of any inscription.
[169] Polz 1997, Tafel 17.
[170] By the New Kingdom the A 28 pose can be found in mourning contexts (see Chapter Four). It was probably this type of scene that provided the transition from the A 28 pose appearing in the dragging scene to it appearing as a mourning gesture.

The aforementioned tomb scenes do not comprise the entire compendium of dragging scenes, but instead provide some parallels to show the scene's longevity and consistency in the Egyptian repertoire of tomb decoration. They also demonstrate the regular inclusion of the A 28 pose in the dragging scene; this and the accompanying inscriptions suggest that the deceased is arriving at the tomb "alive." The A 28 gesture is symbolic of the rebirth of the deceased. The three designations given to the draggers, even if they do not hold the A 28 pose, are: the inhabitants of the sacred Delta localities, all the patricians and all the common folk (see below), and the people of the funerary estate.

Inhabitants of the Sacred Delta Localities

There are differing ideas concerning the identification of the People — or Souls — of Pe.[171] Often this discussion involves the *mww* dancers; for example, in Brunner-Traut's 1937 discussion of the *mww* dancers she associates the People of Pe with her third variety of *mww*, those who dance in pairs and face one another.[172] Reeder notes that the People of Pe are doing the dance of the *mww*, but are not *mww* themselves. This may be confirmed by the fact that in these instances the dancers do not wear the traditional *mww* headdress.[173]

In his 1940 study Junker relates the dance of the *mww* to the Butic burial and illustrates that the funerary voyage originally went to Sais, Tell el-Balamun and Hermopolis Parva,[174] and then back to Buto. Junker states that the *mww* dancers represent the dead kings of Buto, and he associates them with the Souls of Pe.[175] He uses Pyramid Text §1005 to corroborate his theory, which states that the Souls of Pe clap their hands and dance (this being indicative of the actions performed by the female participants in the Old Kingdom tomb scenes mentioned above).

Frankfort equates the Souls of Pe and Nekhen with the Followers of Horus.[176] He remarks that the title "Followers of Horus" refers to the kings of the past, but also that every Egyptian king could be considered a follower of Horus in that he was a worshipper of the god. However, Frankfort clearly notes that the term does not necessarily refer to historical kings, only that the deceased king became a transfigured spirit and merged with a "spiritual force which had supported the living ruler and descendant on the throne of Horus since time immemorial."[177]

[171] For an overview of the differing opinions regarding the Souls of Pe and Nekhen, see Žabkar 1968, 16-17.
[172] Brunner-Traut 1937, 43.
[173] Reeder 1995, 77.
[174] Junker 1940 reads "Heliopolis," followed by Griffiths 1980.
[175] Junker 1940, 23.
[176] Frankfort 1948, 90-91. See also J. Wilson 1955, 236.
[177] Frankfort 1948, 91.

Gardiner calls our attention to a Roman document, which he believes to have roots in the Fourth Dynasty, containing two entries that read, "Souls of Pe, Followers of Horus as Kings of Lower Egypt," and "Souls of Nekhen, Followers of Horus as Kings of Upper Egypt."[178] In his opinion, these Souls are indeed the royal ancestors.

Altenmüller does not believe that the Souls of Pe should be equated with the *mww*;[179] and he shows that the *mww* dancers were divine ferrymen for the deceased,[180] indicating that they helped the deceased cross over to the Other Side.[181]

In his discussion on the dance of the *mww*, Reeder suggests that the World Beyond is based on the geography of the Nile Delta, and therefore when the deceased enters the Hereafter, the People of Pe and Dep logically line the watercourse and take positions in the funeral cortege. They greet the deceased on his voyage to these sacred localities. He further suggests that "what is depicted in the tomb scenes is either actually transpiring in the Next World, or the real-life participants in the funeral rites symbolically represent the people of Pe, their actions in this world magically ensuring that those same actions will take place in the Hereafter."[182] With Reeder's suggestion being the most likely, it can be assumed that the people of Pe, or those who represent the people of Pe in the funeral service, are encouraging the deceased to enter the Next World and are welcoming him there. Reeder's theory accounts for why it is the people of the sacred localities who perform the rite of *ḥꜣi* (the A 28 pose being symbolic of this rebirth).

To conclude, the scene illustrated in the tomb of Hetepherakhti is rare in the Old Kingdom, with parallel scenes appearing in the tomb of Ptahhotep and the Barnûgi tomb. It is likely that the women who appear in Hetepherakhti's dragging scene are affiliated with the *šnḏt* (Acacia House). Through the scenes in the tombs of Debehni, Qar, and Ptahhotep one can see that the women of the Acacia House perform the ritual of *ḥꜣi* and appear in the dragging scene. However, in the Middle Kingdom, a new development occurs: the Souls of Pe — or the people of the sacred Delta localities (or their representatives on earth) — assume the same A 28 pose and walk in the funerary procession in the same manner as the women in the tomb of Hetepherakhti. Their role in the Pyramid Texts confirms that they summon and/or welcome the deceased to the Afterlife. PT §§863b, 1366a, 1947, 2013, and 2239 demonstrate that there is dancing during this joyful event. This provides another parallel for the women illustrated in the Old Kingdom tomb scenes. Likewise, the People of Pe are shown dancing at the tomb in TT 82.[183] In the New Kingdom, the patricians and common folk appear in this position, for example, in the tombs of Amenemhet and Rekhmire. What we may be seeing are attendants at the funeral acting as representatives of the People of Pe – as they are identified as such —according to Reeder's theory. In the tomb of Hui and Kel there is a harkening back to the Middle Kingdom trend of representing the draggers as the People of Pe. Again, it is probable that the *pꜥt* and *rḫyt nbt* were the earthly representatives of the Souls, or People, of Pe during the funeral drama. The Souls of Pe and the common folk were complementary — one group is mythological and one group functions on earth. Since these later funerary scenes are considered to have originated in the Butic tradition, it may also be assumed that the Old Kingdom tomb scenes featuring the ritual of *ḥꜣi* display a Butic ceremony. Predynastic statuettes exhibiting the A 28 pose can provide evidence for the fact that the ritual of *ḥꜣi* is very archaic.[184] (See Chapter Seven below for a discussion of the A 28 gesture.) In the tombs of Paheri, Neferhotep, and Amenmose the men appear in the same position in the procession and with the same gesture; however, they are not identified.

Another pattern that becomes visible is that in the Old Kingdom women originally took charge of the A 28 rite, while as time progressed, men, barring the example in the tomb of Hui and Kel, eventually performed the ritual. The rite exhibiting the A 28 gesture has remained in use during the funeral and has retained its placement in the funerary procession throughout the Old, Middle and early New Kingdoms. In the early Old Kingdom, examples of the A 28 gesture may have been part of a ritual movement or dance (confirmed by the above mentioned Pyramid Texts), but by the time of the Barnûgi tomb the ritual takes on a more solemn expression. This solemnity was maintained. Through the examples preserved in the Middle and New Kingdoms it becomes apparent that the People of Pe, or the pat and *rḫyt nbt*, played an intricate role in the ritual involving the A 28 pose, replacing the women of the Old Kingdom. Additionally, this ritual continues to take place on the day of burial as the procession is reaching the tomb.

---

178 Gardiner 1964, 421. Griffith and Petrie 1889, pl. 9, fragment 10.

179 Altenmüller 1975, 2.

180 Altenmüller 1975, 7-9.

181 Reeder 1995, 74.

182 Reeder 1995, 77.

183 I am not suggesting that the *mww* are related to the people of Pe. I follow Reeder in that I believe that it is only the dance of the *mww* being performed.

184 For example, the female figurine with incurving arms from el-Ma'mariya (Capel 1996, 121-122) and one from Naqada (Lacovara 1988, 70). Ucko (1968, 44-48, 84, 99-101, 181-184, 188-191) catalogues 17 female figurines with both upraised arms and beak noses: nos, 28, 56-69, 72-73.

Sabni: ḥ3(i)tiw

The penultimate Old Kingdom private source is the inscription of Sabni (Figure 17), which provides additional information about who can perform the ritual of *ḥ3i*. First of all, this source confirms that men also performed this rite at an Old Kingdom funeral, in that the determinative used in the writing of *ḥ3(i)tiw* is a man, and the form is masculine plural.[185] Likewise, the inscription implies that the *ḥ3(i)tiw* originated from the embalming house (*pr-nfr*):

> He (also) brought...two embalmers, a senior lector priest, one who is on annual duty, the inspector of the *wabet*, mourners, and the whole of the equipment from the *per-nefer*.[186]

The *ḥ3(i)tiw* were most likely employed by the *pr-nfr*, or at the very least they were functioning as *ḥ3(i)tiw* under the auspices of the *pr-nfr* (see Chapter Six below). Perhaps females were associated with a particular cult and men were associated with institutions connected with a profession, for example, the Acacia House versus the mortuary workshops.

Pepiankh: ḥ3(i)w

Lastly, in the tomb of Pepiankh at Meir a rare variant of *ḥ3i* occurs.[187] One sees a man standing beside a *ḏryt* before a pile of offerings; in one scene he is in front of the purification tent, and then in another scene, in front of the embalming house.[188] This man has his arms raised in the A 28 gesture and is labeled a *ḥ3(i)w* in both cases. In one scene his arms are raised slightly higher than in the other. We have several other examples where a female or a goddess is called a *ḥ3(i)t*, but the masculine version is rare. To the best of my knowledge, aside from the *ḥ3itiw* mentioned previously from the inscription of Sabni, the only other examples of a masculine form appear in CT II 238b and in BD 1.[189] In the Coffin Texts the context is completely different and refers to the bird the deceased is comparing himself to: "my wings are on him as a *ḥ3(i)w*-bird...."[190] In Pepiankh's tomb it appears that the label refers to the ritual title the man holds with regard to the funeral in which he is participating; the term itself is the masculine singular participial form deriving from the word *ḥ3i*. The title describes his function in the scene. This illustration further confirms that men, as well as women, performed the ritual of *ḥ3i* in the Old Kingdom, and that the function of a *ḥ3(i)w* is different from that of a *ḏryt*. At the very least their posts required different titles. Likewise, the *ḥ3(i)w* is one of the seven members of the funeral procession who deals with the rituals of the purification tent, the embalming house, and their associated offerings. Since his personal name is not given, it is his ritual title that is important, and not the man himself. In this caption there is no designation of an organization to which the *ḥ3(i)w* belongs, as there is in the tombs of Debehni and Qar. This may be another example where the male performer of *ḥ3i* is associated with the mortuary workshops. It seems reasonable to assume that a *ḥ3(i)w* who is positioned outside the *wʿbt* and women who *ḥ3i* outside the *wʿbt* perform the same function, only their affiliations may be different based on an acceptable vocational association for each sex.

With regard to provincial tombs, Harpur notes, "tradition was much less a force in later provincial chapels than at Memphis."[191] For this reason it is difficult to compare the southern chapels with those of the north. Likewise, the education, experience, and predilection of the local artist, played a major role in the type of decoration employed in the provincial tombs.[192] Furthermore, the tomb of Pepiankh at Meir is one of the most detailed as far as the funerary scenes are concerned. This fact may provide the explanation as to why there is only one preserved example of the scene where the mummified body is collected by the procession.

Old Kingdom Royal Sources

Pyramid Texts

As far as Old Kingdom royal sources are concerned, there are eight examples of the word *ḥ3i* that can be found in the Pyramid Texts, two of which occur in the same spell. The following subjects either perform the ritual of *ḥ3i* or receive the associated title. Nursing cows, the *wršiw*, Isis, and the deceased king are all associated with the ritual of *ḥ3i*.[193] The references that associate Isis with the *ḥ3it*-bird will be considered separately in Chapter Five.

Nursing Cows

The first example, Pyramid Text §550, speaks of milch-cows and nursing cows "who are in this," *imywt nn*, and who encircle the deceased.[194] These participants, who are imagined as nursing cows, *ḥ3i* the deceased, in addition to crying and lamenting, as they go around him.

[185] However, since these men were being sent abroad the trip may have been too treacherous for females to make and therefore male substitutes were provided. This title should be contrasted with the New Kingdom equivalent that occurs in the BD 1 where the "t" is removed and the title appears as *ḥ3yw*.

[186] Strudwick 2005, 337. "*Il amena des...embaumeurs, un prêtre-lecteur aîné, un droguier et un supérieur [des artisans?] de la place d'embaumement, des pleureuses, et tous les outils de la Maison de l'embaumement.*" Roccati 1982, 218.

[187] Blackman 1935, pls. 42 and 43.

[188] Blackman 1953, plates 42 and 43.

[189] Jones 2000, 495.

[190] Faulkner 2004, 1:127.

[191] Harpur 1987, 116.

[192] Harpur 1987, 123.

[193] PT §§2112 and 2117 are written in the first person, but omit the pronoun.

[194] Ritner (1993, 57) describes the act of encircling as synonymous with purification.

The first bovine reference is written *mhiwt*, with three cows (P) or three heads of cattle (T).[195] The second reference employs the word *mnʿwt* "nurses." Version P includes a cow head determinative for the latter word.

Throughout Pharaonic times cattle cults were important in Egyptian religion and mythology. Although there are sporadic references to cows and cow goddesses in the corpus of early funerary literature, the majority of the information about the significance of the cow comes from later sources that include mythological content.[196]

In general, the cow was the representative animal for maternal and domestic characteristics, and was the sacred animal for the goddesses Mehet-Weret, Bat, Hesat, Neith, Nut, Hathor, Isis, and Shentayet, among others. Since the cow was connected with both Heaven and the Underworld,[197] she became a symbol of life in the Hereafter.[198] There are funerary references to cows that allude to the special function of the bovine in the continuation of life. During the Osirian Mysteries the body of the god was placed in a cow-shaped box with the hope of his being reborn from a cow's womb.[199] This cow-shaped box symbolizes the goddess Shentayet, whose name means "widow." Her origins are obscure; however, she was eventually assimilated with Isis and went by the name Isis-Shentayet. In this form, the goddess was linked with the resurrection of Osiris and was connected with the god's sarcophagus.[200]

The Book of the Dead also speaks of cows. Chapter 148 reads as follows:

> Hail to you, You who shine in your disk, a living soul who goes up from the horizon! I know you and I know your name; I know the name of the seven cows and their bull who give bread and beer, who are beneficial to souls and who provide daily portions....[201]

The names of the cattle are:[202]

> Mansion of Kas, Mistress of All
> Silent One who dwells in her place
> She of Chemmis[203] whom the god ennobled
> The Beloved, red of hair
> She who protects in life, the parti-colored
> She whose name has power in her craft
> Storm in the sky which wafts the god aloft

These seven cows represented the sevenfold form of Hathor, although they have no clear designation other than their function of providing nourishment to the deceased in order to maintain him in the Afterlife.[204]

Additionally, the cow can be a symbol for the mother of the king. There are two passages in the Pyramid Texts that equate the king with a calf. Pyramid Texts §§388-389 (Utterance 271) reads as follows:[205]

> ...I have united the Two Lands, I have joined my mother the Great Wild Cow.[206] O my mother, the Wild Cow which is upon the Mountain of Pasture and upon the Mountain of the *sḥsḥ*-bird...

In Pyramid Text §§1029-1030 (Utterance 485A) the deceased king is also depicted as a calf:[207]

> [...I have come to you, my father,] I [have come] to you, O Re, a calf of gold born of the sky, a fatted calf of gold which *ḥsꜣt* created. O Horus, take me with you, living and enduring; O Horus, do not leave me boatless.

Pyramid Texts §§729, 1370, 1566, and 2003 state that the deceased king is the son of the Great Wild Cow. They appear below in their respective order:

> Your mother is the great wild cow who dwells in Nekheb, white of head-cloth, long of plumes, and pendulous of breasts; she suckles you and will not wean you.[208]

> You are a son of the Great Wild Cow.[209]

---

[195] Faulkner 1991, 113.
[196] Pinch 2002, 123.
[197] The Upper Egyptian goddess, Bat, was one of the first cow goddesses to be associated with the sky. Both Hathor and Nut were thought to be giant cows with stars covering their bodies. The New Kingdom funerary text, the Book of the Heavenly Cow, describes how Nut first lifted the sun god to heaven with her horns. The cow's connection to the Underworld can be seen when the sun god traveled along a river that was sometimes identified with Mehet-Weret (Pinch 2002, 125).
[198] Lurker 1995, 41-42.
[199] Lurker 1995, 42.
[200] Wilkinson 2003, 175.
[201] Faulkner 1994, pl. 35.
[202] Faulkner 1994, pl. 35.
[203] The floating island of Chemmis is where Isis gave birth to her son Horus.
[204] Book of the Dead Chapter 141 provides a parallel passage. In this sevenfold form, Hathor decreed the time and manner of a person's death (Pinch 2002, 139; Wilkinson 2003, 77). This can be seen in *The Doomed Prince* where it is said: "Then came the Hathors to determine a fate for him" (Lichtheim 1976, 2:200).
[205] For hieroglyphs see Sethe 1908, 1:203; and for translation see Faulkner 1998, 79.
[206] *smꜣt ḥmt*, "female wild cow." See also Hannig 2003, 241 and 829 for a possible reading as *idt* here.
[207] For hieroglyphs see Sethe 1908, 2:77; for translation see Faulkner 1998, 172.
[208] For hieroglyphs see Sethe 1908, 1:399; for translation see Faulkner 1998, 135.
[209] For hieroglyphs see Sethe 1908, 2:248-249 for translation see Faulkner 1998, 214.

> It is my mother the great Wild Cow, long of plumes, bright of head-cloth, pendulous of breasts, who has lifted me up to the sky, not having left me on earth, among the gods who have power.[210]

> O King, you have no human father who could beget you, you have no human mother who could bear you; your mother is the Great Wild Cow who dwells in Nekheb, white of head-cloth, long of hair, and pendulous of breasts, she suckles you and does not wean you.[211]

In Pyramid Texts §§531, 1344, and 1375 a cow suckles the king without direct reference to the cow being his mother. They appear below in their respective order:

> ...I have sucked the milk of the two black cows, the nurses of the Souls of On.[212]

> Nut the Great puts her hands on him, (even) she the long-horned, the pendulous of breast, She suckles this King and does not wean him...[213]

> My mother is Isis, my nurse is Nephthys, she who suckled me is the *šḫ3t-ḥr* cow, Neith is behind me, and Selket is before me.[214]

A divine cow suckling the king is a common motif, both in the inscriptional material and pictorially. At the temple of Luxor, Amenhotep III is also shown being divinely conceived and then suckled by a divine cow.[215] Frankfort notes an example at Deir el-Bahri where Amun orders four goddesses (Nekhbet, Wadjet, Selket, and Hesat) to nurse the infant Hatshepsut; he quotes:

> I have commanded (you) to nurse Her Majesty and all her Ka's, with all life and good fortune, all permanence, all health, all joy, and the passing of millions of years on the throne of Horus of all the living, forever.[216]

Strengthening forces and powerful blessings were thought to enter the king with the milk of the divine.[217] And most importantly, the rejuvenation qualities that divine milk possessed provided for a glorious resurrection in the Hereafter.[218] Frankfort remarks, "Health and joy, but also the many years of the reign, are quite concretely regarded as benefits which enter the child with the milk of the nursing goddesses."[219] There are several references in the Pyramid Texts that illustrate the benefit of divine milk for life in the next world. In the Pyramid Texts Isis, Nephthys, Selket, Ipy and the goddess of Elkab, in her variety of forms, nurse the deceased king.[220]

PT §131 (Utterance 211) reads:[221]

> My detestation is hunger, and I will never eat it. My detestation is thirst, and I will never drink it. It is indeed I who will give bread to those who exist, for my foster-mother is *i3t*,[222] and it is she who nourishes me, it is indeed she who bore me.

PT §371 (Utterance 268) reads:[223]

> Isis nurses him, Nephthys suckles him...

PT §381 (Utterance 269) reads:[224]

> O my mother Ipy, give me this breast of yours, that I may apply it to my mouth and suck this your white, gleaming, sweet milk. As for yonder land in which I walk, I will neither thirst nor hunger in it forever.

PT §§622-623 (Utterance 365) read:[225]

> Receive your dignity, for your foot will not be obstructed in the sky, you will not be opposed on earth, for you are a spirit whom Nut bore, whom Nephthys suckled, and they put you together. Arise in your strength...

PT §707-708 (Utterance 406) read:[226]

> Bring me the milk of Isis, the flood of Nephthys, the overspill of the lake, the surge of the sea,

210 For hieroglyphs see Sethe 1908, 2:337 for translation see Faulkner 1998, 236.
211 For hieroglyphs see Sethe 1908, 2:484 for translation see Faulkner 1998, 289.
212 For hieroglyphs see Sethe 1908, 1:271; for translation see Faulkner 1998, 105.
213 For hieroglyphs see Sethe 1908, 2:241; for translation see Faulkner 1998, 211.
214 For hieroglyphs see Sethe 1908, 2:250-25; for translation see Faulkner 1998, 215.
215 Bell 1985, 266.
216 Frankfort 1958, 74; Sethe, *Urk.* IV, 227.
217 Gardiner 1950, 7; Leclant 1951; Feucht 1984, 402-404; Bell 1985, 266, n. 76; Pinch 2002, 125.
218 Leclant 1951, 125.
219 Frankfort 1958, 74.
220 Leclant 1951, 123. In addition to the references listed above, see also PT §§32, 910, 1109, 1118, 2089, 2204.
221 For hieroglyphs see Sethe 1908, 1:77-78; for translation see Faulkner 1998, 40.
222 A milk goddess, for *i3tt*.
223 For hieroglyphs see Sethe 1908, 1:193; for translation see Faulkner 1998, 77.
224 For hieroglyphs see Sethe 1908, 1:198; for translation see Faulkner 1998, 78.
225 For hieroglyphs see Sethe 1908, 1:334; for translation see Faulkner 1998, 120.
226 For hieroglyphs see Sethe 1908, 1:385-6; for translation see Faulkner 1998, 132.

> life, prosperity, health, happiness, bread, beer, clothing, and food, that I may live thereby.

PT §734 (Utterance 413) reads:[227]

> Raise yourself, O King! You have your water, you have your inundation, you have your milk which is from the breasts of Mother Isis.

PT §§911-912 (Utterance 470) read:[228]

> 'O Ruddy One, O Red Crown, O Lady of the lands of Dep, O my mother,' say I, 'give me your breast that I may suck from it', say I. 'O my son,' says she, 'take my breast and suck it,' says she, 'that you may live,' says she, 'and be little (again)', says she. 'You shall ascend to the sky as do falcons, your feathers being those of ducks', says she.

PT §1354 (Utterance 553) reads:[229]

> O King, because you are a spirit whom Nephthys suckled with her left breast...

PT §1427 (Utterance 565) reads:[230]

> Selket[231] has set her hands on me, she has extended her breast to my mouth...

PT §1873 (Utterance 661) reads:[232]

> O my father the King, take this milky fluid of yours which is in the breasts of your mother Isis...

The passages presented above feature the following bovines: the Great Wild Cow — who is also the Female Wild Cow — (PT §§388-389, 1370, 1566), two black cows who are the nurses of the Souls of Heliopolis (PT §531), the Great Wild Cow from Nekheb (PT §§729, 2003), the goddess Hesat (PT §§1029-1030), Nut the long-horned (PT §1344), and the goddess of Elkab in the form of *šḫ3t-ḥr* (PT §1375).

Discerning which cow divinities actually nurse the deceased king in other Pyramid Texts will provide parallels for the milch-cows appearing in PT §550. The texts above show that nursing cows occur in Pyramid Texts §§531, 729, 1344, 1375, and 2003. The Great Wild Cow (Female Wild Cow),[233] the Great Wild Cow from Nekheb, and the goddess of Elkab in the form of sxAt-Hr (PT §1375) are all the same divinity: the goddess Nekhbet.[234] The other two possibilities are: the two black cows (PT §531) and Nut the long-horned (PT §1344). According to Leclant, the goddess of Elkab is known to nurse the king in a variety of her forms, sometimes assimilated with Nut.[235] This would then mean that Nut the long-horned and the goddess of Elkab in the form of *sḫ3t-ḥr* are all manifestations of Nekhbet. This leaves only the example of the two black cows that nurse the Souls of Heliopolis (PT §531) who cannot yet be identified with Nekhbet. According to Mercer, one of the Souls of Heliopolis is the dead king himself.[236]

To conclude, the cow was a symbol of life in the Hereafter. The bovine had a specific symbolism in the process of rebirth as is shown by the use of the cow-shaped box in the Mysteries of Osiris and BD 148 which explains the cow provides nourishment for the soul. Furthermore, it is clear from the numerous Pyramid Texts presented above that it was desirable for the deceased king to drink from a divine breast in order to thrive in the Afterlife. Cattle played a primary role in the mythology of the divine king, and both the living and deceased kings are depicted as being suckled by the divine cow. The milk from the divine cow had rejuvenation qualities that were essential for the well-being of the king in the Afterlife. This iconography and mythology impart a better understanding of PT §550 — the nursing cows provide the essential nourishment for the deceased king to be resurrected and thrive in the Afterlife. In the case of PT §550, the milch-cows are not clearly linked to any particular deity, but may represent a manifestation of the Great Wild Cow of Nekheb, as do the overwhelming majority of the references to a cow who suckles the dead king in the Pyramid Texts. Mercer suggests that these milch-cows represent Isis and Nephthys as heavenly cows.[237] He compares this

[227] For hieroglyphs see Sethe 1908, 1:402; for translation see Faulkner 1998, 136.
[228] For hieroglyphs see Sethe 1908, 1:4-5; for translation see Faulkner 1998, 159.
[229] For hieroglyphs see Sethe 1908, 1:244; for translation see Faulkner 1998, 213.
[230] For hieroglyphs see Sethe 1908, 1:274; for translation see Faulkner 1998, 220.
[231] Nephthys appears in some versions of this spell instead of Selket (Faulkner 1998, 221, n. 7).
[232] For hieroglyphs see Sethe 1908, 1:456; for translation see Faulkner 1998, 272.

[233] Mercer (1952, 2:179) concludes that *sm3t wrt* is the more common way that the Pyramid Texts refer to the Great Wild Cow; however, in PT §389, *sm3t ḥmt*, "female wild cow" occurs. This phrase has a parallel in PT §1370 where *sm3t wrt ḥmt* can be found. He explains that *ḥmt* is redundant in both of these passages and functions as an unnecessary feminine determinative. He also notes that *ḥmt* occurs four times alone to mean, "cow" (PT §§531, 568, 569, and 1708). If this is so, then *ḥmty kmty* in PT §531 may refer to the Great Wild Cow that is referenced in the other Pyramid Texts. See note 178 above for discussion on the reading of *ḥmt*.
[234] Mercer 1952, 2:179-180.
[235] Leclant 1951, 123.
[236] Mercer 1952, 2:254.
[237] Mercer 1952, 2:264-265.

manifestation to the seven-fold bovine form of Hathor appearing in the Book of the Dead. However, the dual form has not been employed in PT §550 and the form *imywt* is the feminine plural. To the best of my knowledge, there is no evidence to support a manifestation of Nephthys as a cow, although she can nurse the king in the Pyramid Texts. Pyramid Texts §550 presents a situation where nursing cows symbolize the continuation of life. They encircle the deceased in order to purify him,[238] and they perform the rite of *ḥ3i* in order to resurrect him and take him to the Hereafter. Their milk will magically provide the deceased king with the essential nutrients for his survival in the Afterlife.

The wršiw

The next text under discussion is Pyramid Text §744 (Utterance 419), where the king is addressed by his son on the day of his funeral. The passage in question reads as follows:

> Hail to you, my father, on this your day when you stand before Re when he ascends from the East and when you are clad with this your dignity which is among the spirits! Arms are linked for you, feet dance for you, hands are waved for you. Isis has grasped your hand and she inducts you into the baldachin.[239] The land is covered,[240] the *wršiw ḥ3i*.[241]

The *wršiw* are the subject of the verb *ḥ3i*. Here the deceased king is entering the next world as Isis receives him and as greeters are dancing for him. In version M the head of a woman is used as the determinative for the word *wršiw*, and in version T there is no determinative. This word appears in *Wb* I 336, 12 and is translated as *Klagefrauen*. Pyr. §744 is the only citation given. Hannig remarks that this group consists of people who are dancers for Osiris.[242] In Zandee's study he translates *wršiw* as "guards," "dignitaries," and "wailing-women" (PT §744), as the circumstances dictate. He also notes that the *wršiw* play a positive role.[243] The verb *wrš* is defined as "spend the day" or "spend time," sometimes used for a person who is awake or watchful. A variant of the word, written without the female determinative, is defined as "sentry" or "watcher."[244] The *wršiw* also appear in PT §§656e, 795d-e, 1013b, 1901b, 1915b, 1945c, and 1947a. In some instances they are referred to in connection with the sacred cities of Buto and Hierakonpolis, and in other examples they are coupled with the Great Ones.

In PT §§795d-e and 1013b the word refers to the Watchers (masculine) of Buto and Hierakonpolis.[245] The passages of PT §§795 and 1013, respectively, read as follows:

> O earth, hear this which the gods have said! Re speaks, he makes a spirit of this King, who receives his spirit-form in front of the gods as Horus son of Osiris; he gives him his spirit which is among the Watchers of Pe, he ennobles him as a god who is among the Watchers of Nekhen.[246]

> O earth, hear this which Geb said when he spiritualized Osiris as a god; the watchers of Pe install him, the watchers of Nekhen ennoble him as Sokar who presides over *Pḏw-š*, (as) Horus, Ha, and Hemen.[247]

These two passages demonstrate that the *wršiw* are not only present when the deceased is ritually transformed into a spirit, but they actually participate in his spiritualization, or divine transformation. Mercer equates these Watchers with the souls (*b3w*) of the deceased kings of the North and the South, the Followers of Horus. He notes that they are in the service of Horus. Mercer points out that in the sun-temple at Abu Ghurob the Watchers of Hierakonpolis carry the king in his sedan-chair, while the attendants cry, "May the Souls of Nekhen give life."[248] This passage is most intriguing; it illustrates that what the watchers are doing is transporting the king to the Hereafter. In the sun-temple it is the Watchers of Hierakonpolis that carry the king in his sedan-chair while in PT §744 the watchers (*wršiw*) *ḥ3i* immediately after Isis has inducted the deceased king into his pavilion.[249] The meaning of *ḥ3i* is quite clear: to ritually transport. Furthermore, scholars have associated the Souls of Pe with the *mww* dancers and earlier kings (see above). The people of the sacred Delta localities appear in related contexts, namely in TT 60.

The following examples demonstrate the pairing of the Watchers with the Great Ones. PT §1901b reads:

> The Great Ones stand up for you, the Watchers sit down for you as Horus, protector of his father.[250]

---

[238] Ritner provides many examples of this purification rite. He also notes that the Demotic word *pẖr* means "to enchant" (Ritner 1993, 57-67).

[239] *ẖnw mnnw* "interior of the rooms." Allen (2005, 86) translates this word as "pavilion."

[240] Faulkner notes that the word *ḏb3* literally means "adorned" or "clad" and perhaps is an allusion to funeral garb.

[241] Faulkner 1998, 138.

[242] Hannig 1997, 207; 2003, 366.

[243] Zandee 1960, 203.

[244] Faulkner1991, 65.

[245] Mercer 1952, 2:372.

[246] Faulkner 1998, 144.

[247] Faulkner 1998, 170.

[248] Mercer 1952, 2:400.

[249] Allen 2005, 86.

[250] Faulkner 1998, 274.

On the one hand, Mercer notes that the Great Ones stand in the presence of the resuscitated king while the lower-ranked Watchers sit and work.[251] On the other hand, he notes PT §656e where "the Watchers arise for you."[252] PT §1915b reads as follows:

> The Great Ones will care for you and the Watchers will wait on you as on Horus, protector of his father.[253]

Mercer further mentions that the *wršiw* are connected with the imperishable stars, who are perhaps the blessed dead, the deceased kings or the deified dead in heaven.[254]

PT §1947a presents an anomaly in comparison to the immediately aforementioned passages. It speaks of the Watchers dancing for the deceased:

> The Watchers dance for you.[255]

This is a noteworthy passage because PT §1947a provides a parallel for PT §744.

The *wršiw* also appear in column 22 of the Funerary Liturgy, where Gardiner translates the word as "the watchers."[256] In this example, however, the man (not the woman) determinative is used. The section in question opens with, "Second time [of circulating around] the mastaba; a summoning in the presence of the crowd of women (*dmḏt*), [they] *ḥ3i*." Column 22 then follows with the word *wršiw*. I believe a purification ritual is taking place in order to prepare the deceased for entering the Afterlife. The *dmḏyt* are performing the ritual of *ḥ3i* (to be discussed below) and the *wršiw* are also present. Little sense can be made of the context beyond this point.

It can be concluded that the *wršiw* were attendants at a funeral, watched over the deceased,[257] and witnessed the rejuvenation ritual of *ḥ3i*. With regard to Pyramid Texts §744, it is likely that it is the *wršiw* who link their arms, dance with their feet, and wave their hands for the deceased. These descriptions are reminiscent of many of the previously discussed scenarios where the term *ḥ3i* occurs.

The Deceased King or Queen

The next passage to be examined is PT §1585 where it is the deceased king/queen that performs *ḥ3i*. This is a solar text that survives mainly in the pyramid of Queen Neith, although the passage that contains the word *ḥ3i* is also preserved in the pyramid of Pepi I.[258] It reads as follows:

> Tell your mother, O *šs3*, that it is the King who weeps for you, it is the King who *ḥ3i*-s you [...] give a hand to the King when he comes.[259]

This utterance is atypical because the person being addressed is not the deceased king or queen. The passage speaks of the god *šs3*, who may be a carpenter god, or chief of the granary city *šnꜥt*, as Mercer describes him.[260] In this text his name is written with a plough and a god determinative. In PT §2080 *šs3* cuts the timbers for the ladder the king uses to reach heaven; he is also mentioned in PT §1329.[261] While it is the god *šs3* who is addressed by the utterance, it is the deceased king/queen who is weeping and magically transporting/revivifying the god. This is corroborated by the usage of the masculine singular dependent pronoun *ṯw*. What is significant is that the ritual of *ḥ3i* occurs prior to the deceased reaching heaven, and that Khnum brings a ladder for the deceased's ascension.

ṯmt

PT §1791 also includes the word *ḥ3i*. This utterance is comprised of only one line: "It is you who *ḥ3i* over him."[262] It has been suggested by Faulkner that the feminine pronoun *ṯmt* probably refers to the goddess Isis. It is possible that the masculine singular suffix pronoun (*.f*) may refer to the deceased as an Osiris. Likewise, Faulkner notes that this pronoun points to the great antiquity of the spell. If this is the case, it is

---

251 Mercer 1952, 3:858.

252 Mercer 1952, 3:858. He translates this passage as follows, "the watchers stand before thee," *ꜥḥꜥ n.k wršiw*. Faulkner (1998, 124) translates "the Watchers wait upon you."

253 Faulkner 1998, 276.

254 Mercer 1952, 2:321; 1952, 3:863.

255 The passage continues, "and the Mourning-Woman calls to you as Isis" (Faulkner 1998, 281). Mercer (1952, 3:878) suggests that the word for mourning woman [*smnt(y)t*] should be taken as a plural, parallel to watchers. I don't believe this is the case. He translates as follows: "The Watchers dance for thee, as the mourning-women of Osiris call for thee" (1952, 1:290). Faulkner's note 4 says to read *3st* for *Wsir* (1998, 282). This mourning-woman who calls, also calls as Nephthys (PT §§1906 and 1928). PT §1997 reads, "The Mourning-Woman calls to you as Isis, the Joyful One rejoices over you as Nephthys" (Faulkner 1998, 288). For the word *smnt(y)t* see Hannig 1997, 707; 2003, 1127. These passages repeatedly demonstrate a single ritual associated with dancing and joy. First a dance is performed and then either following, or simultaneously, the deceased is summoned. The various players include: Isis, Nephthys, the *smntyt*, the *mniwt wrt*, the *wršiw* and "the joyful one." In PT §744, the section under discussion, Isis is inducting the deceased to the Hereafter while the *wršiw* perform the rite of *ḥ3i*. It also states that this rejuvenation rite is accompanied by dancing.

256 Gardiner 1955, 12.

257 A *wršt*-priestess is also known from Akhmim; according to Fischer she watched over the god Min (Fischer 1989, 19; Ward 1986, 7, 73; Jones 2000, 399-400).

258 See Faulkner's supplement (1998, 11-12).

259 Faulkner 1998, 238. He translates *ḥ3i* as "mourn." Mercer (1952, 1:245) organizes the passage as follows, "To say: Great is Atum; the son of a great one is Atum; N. is the *šḥd*-star in the sky among the gods. Thy mother says to thee that *šs3*, like N., weeps for thee; like N. he mourns for thee."

260 Mercer 1952, 3:659, 760.

261 Mercer 1952, 3:760; Faulkner 1998, 209, 297.

262 Faulkner 1998, 262. See also Mercer 1952, 3:832.

unlikely that the feminine pronoun refers to Isis, since texts laden with mythology are later than those without it. Evidence for the cults of Isis and Osiris begins to appear only around the Fifth Dynasty.[263]

First Person Subject

§§2112 and 2117-2118 of the Pyramid Texts both belong to the same utterance, namely, a series of short spells with obvious Osirian overtones; and both include the word *ḥ3i*. The general sentiment of the passage is that the deceased king is an Osiris who is being summoned to rise and live. In both examples the person who is performing the rite of *ḥ3i* is identified as "I":

ḥ3(i).n(.i) ṯw ḥr ḥ3t

I have *ḥ3i*-ed you at the tomb (PT §2112)

iw ḥ3(i).n(.i) ṯw

I have *ḥ3i*-ed you[264] (PT §§2117-2118)

In many cases it appears to have been the dead king who would have recited the utterance.[265] The "you" that both passages speak of refers to Osiris. The first few lines where the deceased king is compared to the god make this clear (PT §§2111-2113).

Summation of Old Kingdom Participants

In summary, there are different groups of people, including both males and females, who perform the rite of *ḥ3i* during the Old Kingdom funeral. Additionally, the titles of *ḥ3(i)w*, *ḥ3(i)t*, and *ḥ3(i)tiw* describe the actors who perform the ritual. A distinction is made between private and royal sources, in that different participants appear exclusively in each class of sources. This dichotomy most likely occurs because separate funerary rituals were performed in each context.

The scenes in the tombs of Debehni, Qar and Hetepherakhti all show women performing the rite of *ḥ3i*. The tomb of Ptahhotep does not include a descriptive label but does parallel the scene in the tomb of Hetepherakhti in that it shows women from the *šnḏt* holding their arms in the A 28 pose and leading a dragging scene. Therefore, it is likely that the women shown in Hetepherakhti's scene are also affiliated with the *šnḏt*. Consequently all four scenes show the women of the *šnḏt* performing the ritual of *ḥ3i*. The *šnḏt*, or Acacia House, symbolizes the force of life and death, and rebirth in the Hereafter. It is stated in the Coffin Texts that the one who comes from the acacia-tree prevents putrefaction in the realm of the dead (CT Spell 755).[266] The women in the tomb of Debehni are magically protecting and assembling the deceased with their chant: "His flesh is complete." In the tomb of Qar this rite is performed outside the *wꜥbt* where the women encourage the rebirth of the deceased through their dancing and singing. Additionally, Qar has just been transported to the *wꜥbt* for his corpse to be embalmed, and thus preserved for eternity. This ritual was essential for attaining rebirth in the Afterlife. In the tomb of Pepiankh the *ḥ3(i)w* stands outside the *wꜥbt* magically reassembling the deceased. The *ḥ3(i)tiw* in the inscription of Sabni come from the *pr-nfr* as part of a group sent to take care of the funeral arrangements. The *ḥ3(i)tiw* were meant to magically protect and transport the deceased, not only from Wawat to Qubbet el-Hawa, but from this world to the next by performing the *ḥ3i* ritual.[267] Therefore, all six participants from the Old Kingdom private sources function as rejuvenators of the deceased while performing the funerary rite of *ḥ3i* or serving in the capacity of a *ḥ3it*/*ḥ3iw*.

In summary, in the Pyramid Texts the performers of the *ḥ3i* ritual include nursing cows, the *wršiw*, the goddess Isis, and the deceased. These participants are not clearly affiliated with any organization or group. The commonality among all of them is that they appear in the Pyramid Texts, and most of them appear in contexts that have obvious Osirian overtones. The two utterances that do not noticeably reflect the Osirian tradition are PT §§1585 and 1791. PT §1585 does clearly deal with the idea of the resurrection of the king, in that the deceased king is brought a ladder that was made by Khnum for the express purpose of ascending to the sky to escort Re. The myth of Osiris and its relationship with the royal cult was intended to achieve the eternal life of the king, as was this spell. The theme of resurrection runs throughout the passages that contain the word *ḥ3i*.

Not many commonalities exist between the participants of the *ḥ3i* ritual in the private sources and those in the royal sources. In both classes, though, female performers are more regular than male. Another commonality is the existence of dancing or (rhythmic?) movement. While performing the ritual of *ḥ3i* the women dance in the tomb scenes, and dancing (or prescribed movement) also occurs in PT §§550 and 744. In PT §550 it is the nursing cows who encircle the deceased. In PT §744 arms are linked, feet dance and hands wave for the deceased, but the actor is not specified in the latter source. However, PT §1947 tells us that the *wršiw* dance for the deceased, thus linking PT §744 with the private sources that feature dancing. Also in PT §744, it is Isis who leads the deceased to the pavilion and initiates his spiritualization into the Next World through ritual transportation. Likewise, in both

[263] Griffiths 1980, 41.
[264] Sethe 1908, 514-515.
[265] Faulkner 1998, viii.
[266] Faulkner 2004, 288.
[267] Frandsen 1992, 52.

Pepiankh's tomb and PT §§1255 and 1280 the *ḥ3(i)t/w* is coupled with a *ḏryt* (these Pyramid Texts are considered separately in Chapter Five). In the former source the title is written without a bird determinative, and in the latter source the title is written with a bird determinative. The royal sources present the ritual in its mythic version, while the private sources still retain the more historical rite. The reason for the different writings may simply be that in the mythological realm a goddess can be imagined as a bird, but in an illustration of a real funeral the performer must be presented as accurately as possible — it would be contradictory to depict a man with a caption that indicates he is a bird.[268]

[268] As the next section of this work will show, the Coffin Texts mention a *ḥ3(i)w*-bird, written with either a bird determinative alone or a bird determinative coupled with a god determinative.

TABLE 5: DRAGGING SCENES WITH A 28 POSE

	Tomb Owner	Date	Oxen	Statue or Coffin	Male/Female
1	Hetepherakhti	Fifth Dynasty	X	Statue	F
2	Ptahhotep[269]	Fifth Dynasty	X	Coffin	F
3	Barnûgi tomb[270]	OK	X	Coffin	F
4	Hery (TT 12)[271]	Seqenenre-Tao II – Amenhotep I	X	?	M/F
5	Renni272	Amenhotep I	X	Coffin	M/F
6	Amenemhet (TT 82)[273]	Hatshepsut/Thutmose III	X	Coffin	M
7	Paheri[274]	Thutmose III	X	Coffin	M
8	Rekhmire (TT 100)[275]	Thutmose III – Amenhotep II	X	Coffin	M
9	Suemnut (TT 92)[276]	Thutmose III/ Amenhotep II	X	Coffin	M
10	Nebamun (TT 17)[277]	Thutmose III/Amenhotep II	X	Coffin	M
11	Amenemhab (TT 85)[278]	Thutmose III – Amenhotep II	X	Coffin	F

[269] *LD* II, 101b.
[270] Maspero 1907, 116, fig. 15.
[271] *PM* I.i, 24-25.
[272] Tylor 1900, Tafel 9-13, 15.
[273] Davies 1915, pl. XI.
[274] Tylor and Griffith 1894, pl. V.
[275] Davies 1943, pl. XCII.
[276] *PM* I.i, 187-189.
[277] Säve-Söderbergh 1957, pls. 24-25.
[278] Virey 1891, 224-285.

Chapter Three

Introduction

Many of the participants that appear in the Middle Kingdom sources reflect precursors found in the Old Kingdom sources. The avian connection is explored in Chapter Five; however, there are many other similarities that are examined here.

Funerary Liturgy

The very informative Funerary Liturgy published by Gardiner presents some of the most intriguing parallels.[1] Gardiner's Funerary Liturgy is likely to be a royal text, however, it has been suspected that it dates to the Old Kingdom since it includes various archaic references. There are some similarities between this document and the Old Kingdom private sources discussed above.[2] As has already been noted, this liturgy includes five possible occurrences of the word *ḥ3i*, the first occurrence (col. 7) being somewhat sketchy. In column 14a-16 the text reads, "second time [of circulating around] the mastaba; a summoning in (the) presence of the *dmḏt*, [they] *ḥ3i*-ing."[3] The definition of the word *dmḏ(y)t* is discussed below;[4] however, here the *dmḏ(y)t* is actually a single woman. In this example, the *dmḏ(y)t* is performing the ritual of *ḥ3i* and calling to the deceased to revive in the form of a newly rejuvenated god/king. According to Gardiner, this part of the text occurs in the first section of the liturgy (of which there are four) where he sees evidence for ritual action.[5]

The next example of *ḥ3i* occurs in column 44 which reads, "Arises *ḥ3i*-ing; circulation around the magistrates."[6] There is not much to note with regard to the actors in this example except that the *dmḏ(y)wt* appear to be in motion in columns 47-48,[7] and may still be performing the rite of *ḥ3i* here.

The third example of *ḥ3i* occurs in columns 64-65, which are badly damaged. Gardiner has managed to decipher the word *ḥ3i* at the beginning of column 64 and the word *dmḏ(y)t*, again, in column 65.

The fourth and last example of the word *ḥ3i* in this text occurs in column 84. Here Gardiner reconstructs the signs to read *rḫyt nbt* "All the common folk." It would seem that this last example of *ḥ3i* might be taking place in the embalming workshop (*wꜥbt*).[8]

To recapitulate, in this funerary liturgy there are two separate actors who are performing the ritual of *ḥ3i*, or are in some way associated with it: *dmḏ(y)t*[9] and *rḫyt nbt*. Neither of these participants occurs in any of the Old Kingdom sources as the actor in the *ḥ3i* ritual. However, there are New Kingdom tomb scenes which can be compared to this Liturgy with regard to the term *dmḏ(y)t*. These later references will be discussed at the end of this section.

dmḏ(y)t

It was initially thought by Gardiner, and followed by Faulkner, that the *dmḏ(y)t* was related to the *dmḏw*. The word *dmḏw* is commonly translated as "crowd" and is far more common;[10] however, in this source it is the feminine form that appears five times. In his dictionary entry Faulkner cites examples of *dmḏ(y)*t only from this text.[11] The entry for the word *dmḏ(y)t* in Wb V 462, 12 reads *"von der Klagefrau."* The *Belegstellen* lists two references from the tomb of Amenemhet (TT 82) (see below). In the funerary liturgy this designation is used both in the singular, *dmḏ(y)t*, and in the plural, *dmḏ(y)w*t. According to Gardiner, the word *dmḏ(y)t* also refers to a crowd and is "possibly identical with the collective *Wb* V 461, 12" — there transliterated *dmḏ.w*t.[12] Gardiner's assumption is based on the word's supposed connection with *dmḏw* and its reference to a crowd of people. With that, Gardiner points out that Coffin Text IV 371 features the "corresponding masculine word" (*dmḏw*) in "the crowd at the burial of Osiris."[13] Note that the word *ḥ3i* appears in this same spell, although it is not clear who exactly is performing the ritual.

In the New Kingdom, *dmḏ(y)t* is used as a title for a single woman (see below). Therefore, it appears that when the singular form is used in the Liturgy, it refers to a single woman; and when the plural form is used it refers to a group of women. In actuality *dmḏ(y)t* and *dmḏw* are two different words with entirely different meanings that are derived from the same root. The root of the two words is *dmḏ*, which in the Old Kingdom can mean "to collect or put together (the limbs of Osiris)."[14] This signification can be seen in the following Pyramid Texts:

[1] Gardiner 1955.
[2] See Chapter Eight for more information on the funerary liturgy and the evidence for its early date.
[3] Gardiner 1955, 12. In this article Gardiner translates *ḥ3i* as "wailing."
[4] See Diamond 2008a.
[5] Gardiner 1955, 11.
[6] Gardiner 1955, 13.
[7] Gardiner 1955, 13.
[8] Gardiner (1955, 14-15) suggests that the end of the section (col. 90) is completed with the word *wꜥbt*, without the house determinative. He reads the column, "in (or 'from') ...the place of embalmment of this So-and-so."
[9] The word *dmḏ(y)t* occurs in columns 16, 20, 47, 65 and 117. In columns 47 and 117 the word is written as a plural. All examples are written with a female determinative (Gardiner 1955, 12, n. 2). See below for more examples of this title.
[10] *Wb* V 461, 12; Faulkner 1991, 313; van der Molen 2000, 797.
[11] Faulkner 1991, 313.
[12] Gardiner 1955, 12, n. 2.
[13] Gardiner 1955, 12, n. 2. Faulkner (2004, 1:280) translates it entirely differently, namely, "on that day when all the gods were clothed at the burial of Osiris."
[14] Hannig 1997, 979-981; 2000, 1476-1477.

PT §318a: My limbs which were in concealment are reunited...[15]

PT §617b: He has put you together.[16]

PT §1036c-1037a: ...that you may assemble my bones and collect my members. May you gather together my bones...[17]

PT §1514b: This King's bones shall be reassembled, his members shall be gathered together.[18]

PT §1890a: O Osiris the King, knit together [your] limbs, reassemble your members, set your heart in its place![19]

These passages demonstrate that in the Old Kingdom the root *dmḏ* is intimately connected to the revivification process of Osiris. The word *dmḏw* is a masculine passive participle that means "those who are collected/assembled," and thus form "a crowd" (at the burial of Osiris). The word *dmḏ(y)t* is a feminine active participle that means "she who collects/assembles" (the limbs of Osiris); the corresponding plural *dmḏ(y)wt* means "those (f.) who collect/assemble" (the limbs of Osiris). This is significant because the *dmḏ(y)t*/*dmḏ(y)wt* perform the rejuvenating rite of *ḥ3i* at the funeral service in the liturgy. Likewise, the rite of *ḥ3i* is performed in CT IV 371 where the *dmḏw*, "crowd" gather at the burial of Osiris (with no further specification of their identity or role).

From the Funerary Liturgy, the following conclusions can be made about the *dmḏ(y)wt* "the collectors of Osiris' limbs." They attend the service at the mastaba on the day of burial; they attend the entire funeral service since they appear from beginning to end in the liturgy. The summoning of the deceased for revivification occurs in conjunction with their participation. If they themselves do not circulate around the mastaba, then at least they witness the circulation. They may move in opposite directions simultaneously, which may refer to dance movement (see above). The speech of the *dmḏ(y)wt* at the funeral service is introduced by *ḏd md*w. According to Ritner, the term *ḏd mdw* can be translated as "magical words to be said."[20] It is beyond doubt that what the *dmḏ(y)wt* are doing cannot be described as mourning. They are participating in an important part of the funeral service, namely, a ritual purification that includes magical recitation. This description is reminiscent of the scene in the tomb of Debehni where female dancers are accompanied by a caption explaining that they are performing the rite of *ḥ3i*. These women dance with their arms in the air and they speak the magical words, "His flesh is complete," which refers to the deceased's reconstructed body, in preparation for his subsequent rebirth.

The later New Kingdom references to *dmḏ(y)t* mentioned above occur in the tombs of Amenemhet (TT 82),[21] Rekhmire (TT 100)[22] (with two occurrences in each case), Mentuherkhepeshef (TT 20)[23] and Hekmaatre-nakht (TT 222).[24] The contexts do not give the impression that the word refers to a feminine plural noun, but rather a female individual. The word is a title and appears in the same two scenes in both TT 82 and TT 100, although one scene (plate XIII) in TT 82 is damaged.

In the first scene, two women — depicted one above the other — kneel before four tanks of water in the *s(my)t*, "desert necropolis,"[25] offering *nw*-jars. The area of this performance is the Sacred District or *t3 ḏsr*. These women have their hair cut short, and wear a fillet.[26] Robins describes the attire of these women as consisting of a cap of short black hair that leaves the ear uncovered. She acknowledges that there is no evidence as to whether the women's natural hair was cut for the occasion or whether she was wearing a wig.[27] Robins recognizes that short hair is not the norm for Eighteenth Dynasty women and concludes that its use was designed to mark the performance of a cultic role by a woman. The change in hairstyle shifts her identity from a secular one to a religious one. She also notes that the dress worn by the *dmḏ(y)t* and *knwt* is a more traditional garment no longer worn by women in secular contexts.[28] In TT 82 one woman is labeled *mnknw* and the other woman *dmḏ(y)t* (Figure 18). Gardiner suggests that *mnknw* is an epithet of Isis and *dmḏ(y)t* a name applied to Nephthys, based on a parallel scene in the

[15] Faulkner 1998, 69.

[16] Faulkner 1998, 119.

[17] Faulkner 1998, 173.

[18] Faulkner 1998, 232.

[19] Faulkner 1998, 274. Additional examples can be found in PT §§ 70a, 577b, 623b, 635a, 645a, 828b, 835b, 980b, 1789, 1801b, 2283 supplement.

[20] Ritner 1993, 50. He also states, "(these) terms conclude most magical recitation, serving to introduce the directions for the accompanying rite. Despite this fixed idiomatic usage, the phrase is by no means limited to purely 'magical' practice (as traditionally defined), and appears commonly as the introduction to both ritual responses by deities on temple walls and to cultic recitation. It is perhaps significant that this simple phrase, often encountered yet rarely analyzed, occurs in just those environments in which the traditional distinction between magic and religion is the most tenuous" (1993, 41).

[21] Gardiner 1915, pls. X, XIII.

[22] Davies 1973, pls. LXXXVIII, LXXIX.

[23] Davies 1913, pl. XIV.

[24] *PM* I.i, 323.

[25] Faulkner 1991, 227.

[26] This same scene also appears in TT 17, 21, 39, 81, and 123, although the labels are not the same. Settgast (1963, 64-65) offers a brief discussion on *Der Heilige Bezirk* and *Die vier Bassins*. See also Diamond 2009.

[27] Robins 1999, 67-68.

[28] Robins 1999, 68.

tomb of Paheri (see below).[29] In TT 100 the women are dressed in the same fashion, but they have switched positions with one another. One is labeled *dmḏ(y)t* and the other *knwt*.[30] This same scene appears in the tomb of Paheri at Elkab, but the labels are different. In the tomb of Paheri the two women are assumed to impersonate Isis and Nephthys by their respective titles: *ḏr(y)t wrt* and *ḏr(y)t nḏst* (Figure 19).[31]

The second scene, appearing in both TT 82 and TT 100, is more difficult to interpret. The scene in TT 82 is damaged, and all that is left is a woman standing facing left, her right arm bent in front of her with her right hand in a fist, and her left arm bent at her side with her hand in a fist. The caption reads, *ḏr(y)t wrt dmḏ(y)t*. In front of her there is the bottom portion of a wall or column resting on a plinth, probably the remains of a shrine. Above her is an identical woman, although only partly preserved; her label has been destroyed (Figure 20). Most likely she would have been the counterpart to the remaining figure. In TT 100 an identical woman appears before a shrine with the accompanying caption: *dr(y)wt dmd(y)wt*.[32] There is no second woman above her.

The two references to a *dmḏ(y)t* in TT 20 are different from the scenarios presented above (Figure 21). Davies describes this scene as depicting an ox bound for sacrifice followed by four female ministrants. We are concerned with the last two women who are labeled *dmḏ(y)t* and have their hand raised in adoration. Davies compares their costumes to the short dresses worn by women who dance and shake sistra in numerous other tomb scenes. He suggests the caption reads: "Offering carob-beans (?)." He associates the *dmḏ(y)t* with the funerary rites at the burial. This scene also includes various elements that we have seen before in this study: the tekenu and the mention of hair.[33]

The assumptions that can be made about the *dmḏ(y)t* from these later texts are that the *dmḏ(y)t* and *knwt/mnknwt* regularly appear together; that both of these individuals participate in funerary rituals beginning at least as early as the Middle Kingdom, depending on the date of the Funerary Liturgy and the traditions it reflects; and that in the New Kingdom there is an association between the *dmḏ(y)t* and *knwt/mnknwt*, and the two *ḏr(y)ty*. This latter connection should not at all be surprising considering the fact that Isis, who in her bird form, collects the pieces of Osiris' slain body and reassembles them to rejuvenate her husband. This is a significant example of a myth, in this case the Osirian myth, being used to explain an earlier ritual, namely the participation of a female "bone collector" in the funerary ritual.[34]

rḫyt nbt

The second title given to the performers in the Funerary Liturgy is "All the common folk." This popular appellation includes the word *rḫyt* meaning, "plebeians," "mankind," or "common folk."[35] This designation was noted above in regard to the participants in the New Kingdom dragging scene. Gardiner, in his discussion of the *rḫyt* in relation to the *rmṯw*, *pʿt*, and *ḥnmm(t)* states that these words frequently occur in the same order in magical texts and cover all areas of humankind. In this scheme, *rḫyt*

---

[29] Gardiner 1915, 52. He suggests that this ritual represents the fertilization of the barren desert in order to make it suitable for Osiris.

[30] It can be assumed that the label *mnknw* (TT 82) and *knwt* (TT 100) refer to the same title. In the tomb of Rekhmire (TT 100), the second section of the western half of the south wall of the passage shows a man and woman at either end of a boat, tying it to two mooring-posts. The man is labeled *ḥry-wr*, the woman is labeled *knwt*, and *mnit* is written above the post (Davies 1973, pl. LXXXII). Additionally, a *knwt* is represented twice sitting behind the *ḥry-wr* who is offering two *nw*-jars to the mooring-posts at the prow and the stern; she is labeled *ḥms(i)t knwt* (Davies 1973, pls. LXXX, LXXXI). The *knwt* in these two scenes is depicted differently from the *knwt* who kneels with the *dmḏ(y)t* before the tanks of water. It is possible that the label in TT 82 is attempting to incorporate the words *mni* "to moor" (Faulkner 1991, 107) and the title *knwt*; the title may actually be *knwt*, not *mnknw*. However, Settgast (1963, 65) points out that a *knwt* also appears in column 13 of Gardiner's Funerary Liturgy. Because the text is broken and an "n" occurs before *knwt*, it is possible that the word is *mnknwt*. Gardiner (1955, 12), in his description of the text, was unable to recognize the title or make any sense out of it: "Col. 13 refers to a priestess or some other woman in a way which I do not understand." There is also a third possibility. Hannig (1997, 884) notes that *kni* means to do something in a weepy sort of way and states that *knwy* means "mourning women," and *knwt* "mourning woman." Faulkner (1991, 286) suggests "be sullen(?); sullenness(?)." It is possible that the term *knwt* may also have something to do with complaining or lamenting. Through personal communication, Lanny Bell has suggested that the label may have read *mnk*, with the meaning of "one who cares for." His suggestion is based on a First Intermediate Period stela from Dra Abu el-Naga (Clère and Vandier 1948, 14, line 3). If this is the case, then the New Kingdom source has confused the words and misinterpreted the original meaning to have something to do with the nw-jars that the women are holding. It has also been suggested that *mnknw* may have a connection to the word "garden" (Tylor and Griffith 1894, 22; Gardiner 1915, 52). During my field work on the west bank of Thebes in early 2009 I discovered yet another example of a *knwt* in the tomb of Duauneheh (TT 125) (unpublished), or in this case the scribe had written *ktnw*. In the case of TT 125 the *ktnw* is mooring the funeral barque to a post in a similar scene to the one appearing in TT 100. There is no doubt that the same appellation is being employed here. However, I believe the existence of an additional misspelling of the word indicates its lack of usage in the 18th Dynasty. Most likely it is a holdover from an earlier tradition that has been included in these few tomb scenes for its value as an antiquated ritual, or historical scene.

[31] Tylor and Griffith 1894, 22, pl. V.

[32] See Davies 1973, plate LXXXVIII.

[33] Davies 1913, 15-18.

[34] See Hendrickx *et al.* 2010, 24-25. The authors describe evidence for religious and ritual activity at the Naqada II-III burials at Hierakonpolis. In particular, there were some individuals with cut marks found on the neck vertebrae which indicate that their throats had been cut or that they had been decapitated (also found at Adaïma). There is the possibility that these throat cuttings were part of a post-mortem ritual involving dismemberment and recreation.

[35] *Wb* II 447, 9-13; Gardiner 1947, 2:98*-112*; Faulkner 1991, 152.

signifies "plebeians." However, Gardiner believes that these terms are not necessarily mutually exclusive. He also stresses that "in the later and wider sense" all four words generally mean "mankind."[36] In early texts these four words are never found together. A contrast first occurs in the Middle Kingdom, where *pꜥt* and *rḫyt* are always written in this order (see below for a description of the tomb of Amenemhet, TT 82). Gardiner finishes his commentary by listing five contexts in which *rḫyt* occurs: as enemies of the king, as subjects of the king, as common people, in titles, and in phrases contrasting *rḫyt* and *pꜥt*. In the end, he concludes that *rḫyt* is a term of Lower Egyptian origin and that the lapwing bird is used to determine the word. One might assume that in this case the term is being applied generally to people attending the funeral with no particular affiliation or ritual identification.

Coffin Texts

The second major source for Middle Kingdom references to *ḥ3i* is the Coffin Texts. The Coffin Texts present many contexts for the word *ḥ3i* that are not seen in the other sources. In addition, the Coffin Texts demonstrate that many different people can perform this ritual. There also seem to be two cases where a bird carries out the rite (not to be confused with a bird doing bird activity – see above). Table 6 illustrates the frequency of the appearance of the different performers of *ḥ3i* in the Coffin Texts. CT IV 331g and IV 336g are left out of this study because the word *ḥ3(i)t* refers to a locality and does not offer a participant to examine. All Coffin Texts that include the avian motif are considered separately in Chapter Five. However, there are some references to *ḥ3i* that are written with a bird determinative; when no other evidence for the avian motif is present the text is discussed here.

Certain passages that include the word *ḥ3i* listed in Table 6 below are of little use for this study on the participants in that they read in circles. For example, CT III 307a-b and CT III 317e present expressions comparable to: A cook who cooks. The title is a derivative of the original word. What these passages can tell us is that one who bears the title *ḥ3(i)t* performs the rite of *ḥ3i*.

The performers of *ḥ3i* can be categorized under the heading: those who assume the title *ḥ3it* (fem. sing.) or *ḥ3itiw* (masc. plur.). There are eight examples to consider. In these cases the subject is not otherwise clearly identified.

In CT II 177h the title denotes a masculine plural subject. This particular spell is for assembling the deceased's family in the realm of the dead. In the single copy of this text, *ḥ3itiw* is written with a god determinative. Faulkner translates *ḥ3itiw* as "mourners";[37] however, there is nothing in the context to corroborate this translation — in fact, the divine determinative implies that the *ḥ3itiw* were godly – or born again.

CT III 22a also mentions a *ḥ3(i)t*, this time in the singular. Faulkner is perplexed by this text.[38] In five of the copies the god determinative is used, in four the woman determinative is used, and in one, the book roll is employed. Unfortunately, there is no other information regarding the identity of the *ḥ3(i)t*.

CT III 297i provides a further example of this title. In this case it seems that the Lady of Goodness (*nbt nfrw*) is the one who assumes this title and performs the ritual of *ḥ3i* over Osiris in the Pure Place (*wꜥbt*). There is no mention in this context of any bird-related activity, yet the G 41 determinative is employed in both copies.

CT III 307a-b reads, "*ḥ3(i)t* of Osiris who *ḥ3(i)*-s the limp Great One." In this example of *ḥ3(i)t*, the woman determinative and the god determinative are used. In the second example, the A 28 pose is coupled with the G 38 bird, or this bird appears alone. Copy T1Be lacks determinatives in both cases, and copy T2L adds a forearm determinative in the second example. CT III 308d is part of the same spell; therefore, the epithet pertains to the same person in both sections. There are no determinatives in any of the four copies of this spell, except for copy A1C, which is written altogether incorrectly. CT III 311h is identical to CT III 307a. It is known from the Pyramid Texts that Isis is called a *ḥ3(i)t* while she attends to Osiris. It is reasonable to assume that the title refers to Isis in this spell as well.

CT III 317e also has two examples of *ḥ3(i)t*, both of which represent the subject. Aside from being the person who performs *ḥ3i* for Osiris, she is also his attendant and the Mistress of the *Pr-nw*. *Pr-nw* is the national shrine of Lower Egypt located at Dep.[39]

In CT VII 28o, Isis, also called the Mistress of Thrones, performs *ḥ3i* for Osiris. There is no determinative.

Lastly, the *dmḏw* appear to be involved with the *ḥ3i* rite at the burial of Osiris in CT IV 371a-373a. Faulkner's translation does not name this group of people;[40] however, Gardiner supplies the transliteration and translation, *dmḏw r ḳrs Wsir* "The crowd at the burial of Osiris."[41] In the Coffin Texts example *dmḏw* is written with a god determinative and/or the book roll

[36] Gardiner 1947, 2:99*.

[37] Faulkner 2004, 1:122.

[38] Faulkner 2004, 1:144.

[39] Faulkner 1991, 89.

[40] Faulkner 2004, 1:280. See note 297 above.

[41] Gardiner 1955, 12, n. 2.

determinative.[42] (See above for a discussion on the *dmḏw* and *dmḏ(y)t*.)

Summation of Middle Kingdom Participants

To conclude, it is evident that someone who holds the title *ḥ3(i)t* (and its variants) can perform the rite of *ḥ3i*. By analogy with the Pyramid Texts it is reasonable to assume that the *ḥ3(i)t* is Isis in at least three of the four spells (CT III 307-8, III 317e, VII 280). Already in the Pyramid Texts Isis is called a *ḥ3it*; the Coffin Texts confirm this appellation, and also apply the label to the goddess Nephthys (CT I 303g). There are many examples of the title *ḥ3(i)t* in the Coffin Texts; and even when the title does not designate Isis, the Osirian allusions are clear (Table 4 in Chapter One). Likewise, both males and females perform the rite in the Coffin Texts. They can *ḥ3i* in groups or individually. Furthermore, when the term *ḥ3it* is written, a bird determinative is regularly employed. This may mean the performer is imagined as a bird, or the title is somehow symbolic of a bird. Likewise, it may infer that the holder of the title performs an act indicative of a bird – namely, transport the deceased to the Hereafter (See Chapter Five). Different determinatives were used for the same word in the various copies of the same spell. This may indicate that the scribes were not exactly sure of the word's significance. Nevertheless, there is a strong connection between *ḥ3i* and birds, while the popular A 28 determinative rarely occurs in the Coffin Texts.

[42] The one exception is copy S5C, which does not have a determinative.

TABLE 6: PERFORMERS OF *ḥ3i* IN THE COFFIN TEXTS

Source	Isis and/or Nephthys	The Two Sisters	*dmḏw*	Bird	Deceased	*ḥ3i* used as title	*ḥ3i* as verb with *ḥ3(i)t* as subject	Other
CT I 73d				X				
CT I 74e	X			X[43]				
CT I 303g	X							
CT II 177h						X		
CT II 238b					X			
CT II 239a					X			
CT III 22a						X		
CT III 297i						X		
CT III 307a						X		
CT III 307b							X	
CT III 308d						X		
CT III 311h						X		
CT III 317e						X		
CT III 317e							X	
CT III 317l		X						
CT IV 373a			X					
CT IV 373a			X					
CT V 332c				X				
CT VI 360j								X
CT VI 385o		X						
CT VII 28o						X		
CT VII 51s								X

[43] For CT I 74e I put an X in two columns because Isis and Nephthys perform *ḥ3i* as the *ḏr(y)ty*.

Chapter Four

Introduction

This next section will examine the New Kingdom participants who perform the ritual of *ḥ3i*. There are six different sources: the tomb of Amenemhet (TT 82), Book of the Dead Chapters 1 and 172 (including TT C4), Louvre stela C 286 (BD 185 A),[1] the Book of Gates, and the Amduat. As was the case with the last two chapters, Louvre stela C 286 will be considered separately in Chapter Five because of the apparent avian motif.

TT 82: smr and ẖry-ḥbt

In the tomb of Amenemhet, *ḥ3(i)t* appears in the caption translated by Gardiner as "Rejoicing in faring upstream."[2] The caption appears above a skiff carrying a white naos (Figure 22). It appears that the *smr* and *ẖry-ḥbt* are traveling toward the necropolis while performing the rite of *ḥ3i*. Gardiner has obviously translated the word as *ḥ'i* "to rejoice," instead of *ḥ3*i. The two words have the same determinative, and he must have assumed that the context called for rejoicing. There is sufficient evidence to show that an action that looks like rejoicing took place during the rite of *ḥ3i* (see Old Kingdom evidence above). This is the only reference that shows *ḥ3i* being performed on water; however, the skiff is arriving at the necropolis, which is a more fitting location according to earlier examples (see Chapter Six). It is not the only example, however, that links *ḥ3i* with transportation. We can see this parallel in the dragging scene in the tomb of Hetepherakhti, PT §744, and the avian notion inherent in the ritual of *ḥ3i* (Chapter Five) – the common element being the transfer of the body to a place of rejuvenation. After all, the cemetery was a place of transformation. Rites and rituals changed over time, and this depiction may represent a new variation of the original ritual. This scene is associated with the scene to the right of it that appears at the top of plate X,[3] where a courtier brings the oars to land. This courtier moves toward a shrine, behind which are the two kneeling women discussed above (Figure 18), who are labeled *mnknw* and *dmḏ(y)t*. This information is important because it provides the larger context in which the rite of *ḥ3i* appears. A scene parallel to the one depicting the skiff can be found in the tomb of Paheri at Elkab (Figure 23). Unfortunately, there is no inscription accompanying the scene in this tomb. Griffith suggests that the person sitting at the front of the skiff is a mourner, a designation possibly reliant on the misconception that *ḥ3i* means "to mourn."[4] In TT 82, this person is clearly labeled a lector (*ẖry-ḥbt*). The tomb of Rekhmire (TT 100) offers another parallel scene. The people on the skiff in this tomb are labeled *smr* and *ẖr(y)-wr*.[5] It can be ascertained that the people riding on the skiff are intimately connected with the funeral rituals for the deceased. Sigrid Hodel-Hoenes describes this scene as part of the rituals performed for the Mooring Post.[6]

In the New Kingdom the Mooring Post is associated with the rite of *ḥ3i*, as it was in the Old Kingdom. In the Old Kingdom, titles appearing on ostraca equate the overseer of the *šnḏt* with the *mni(w)t wrt* (the Great Mooring Post) (see above).[7] The women of the *šnḏt* perform the rite of *ḥ3i* in private funerals, and the Great Mooring Post is the overseer of the Acacia House. This connection may indicate that the same entity, or organization, that was responsible for the *ḥ3i* ritual in the Old Kingdom is still responsible for it in the New Kingdom.

The caption above the skiff, which is on its way to the necropolis, tells us that the men onboard are doing the rite of *ḥ3i*. This was done in preparation for the spiritualization of Amenemhet, and was part of the rites performed in conjunction with the Mooring Post.

The Book of the Dead

BD 1: *ḥ3yw*

The Book of the Dead offers three subjects for discussion. In Chapter One of the Book of the Dead the *ḥ3yw* appear. Here the word is being used as a title (in participial form) to refer to a group of men, in contrast to the group of women who are lamenting (*i3kb*) in the same context. This word is written with a man determinative, while the following title *i3kbywt* is written with the woman determinative. Both groups are performing their respective functions for Osiris. The text states that the deceased was reborn in Busiris when he was with the men who performed the rite of *ḥ3i*.[8] This is a clear and concise example showing that *ḥ3i* means to ritually transport the deceased to immortality.

BD 172: The Deceased

In Chapter 172 of the Book of the Dead[9] the sentences with the word *ḥ3i* are written in the passive voice. Although we know that the rite of *ḥ3i* is being performed for the deceased, we do not know who is responsible for the ritual. The relevant passage reads: *i mk ḥ3(i).t(w).k sp sn*. In Faulkner's publication of the papyrus of Ani, he translates this as, "See, you are doubly mourned" and

---

[1] T.G. Allen 1974, 203. In the hymn to Osiris on Louvre stela C 286 (BD 185A), the text clearly states that the individual portrayed as a *ḥ3yt*-bird is Isis. She traverses the land to find and save Osiris, and then rejoices at his rebirth (see translation of passage in Chapter Eight).

[2] Davies and Gardiner 1915, 52, pl. XI.

[3] Davies and Gardiner 1915.

[4] Tylor and Griffith 1894, 21.

[5] Davies 1973, plate LXXXI.

[6] Hodel-Hoenes 2000, 168.

[7] Saad 1947, pls. 42 and 43.

[8] T.G. Allen 1974, 5; Faulkner 1994, pl. 5.

[9] The four known sources are: the papyrus of Nebseni, TT C4, the linen shroud of Princess Ahmose (Turin 5051), and a late Ptolemaic version of the Book of the Dead (BM 10209). I thank Professor Leonard Lesko for bringing the latter two examples to my attention. See L. Lesko, 2007.

places it at the beginning of each stanza.[10] T. G. Allen, on the other hand, writes the phrase out twice (*sp sn*) and translates, "Behold, thou art mourned, thou art mourned"; he places it at the end of each stanza.[11] I prefer Allen's placement at the end of each section because it encapsulates the description presented in each stanza by plainly stating that the deceased has been resurrected in the Hereafter. Therefore, this sentence reiterates the sentiment presented in each full stanza. Examples of statements made in this spell that corroborate this assumption are the following: "Thou art lifted," "Thy nose is (provided) with breath; [the air in] thy nostrils is like the winds in the sky," and "Re blesses thee in his pure abode." The entire spell speaks of the deceased's rejuvenation. In stanza six, the deceased is asked to lift himself up, in order to hear the blessings of his family. This is immediately followed by *i mk ḥ3(i).t(w).k sp sn*, "thou art spiritualized (ritually transported), thou art spiritualized (ritually transported)." The concluding statement refers to the rebirth of the deceased.

Book of Gates: Four Goddesses

The penultimate example of *ḥ3i* is from the twelfth hour of the Book of Gates. Isis and Nephthys guard this final gate in the Netherworld, through which the sun god will enter the horizon. This can be equated with the rebirth of the king. The inscription appears above four goddesses and states:

> "They *ḥ3(i)* with their hair before this great god in the West."[12]

This passage is reminiscent of CT III 22a where a *ḥ3(i)t* prepares her hair/scalp – for what? We are not told. Likewise, the determinative used in the word *ḥ3i* in the inscription in TT C4 (BD 172) is a woman with her hair flung forward. This repetition may be coincidental but it is worth noting (see above). Hair was of immense importance to the ancient Egyptians, and was symbolic of status.[13] Perhaps the significance of hair in this case lies in its presence rather than its absence. There is no doubt that there is symbolism in the manner that hair is depicted on mourners in New Kingdom tomb scenes, for example. However, because the king is on the verge of being reborn in the Twelfth Hour of the night mourning is not an appropriate response. It is more likely that the reference to hair may signify new life and rebirth; or at the very least the end of the mourning period. The Pyramid Texts state that new life springs forth from the tresses of the goddess Yusas (see above), which were compared to the branches of the acacia tree. Additionally, PT §1363 tells of the resurrection of Osiris and equates the mummy bandages of the deceased with the locks of hair of Nephthys. The mummy bandages can also be associated with new life in that they are holding together the corpse of the deceased so that it will be preserved for use in the Next World. The notion of resurrection is of utmost importance at this part in the Book of Gates: the sun god is about to enter the horizon, which signifies new life. The presence of Isis and Nephthys at the final gate before resurrection provides a tangible connection between the participants in the Book of Gates and those in the other sources.

Amduat: A Goddess?

Another book of the Afterlife that gives an example of *ḥ3i* is the Amduat. In this source *ḥ3yt* refers to a single female in the upper register of the third hour. As is noted in Chapter Eight, Budge suggests that *ḥ3yt* is the name of a goddess as a professional mourner.[14] Hornung suggests that the woman is also a goddess, whose name as a mourner is *"Die sich entblößt."*[15] Regardless of their interpretations, *ḥ3yt* refers to a woman of divine status who in this case resides in the Waters of Osiris. She appears to symbolize a particular ritual that is performed in conjunction with weeping (*rmi*), lamenting (*i3kb*) and praising (*m3tyt*). The illustrations seem to indicate that these women have a connection with Osiris, as he manifests himself several times in the bottom register of the third hour. There are two significant reasons to suggest that this goddess is called "she who ritually transports/resurrects." First of all, this function fits well with the other three mentioned as concerns funerary ritual; and second, Osiris, as a symbol of regeneration, requires this fourth aspect to reflect the process of rebirth which he embodies.

Summation of New Kingdom Participants

To summarize, a *smr* and *ḥry-ḥbt*, a group of men called *ḥ3yw*, Isis as a *ḥ3yt*-bird, a goddess identified only by her title *ḥ3yt*, and a group of four goddesses all perform the ritual of *ḥ3i* in the New Kingdom. The only goddess to be clearly identified as a *ḥ3yt*-bird is Isis. The goddesses in the books of the Afterlife are not named, are not in bird form, and their titles do not possess a bird determinative. The sources that feature the ritual of *ḥ3i* in the New Kingdom are diverse and do not show the consistency that they do in the Old Kingdom, and to some extent in the Middle Kingdom. However, these later sources do confirm the Osirian nuances of the ritual. In this later stage of the ritual the common thread does not lie in the participants, as the selection of New Kingdom performers cannot unequivocally establish any characteristic of the ritual of *ḥ3i*. It is still common, though, for the participants to be predominantly female. Possibly the maternal characteristics of women - their

[10] Faulkner 1994, 129.
[11] T.G. Allen 1974, 179-180.
[12] Zandee 1960, 112.
[13] See Shaw and Nicholson 1995, s.v. "hair"; Fletcher and Montserrat 1995; Green 2001; Robins 1999; and for hair in general see Robins 1999, 55, note 2.
[14] Budge 1906, 53.
[15] Hornung 1972, 85.

natural role as child-bearer, nurse, and care-giver - make them an obvious choice for securing life in the Hereafter for the deceased. By the New Kingdom the rite of *ḥ3i* may be an anachronistic ritual, one containing vestiges of the past and one that is recorded only for the sake of tradition.

Developments Over Time

The sources from the three Kingdoms present a variety of participants for the *ḥ3i* ritual. These references provide parallels that allow several patterns to be established. First, women are the predominant participants in all periods, performing the ritual both individually and in groups.

In the Old Kingdom the women are associated with the *šnḏt* (belong to the Acacia House). This organization symbolized the forces of life, death, and regeneration. The scenes from TT 82 may indicate that the Acacia House is still functioning in the New Kingdom, or that its successor is now responsible for the *ḥ3i* ritual. One can see that in the New Kingdom the Osirian overtones are paramount, which corresponds to Osiris' increased association with the acacia tree over time. In TT 82 the rites for the Mooring Post (and the Sacred District in general) are associated with the spiritualizing ritual of *ḥ3i* - a connection visible already in the Old Kingdom sources where the sources implies a relationship between the Great Mooring Post and the Acacia House.

Second, the *dmd(y)t* is another significant participant. First seen in the Funerary Liturgy performing *ḥ3i*, she later reappears in a New Kingdom context within the Sacred District.[16] Her role as "bone/limb collector" begins in a non-Osirian context (Funerary Liturgy); however, there is no doubt that her later merging with Isis in the New Kingdom tomb scenes is associated with the superimposition of the Osirian characters on earlier ritual ministrants. It may also be significant that Isis is a *ḥ3(i)t*-bird who essentially performs the same function as the *dmḏ(y)t*.

Third, when deities are involved in the ritual, they are also female (see Chapter Eight).

There are a few examples where men participate in the ritual; however, the evidence does not show that they are in bird form, nor does it indicate that they might be divine. When men perform the ritual in the Old Kingdom they are associated with the mortuary workshops and seem to carry the title in their professional capacity. Women, on the other hand, are associated with the cultic realm – the Acacia House – for example.

Table 7 presents an overview of the participants who perform *ḥ3i*. More specifically, the table shows that *ḥ3i* can appear as a transitive or intransitive verb. In the first column the source of the example is listed, in the second column the performer or subject is listed, and in the third column the recipient or object of the action is listed. The fourth column, entitled "impersonal," refers to those examples that present a reference to *ḥ3i* occurring as an intransitive verb or as a title — *ḥ3(i)w*, *ḥ3(i)t*, *ḥ3ywy*, *ḥ3yty*, and *ḥ3(i)tiw*. In these cases the person (or people) who is given this label is identified under the performer heading.

[16] Diamond 2009.

TABLE 7: ACTORS INVOLVED IN THE PERFORMANCE OF *ḥ3i*

	Source	Performer	Recipient	Impersonal
1	Tomb of Debehni	4 or 7 women belonging to the *šnḏt*	Deceased	
2	Tomb of Hetepherakhti	4 women who probably belong to the *šnḏt*	Deceased	
3	Tomb of Qar	4 women belonging to the *šnḏt*	Deceased	
4	Inscription of Sabni	Masculine plural noun	Deceased	Title — *ḥ3(i)tiw*
5	Tomb of Pepiankh	1 man	Deceased	Title — *ḥ3(i)w*
6	PT §550	Nursing cows	Osiris = Deceased	
7	PT §744	*Wršiw*	Deceased King	
8	PT §1255	Isis	Osiris = Deceased	
9	PT §1280	Isis	Osiris = King[17] = Deceased	
10	PT §1585	Deceased King or Queen	the god *šs3*	
11	PT §1791	"you" = Isis ?	"him" = Osiris ?	
12	PT §2112	First Person - Deceased	Osiris	
13	PT §2117[18]	First Person	King	
14	Funerary Liturgy col. 16	*dmḏ(y)t*		No Direct Object
15	F.L. col. 44-45	*dmḏywt?*[19]	Deceased?	
16	F.L. col. 64	*dmḏywt?*[20]	Deceased?	
17	F.L. col. 84	All the common folk ?[21]	Bearer of skins?	
18	CT I 73d	The Falcon	Second Person = Deceased	
19	CT I 74e	The Two Kites: Isis and Nephthys	Second Person = Deceased	
20	CT I 303g	Isis	Osiris = Deceased	
21	CT II 177h	Masculine, Plural Noun	Deceased's fire is quenched by subject	Title — *ḥ3(i)tiw*
22	CT II 238b	First Person – Deceased		Title — *ḥ3(i)w*
23	CT II 239a	First Person - Deceased		Title given to the deceased's "wing's" — *ḥ3ywy*
24	CT III 22a	Two Women		Two Women are called *ḥ3yty* and asked to do their hair for the First Person.
25	CT III 297i	Lady of Goodness (*nbt nfrw*)	Osiris	
26	CT III 307 a-b[22]	A *ḥ3(i)t* performs the action of *ḥ3i*.[23]	Osiris (the limp Great One)	*ḥ3(i)t* in CT III 307a is written as a title.

[17] I have included the word "King" in the chart only if the text specifically refers to him. However, in the Pyramid Texts the recipient was the deceased King, often referred to as Osiris.

[18] This is in the same utterance as the one listed above it.

[19] The text is unreadable at this point although the *dmḏ(y)wt* are mentioned in column 47 and may be related (Gardiner 1955, 13).

[20] Column 65 also mentions the *dmḏ(y)t* (Gardiner 1955, 14).

[21] Column 83 is completely destroyed so the translation of this section also proves difficult. I am not sure if column 85 is a continuation of column 84. It appears that column 84 reads: *rḫyt nbt ḥ3(i).sn*. The top of column 85 reads: *ẖr* followed by the hieroglyph F 27, plural strokes and a man determinative.

[22] I included both CT III 307a and 307b together because the two examples of *ḥ3i* occur in the same sentence and are related to one another.

27	CT III 308d[24]	Lady of All	Her Lord	
28	CT III 311h[25]	Unidentified Female	Osiris	Title — *ḥ3(i)t*
29	CT III 317e (x2)	Unidentified Female in both cases	Osiris	Title — *ḥ3(i)[t]*
30	CT III 317l	The Two Sisters		No Direct Object
31	CT IV 331g	Two Banks		Title of Two Banks
32	CT IV 373a	Masculine plural third person referring to previously mentioned *dmḏw*	Osiris	
33	CT IV 373a	Masculine plural third person referring to previously mentioned *dmḏw* (same subject as above)	Second Person	
34	CT V 332c	The fowl of the dwellers of the Netherworld	Deceased	
35	CT VI 360j	"They" (masc. plur. suffix)	Osiris	
36	CT VI 385o	Two Sisterly Companions	The Great One, their father, and their son	
37	CT VII 28o	Mistress of Thrones[26]	Osiris	
38	CT VII 51s	Your (pl.) Great One	"Woe!"	
39	Tomb of Amenemhet	*ẖry-ḥbt* and a *smr*		No Direct Object
40	BD 1	Masc., Plur. Noun	Osiris	Title — *ḥ3yw*
41	BD 172	No Subject	Second person masc. singular	
42	Louvre Stela C 286 (BD 185A)	Isis	Osiris	
43	Book of Gates	Third person plural		
44	Amduat IV 34	One woman; some suggest the goddess Isis		Title — *ḥ3yt*

[23] The subject is feminine singular and is written with a god determinative. Possibly the subject is Isis.
[24] Both examples of *ḥ3i* in this passage are included as one entry in this chart for the same reason as above.
[25] This is the same passage as CT III 307a.
[26] The text reads, "*ḥ3(i)*t of Osiris." The subject is a single female. In the following line the Mistress of thrones is mentioned, and then in the line after that the Mistress of All is referred to. These feminine titles, the feminine singular pronoun that is used in the first line, the phrase "I come that I may greet you," and the feminine form of *ḥ3(i)t* all point to a single female.

Chapter Five

Introduction

Throughout the Old, Middle, and New Kingdom textual sources there is continuous reference to a *ḥ3(i)t*-bird. These citations need to be considered separately in order to fully appreciate the evolution of this avian motif. Many references to the deceased turning into a bird have been made thus far in this work, although without direct reference to *ḥ3i*. There are references in the Coffin Texts to the deceased being a *ḥ3(i)t*-bird; however, most reference to this phenomenon can include any type of bird. In considering all references together one can obtain a better perspective on the connection between *ḥ3i* and the avian motif. There was a practical purpose to the deceased transforming into a bird. Hoffmeier briefly mentions this issue in his work where he states that a man was not transformed into a heron simply because of the sensation to fly like bird but because the man needed to fly to various locations and partake in rites to assist his becoming a god.[1]

The ḥ3it-Bird: Old Kingdom Royal Sources

The earliest textual sources connecting the term *ḥ3i* with an avian notion are the Pyramid Texts and the reliefs from Niuserre's Sun Temple at Abu Ghurob. The Pyramid Text utterances devoid of this motif are discussed above in Chapter Two. The following section will discuss all of the sources where this avian concept is present. One important distinction needs to made, namely, natural bird activity must be distinguished from ritualized activity. In certain cases the references appear to be referring to an actual bird. For example, the two examples from Niuserre's Sun Temple mention only a bird and in each case the text functions as a label.[2]

The next two Old Kingdom examples of the word *ḥ3i* appear in PT §1255 and PT §1280, where the goddess Isis is imagined as a *ḥ3(i)t*-bird. Her counterpart, Nephthys, is imagined as a *ḏryt*, usually translated into English as "kite." Here the passages follow in numerical order:

> Isis comes and Nephthys comes, one of them from the west and one of them from the east, one of them as a *ḥ3(i)t*, one of them as a kite.[3]
>
> Thus said Isis and Nephthys: The *ḥ3(i)t* comes, the kite comes, namely Isis and Nephthys.[4]

In his translation, Faulkner renders *ḥ3(i)t* as "screecher." He notes that the bird is a falcon or a similar raptor.[5] He has based his translation on the assumption that *ḥ3(i)t* is derived from the word *ḥ3i*, which he defines as "screech." Mercer leaves the Egyptian untranslated and employs "*ḥ3t*-bird" in his translation.[6]

The two goddesses Isis and Nephthys are consistently referred to as a pair who prepares the deceased king for his resurrection in the Hereafter. They perform a variety of actions such as locating, collecting, protecting, reassembling, and calling to the deceased king.

According to Fischer, beginning in the Pyramid Texts, Isis and Nephthys are called *ḏrty*, the two mourning birds.[7] However, there is not one example in the Pyramid Texts where Isis is called a *ḏryt*. The two examples where Nephthys is called a *ḏryt* are PT §§1255 and 1280, the two passages under discussion. The goddess Tait is called a *ḏryt* in PT §741, and the deceased king flaps his wings like a *ḏryt* in PT §§463 and 1484.

In both of these Pyramid Texts passages (§§1255 and 1280) the two goddesses are searching for their brother Osiris, with whom the dead king is associated. The purpose of their action is to prevent the putrefaction of Osiris' corpse, who has been killed by Seth. This intent is demonstrated in the following passages that occur in the same utterances as PT §§1255 and PT 1280 respectively:

> They [Isis and Nephthys] prevent you from rotting ... they prevent your putrefaction... they prevent the smell of your corpse from becoming foul.[8]
>
> You [the deceased king] shall have no putrefaction.[9]

The "two kites" (*ḏryty*) are mentioned in PT §§230, 308, 312 and 1254; however, these passages never state that this title specifically refers to Isis and Nephthys. In fact, neither Isis nor Nephthys is mentioned in any of these sections. Consequently, *ḥ3(i)t* is the only bird title given to Isis in the Pyramid Texts, where she functions as one who rejuvenates, not one who laments.

In the tomb chapels of the Fifth and Sixth Dynasties two female mourners assume the title *ḏryty* and appear at the bow and stern of the boat that conveys the coffin.[10] It has been suggested that when PT §1255 speaks of one of them as coming from the west and one of them as coming from the east, it most likely refers to their positioning on either end of the bier.[11]

[1] Hoffmeier 1985, 96.
[2] Edel 1961, Abb. 11.
[3] Faulkner 1998, 199-200.
[4] Faulkner 1998, 203.
[5] Faulkner 1998, 198.
[6] Mercer 1952, 1:207, 210.
[7] Fischer 1976, 39; See also Münster 1968, 1, 53-55, 61, 111, 113, 114, 149f, 193, 201.
[8] Faulkner 1998, 200.
[9] Faulkner 1998, 203.
[10] Fischer 1976, 39.
[11] Münster 1968, 55. See Fischer 1976, fig. 6.

The one connection that has already been referred to above and will be elaborated on below is that Isis can lead the deceased into the Hereafter and the bird is the prime mode of transportation used to reach the Hereafter. So Isis as a *ḥ3it*-bird is a logical and expected construct.

Birds and ḥ3i in the Coffin Texts[12]

From the Middle Kingdom Coffin Texts there are several passages that contain reference to *ḥ3i* or its variants: the *ḥ3it*-bird or the *ḥ3iw*-bird, the latter term being the masculine counterpart.[13] By the Middle Kingdom one can see the masculine form becoming much more common than before. There are some passage that can be compared to Old Kingdom examples, such as CT I 303g where Nephthys is imagined as a *ḥ3(i)t*-bird instead of Isis, although the context is the same as PT §1255. Conversely, the *ḥ3iw*-bird featured in CT II 238b appears in circumstances completely different from the earlier texts. Here the deceased is depicted as a vicious bird who possesses the wings of a *ḥ3(i)w*-bird in order to have power over his enemies in the realm of the dead. Additionally, reference is made to qualities that actually refer to the bird, as opposed to the ritual.

There are three passages (CT I 73d, 74e, and CT V 332c) where the subject of the verb *ḥ3i* is a bird (or birds);[14] in the first case, a falcon (*bik*), in the second case, Isis and Nephthys as *ḏr(y)ty*, and in the third case, fowl (*3pdw*). The *ḥ3i* ritual performed by the falcon in CT I 73d (determined by the A 28, D 40 and G 41 signs) appears to be a prerequisite — along with various other actions — for ascending to the sky. This spell over-emphasizes the bird symbolism. This may be for literary purposes, metaphorical or otherwise.

The bird determinative is not used in CT I 74e; instead A 28 and D 40 are used in separate copies. CT I 74e has a connection to the two previous citations (CT I 73d and CT V 332c), in that Isis and Nephthys each take the form of a kite (*ḏryt*). Isis and Nephthys, as the Two Sisters and as the Two Sisterly Companions, are connected with the rite of *ḥ3i* in CT III 317l and CT VI 385o, respectively. In the latter example they perform the ritual of *ḥ3i* for the Great One, their father, and their son, in order to prevent the putrefaction of the corpse in the realm of the dead. This writing of *ḥ3i* is determined by the book roll sign (Y 2).

CT III 317l is more difficult to analyze. Faulkner believes that *ḥ3i* is a corruption of *ʿḥʿ*. Below in Chapter Eight I have clearly illustrated that this is indeed an example of *ḥ3i*. Isis and Nephthys stand behind Anubis and perform the rite. The action in this case is determined by the forearm sign (D 36).

CT V 332c recounts that the fowl belonging to the dwellers in the Netherworld shall not *ḥ3i* (with G 38 determinative) over the deceased. The purpose of this spell is not to die a second time in the realm of the dead, so presumably the deceased wishes to keep his corpse intact in order to live in the Hereafter. Obviously this is one instance where the term *ḥ3i* has its original meaning — that is the avian meaning that refers to the action of the bird.

The passage in CT V 332c may be interpreted in light of Anthes's supposition that some birds may have waited either for a serpent or for the offal from the preparation of the corpse (this idea is discussed above). Anthes points out that these birds may have been permanent attendants of the body before its interment, and hence the development of the bird forms of Isis and Nephthys was initiated.[15] There is no doubt that certain sources depict the *ḥ3iw*-bird as a vicious, ferocious bird that has predatory tendencies (CT II 238b, 239a, and Thutmose I's Tombos inscription – *Urk* IV 84, 10). Perhaps the instinctual activity of the *ḥ3(i)t*-bird, namely, pecking, gnawing at, and eventually flying away with pieces of a corpse led the ancient Egyptians to formulate a story surrounding the ascension of the deceased to the Hereafter. Eventually culminating is the king transforming into a bird and flying there himself (see below).

Additionally, there are the two examples where the deceased is described as a *ḥ3(i)w*-bird, both of which occur in Spell 149 (CT II 238b, CT II 239a). The spell is entitled, "BECOMING A HUMAN FALCON, MAKING A MAN A SPIRIT IN THE REALM OF THE DEAD, GIVING A MAN POWER OVER HIS FOES, AND SAYING <TO> A MAN: BE SHOD WITH A PAIR OF WHITE SANDALS <AND BE CLAD IN> A KILT AND SASH(?) OF RED LINEN."[16] The first section reads as follows:

> I have appeared as a great falcon, I have grasped him with my talons, my lips are on him as a gleaming knife, my talons are on him like the arrows of Sakhmet, my horns are on him as the Great Wild Bull, my wings are on him as a *ḥ3w*-bird, my tail is on him as a living soul.

The first citation (CT II 238b) is written with either a bird determinative (G 38, G 40) or with both a bird determinative and a god determinative. The choice of determinative may be indicative of the fact that the

[12] All passages are presented in full in Chapter Eight.

[13] Van der Molen 2000, 307. CT I 303g is the equivalent of PT §1255. CT I 303g and CT IV 331g contain the word *ḥ3yt*. CT II 238b mentions a *ḥ3(i)w*-bird, and CT II 239a employs the dual of this form.

[14] Please note the need to differentiate between the deceased being described as a *ḥ3iw*-bird and a bird performing *ḥ3i*.

[15] Anthes 1959, 207.

[16] Faulkner 2004, 1:127.

Egyptians identified the realization of eternal life to be like the gods. Additionally, the answer may be found in the title of the spell – "a man is becoming a spirit." The means of which is symbolized by the bird determinative and the outcome by the god determinative.

The second citation (CT II 239a) is more complicated in that the spell describes the deceased's arms as two *ḥ3(i)w*: "My pinion are on him as two *ḥ3(i)w*-birds." This reference in CT II 239a is also written with a bird determinative (G 38). This spell is unlike the other texts that include the word *ḥ3i*, which makes it difficult to compare with the others. The only commonality that exists is the bird form assumed by the deceased (for example, refer to the form of Isis in PT §§1255 and 1280). In this case the focus is on a characteristic held by the *ḥ3iw*-bird.

The Coffin Texts also provide an example where Nephthys alone performs the ritual of *ḥ3i*. CT I 303g provides a parallel to Pyramid Text §1255 (Utterance 532). Both texts read, "Isis comes and Nephthys comes, one of them from the west and one of them from the east...." In the next sentence the sources differ from one another. In the Pyramid Text, Isis is a *ḥ3(i)t* and Nephthys is a *ḏr(y)t*; in the Coffin Texts it is reversed — Isis is the *ḏr(y)t* and Nephthys is the *ḥ3(i)t*. This comparison is, of course, assuming that parallelism is present in these passages. In the various copies, Nephthys' title is determined by the G 38 determinative accompanied by the woman determinative, the G 41 determinative accompanied by the woman determinative, or just the G 38 sign.

Birds and ḥ3i in the New Kingdom

From the New Kingdom, there are four sources where the *ḥ3it*-bird occurs, although a double reed leaf is written out and *ḥ3(i)t* now appears as *ḥ3yt*. [17] The first instance is in Papyrus Sallier IV, verso 4, 8 (BM 10184) and the reference to the *ḥ3yt*-bird occurs in the text called *A Letter Concerning the Wonders of Memphis*. Caminos states that the bird is unidentifiable.[18] The second reference to the *ḥ3yt*-bird is in Papyrus Chester Beatty III from Deir el-Medina,[19] and appears in the context of a Dream Book that dates to the late Nineteenth Dynasty.[20] The third example appears in Gardiner's *Onomastica*.[21] Gardiner compares this entry to the same word also occurring in Papyrus Sallier IV (*Wb* III 16, 1) mentioned above. The previous three examples are in reference to an actual bird called a *ḥ3yt* without any affinities to a deity. The last example occurs in a hymn to Osiris that dates to the first half of the Eighteenth Dynasty.[22] The word in question appears on Louvre stela C 286 belonging to the official Amenmose and his wife Nefertari. Other than PT §§1255 and 1280, this is the only example of a *ḥ3yt*-bird referring to the goddess Isis:

> Isis, the sorceress, the protector of her brother,
> who searches for him ceaselessly,
> who traverses this land as a *ḥ3yt*-bird,
> she does not stop until she has found him;
> she who makes shade with her feathers,
> who creates air with her wings,
> who does (the rites) of jubilation
> and moors/revives her brother.[23]

This passage demonstrates the continuity of the idea of the goddess Isis manifesting as a *ḥ3yt*-bird. In fact, Isis is performing the same function in this text as she is in the Pyramid Texts, namely, revivifying Osiris. Here it is also plainly stated that she is doing the rites of jubilation in conjunction with reviving him, therefore emphasizing the celebratory sentiment of the action.

Analysis

There is no agreement amongst scholars as to which bird is referred to by the word *ḥ3(i)t* in the Egyptian texts. The bird's existence seems to be verified by its depiction in the Sun Temple of Niuserre at Abu Ghurob, where its images are accompanied by captions that identify it as such.[24] According to Edel, the *ḥ3(i)t* bird is the German *"Seeschwalbe,"* the English "tern."[25] The tern is from the subfamily *Sterninae* and is like a gull but usually smaller with a long forked tail.[26] In Faulkner's translation of CT IV 331, he translates *ḥ3(i)t* as "kite," and notes that the word refers to "a screeching bird (falcon, kite or crow?)." He notes Edel's suggestion "tern," but disagrees with this designation because he states that the cry of a tern cannot be called a screech.[27] However, some terns do exude a harsh high-pitched screeching.[28] Unfortunately, Faulkner offers no suggestion of his own.

Houlihan, in his book, entitled *The Birds of Ancient Egypt* does not contribute substantially to this subject. He states that both Isis and Nephthys are associated with

---

[17] See Chapter Eight for a more detailed discussion on these sources.

[18] Caminos 1954, 349.

[19] Gardiner 1935, 17; Gardiner 1947, 2:257*-258*.

[20] In his 1935 publication of the Dream-book, Gardiner translates the passage, "folding wings around himself(?)." In note 11 he states that *ḥ3yt* is probably the same verb as *Wb* III, 13. This author corrects himself in his later publication of the *Onomastica* where he presents the translation used here (1947, 2:257*-258*).

[21] Gardiner 1947, 2:257*-258*.

[22] See de Buck 1948, 110-113 for hieroglyphs, Moret 1931 for transcription, and Lichtheim 1976, 81-86 for translation. See also Chabas 1857, 65-81, 193-212; Chabas 1899, 95-139; Hassan 1928; Assman 1975; 1999.

[23] Author's translation. See also Moret 1931, 741; de Buck 1948, 111; Assmann 1975, 443-448; 1999, 477-482.

[24] Edel 1961, Abb. 11; *PM* I.i, 319-324.

[25] Edel 1961, 216.

[26] *The Canadian Oxford Dictionary* 1998, 1496-7.

[27] Faulkner 2004, 273, n. 2.

[28] www.enature.com

the Black Kite (*Milvus migrans*),[29] and the Lesser Kestrel (*Falco naumanni*) or Kestrel (*F. tinnunculus*).[30] Assuming the birds depicted in the Abu Ghurob relief are reliable renditions of what the *ḥ3it*-bird looked like, one can then determine that the *ḥ3it* is neither the black kite nor the kestrel (or lesser kestrel). The birds from the Sun Temple have a forked tail, but neither of the two aforementioned species possesses this physical characteristic. Likewise, the black kite and the kestrel have a hooked bill, while the Abu Ghurob *ḥ3(i)t*-birds have a straight bill.[31] The kestrel is also distinguished by the fringed boots and barred tail; neither of these two features appears on the *ḥ3(i)t*-birds.

In summary, with the current sources available it is difficult to determine the specific species of the *ḥ3(i)t*-bird. Consequently, one is left with Edel's suggestion of the tern which at this stage seems to be the best choice. Although there are many varieties of the tern, the bird commonly possesses a forked tail, a straight bill, and plumage that reflect the depictions in the Abu Ghurob scenes; however, the tern shows off both breeding and non-breeding plumage. In modern times the tern can be found in the Nile Delta, around the Suez Canal, on the Red Sea Mainland coast, and in the southern tip of the Sinai.[32]

Several theories have been postulated by scholars as to the connection between the *ḥ3(i)t*-bird itself and its ritual symbolism. It is possible that the term *ḥ3yt* is a result of the sound that the particular bird made. In other words, the name is onomatopoeic. Penelope Wilson suggests that the original verb *ḥ3y* may have been onomatopoeic and may have been derived from the wailing sound made by either mourners or birds.[33] Since it has now been established that this word is not directly linked to mourning, the former source for the derivation of the term is no longer credible. There is no evidence to support the theory that the *ḥ3it* made a high-pitched screeching sound; this idea has resulted only from the false association between the term *ḥ3i* and mourning.

The association of women, or goddesses with birds dates as far back as the Naqada II period, where some Predynastic figurines are distinguished by a beak-like nose.[34] These same figures have their arms raised in the A 28 pose, which is held by the women in the Old Kingdom tomb scenes who are accompanied by the label: *ḥ3(i)t* (see Chapter Seven below).

It is not obvious why Isis and Nephthys may take bird form in their role as attendants of Osiris. According to J. Gwyn Griffiths, the figures of Isis and Nephthys were superimposed on the pre-Osirian "mourning" birds,[35] assuming that the myth of Osiris had merged with a pre-existing set of royal funerary rituals where the living king was associated with the god Horus.[36] He explains this phenomenon as follows: "What has happened is that the god [Osiris], through identity with the dead King, has attached to his person the stock-in-trade of current funerary practice and iconography and that a process of myth-making has proceeded therefrom."[37] Therefore, the role of these birds in the funeral ceremony had a pre-Osirian origin.[38] Isis' original signification had nothing to do with the bird; she was originally the deified throne.[39]

Various scholars have posited explanations for the "mourning" birds.[40] As noted above, Anthes suggests that pairs of birds may have been attracted to the embalming waste, and thus have become common attendants at the funerary proceedings.[41] While it does not seem desirable to imitate a bird whose intention was to destroy the corpse and to create a nuisance during the embalming proceedings, there is a precedent for this in Egyptian thinking. The jackal, who regularly roamed the cemeteries for food, and consequently destroyed the burials, became the symbolic guardian of the necropolis. As Černy points out, the animal of Anubis was a god of the dead and protector of burials, and his cult was a kind of *captatio benevolentiae*.[42] Frankfort's theory – with which Griffiths agrees[43] – is that the relevance of the bird form has to do with the falcon shape of the god Horus. Frankfort also points out that the sound of Isis and Nephthys mourning Osiris

[29] See Black Kite in Houlihan 1986, 37, figure 52.
[30] See Kestrel in Houlihan 1986, 45, figure 60. Houlihan and Goodman 1986, 36-40; 45-46; Houlihan 1996, 156, 161.
[31] Houlihan 1986, 36, 45.
[32] Goodman and Meininger 1989, 287-302.
[33] P. Wilson 1997, 611.
[34] Needler 1984, 336-344 (see note 167 for Ucko reference); Graff, 2008. See Chapter 7 below.

[35] With reference to page 171 in S. Schott, *Die Deutung der Geheimnisse des Rituals für die Abwehr des Bösen,* Abh. Mainz 1954, 5. Griffiths (1980, 60) suggests that the mourning birds originally belonged to the Butic funerary tradition.
[36] Griffiths 1980, 35.
[37] Griffiths 1980, 34 following Kees in Mercer 1952, 4:125.
[38] Griffiths 1980, 49.
[39] See Frankfort (1958, 43) for a discussion on the origin of the name Isis and her connection with the royal throne.
[40] Scholars have assumed that when Isis is in bird form she is mourning Osiris. There would appear to be no doubt that mourning is indeed one of Isis' many functions. However, Griffiths incorrectly states that this is the only scenario where Isis is imagined as a bird (Griffiths 1980, 49). But Isis appears as a bird in other circumstances, as well. In the *Contendings of Horus and Seth* Isis is playing a trick on Seth whereby she fools him into confessing that Horus should inherit the office of his father Osiris in preference to himself. After she has succeeded she turns herself into a *ḏryt* and flies to the top of an acacia tree (*LES* 45, 9). Likewise, in a relief from the temple of Seti I at Abydos, Isis, who appears as a bird, probably a kestrel, conceives Horus on Osiris' bier. This scene reflects an event in the myth of Osiris, of which Plutarch records the fullest account (Frankfort 1958, 40, fig. 18).
[41] Anthes 1959, 206.
[42] Černy 1952, 22.
[43] Griffiths 1980, 50.

would have mimicked the shrill plaintive cry of the *Falco milvus* when circling above.[44]

The connection with Horus may have been attractive; however, I believe that the real association had to do with something the birds were doing that was specifically related to the funeral. Maybe the bird the Egyptians called the *ḥ3it* did come down to scavenge the rotting corpse and then took it with them up to the sky. The Egyptians could have associated this act with the ascent to heaven. Furthermore, the idea of sustaining life, or creating new life through ingesting the old one may have signified rebirth and been appealing to the ancient Egyptians.[45] Can one see a similar phenomenon is the Eucharist? Some Christians see the bread and wine as the body and blood, respectively, of Jesus. E. O. James writes that the Eucharist is "the perpetual memorial of the supreme recreative event in the history of the world...".[46]

A comparison may be made with the Tibetan Sky Burials. Some believe this practice is related to the mortuary practice of the Zoroastrians of Persia; however, this assumption is questionable.[47] This death ritual involves the body of the deceased being either left in a remote location to decay and be eaten by prey, or dismembered into small pieces and mixed with flour. This latter addition reinforces the alms-giving nature of the ritual.[48] The sky burial is considered an act of generosity on the part of the deceased, since the deceased and his/her surviving relatives are offering food to sustain other living beings. With this mode of corpse disposal the vultures nourish their bodies by re-cycling the remains of those whose souls have passed. The sky burial returns the remains to the cycle of life.

Although it has been suggested that *jhator*[49] is also meant to unite the deceased person with the sky or sacred realm, this does not seem consistent with most of the knowledgeable commentary and eyewitness reports, which indicate that Tibetans believe that at this point life has wholly left the body and that it contains nothing more than simple flesh.[50]

The origin as well and its import are unknown.[51] In Tibet, vulture-disposal is only one of five options to dispose of a corpse. For the most part geography plays a role in the selected method, in that certain regions are mountains and do not allow for burial and where trees are scarce and cannot provide firewood for cremation.[52] This scenario does not fit the Egyptian situation well, as the natural sand dried the body quite adequately, rendering vulture disposal unnecessary. When looking at the bones of predynastic burials it has been deduced that either humans or animals had done some damage.[53] It has been suggested that this may have taken place during the bones exposure prior to interment. This topic can be discussed in conjunction with the dividing of the body, or the body's dismemberment, a practice that has been well-established for predynastic times.[54]

Likewise, it is well documented that the ancient Egyptians needed their bodies for their survival in the hereafter.[55] Essentially, the body was not considered an empty vessel suitable for nourishing birds of prey.

One cannot ignore the ferocious qualities assigned to the *ḥ3iw* bird in the Coffin Texts and elsewhere. Perhaps this ferociousness was a distinguishing characteristic as it directly related to the importance of the bird in Egyptian mythology.

To conclude, in the Pyramid Texts Isis appears as a *ḥ3(i)t*-bird and functions as a rejuvenator,[56] particularly one who revivifies the deceased king as Osiris. Throughout the Pyramid Texts Isis is involved with the deceased king's ascension to the sky, although she is not always described as being in bird form.[57] This same connection continues into the New Kingdom, as evidenced by the Hymn to Osiris on Louvre Stela C 286. The *ḥ3(i)t*-bird's connection with the funerary rites must have originated in a pre-Osirian tradition, since there is no apparent connection to the early royal religious dogma. The relevance of the bird lies in its ability to take the deceased to heaven, since resurrection is synonymous with ascension to the heavens.[58] Most likely, this notion originated from the birds' picking at the corpse and then flying away with it. Isis may appear as a *ḥ3it*-bird in her job of revivifier because the bird form allowed for ascent to the sky with the newly reborn king. It was Isis' job to resurrect the deceased, and it makes more sense that her imagery was in line with her function, instead of her bird form relating to the sound made by mourning women. In the mythological world it is possible for a deity to take the form of a bird in order to achieve the deceased's rebirth. In PT §741 the goddess Tait lifts the deceased

[44] Frankfort 1958, 40-41.
[45] Personal communication with Susan Tower Hollis.
[46] James 1948, 135.
[47] Wylie, 1965, 232.
[48] www.yoniversum.nl/dakini/jhator.html
[49] Tibetan Sky Burial – literally "giving alms to the birds"
[50] Faison, Seth (July 3, 1999) "Lirong Journal; Tibetans, and Vultures, Keep Ancient Burial Rite." New York Times, nytimes.com.
[51] Wiley 1965, 232.
[52] "region, reason, and rank" (Wiley 1965, 242)
[53] Wengrow 2006, 119.
[54] Wengrow 2006, 116-119.
[55] Quirke 1992, 143; Taylor 2001, 46-47. These are only two of many references to the practice of body preservation and its religious significance.
[56] She does not appear as a *ḏryt* in the Pyramid Texts, so it is unnecessary to compare the two roles in this context.
[57] For example, see PT §§210, 379, 741, 939, 996, 1089.
[58] Zandee 1960, 78.

king up to the sky in her manifestation as a kite, and in PT §463 the king himself is imagined as a bird who flaps his wings like a goose or a kite. Additionally, PT §1484 envisages the king as a bird escaping from the hand of the fowler and flying to the sky.[59] Furthermore, Mercer confirms that a goose, heron, or falcon can also act as an alternative to a ladder – a separate method of ascension – as a means of reaching heaven.[60] Sometimes, especially in the later periods, Isis performed her job as a *ḏryt*. Originally these birds must have served different functions in the funerary realm, but as time went on the role of *ḏryt* became popular and the confusion surrounding *ḥ3it* increased. Finally, the *ḥ3(i)t*-bird does appear to be a real bird, as opposed to a mythological bird; however, it is impossible to determine its exact species with any degree of certainty.

As a *ḥ3(i)t*-bird in PT §§1255 and 1280, Isis also participates in the spiritualization of her brother Osiris. *ḥ3(i)*t and a *ḥ3(i)w* are both terms for someone who protects and assembles the deceased's corpse for transference into the Hereafter. This is clear from Isis' role in the Pyramid Texts and in the New Kingdom version of the myth of Osiris.

Both Isis and Nephthys in their roles of rejuvenators of Osiris are called a *ḥ3it*. In these cases the divinities are usually, but not always, in bird form (see Chapter Eight). In contrast, the Old Kingdom private sources show no connection to an avian motif. The royal sources demonstrate that the bird form was primarily related to the myth of Osiris and its *dramatis personae*. That the bird form was adopted for Isis (and later Nephthys) at an early age perhaps corresponds to the form assumed by the falcon god Horus who was the king incarnate. The names "Isis" and "Nephthys" reveal their early association to the royal house. On the contrary, it would have been very un-Egyptian for a private individual to be portrayed as a bird.

Some Coffin Texts reference a *ḥ3it* but do not specify with which divinity the passage is concerned. The only New Kingdom example that preserves the avian association is the Hymn to Osiris where Isis rejuvenates Osiris in her form of a *ḥ3yt;* this passage is evidently only a later version of the same myth that is presented in the Pyramid Texts. There are other instances where Isis is called a *ḥ3yt* but she is not imagined as a bird. The reason for this may lie in the fact that by the New Kingdom, in such sources as the Amduat, Book of Gates, Book of Caverns, the Hereafter, or Realm of the Dead lies beneath the earth (under it, or in it), not above.[61] This concept renders the avian symbolism useless.

The Coffin Texts may disclose the possible origin of the word by revealing that real birds can also *ḥ3i*. Using the Coffin Texts one can discern that what the birds do has a negative connotation in real life (as opposed to the mythological realm) and that their actions were predatory.

[59] See additional reference in Introduction
[60] Mercer 1952, 4:5.
[61] Te Velde 1988, 32.

Chapter Six

Introduction

It has been demonstrated that the sources containing the word *ḥ3i* relate specifically to a funerary context. This chapter focuses on the location and the time in which the ritual of *ḥ3i* occurred within the funerary program. These two factors are intimately related to one another, for example, if the ritual of *ḥ3i* was performed near the tomb it can be understood that the time was on the day of interment. If the rite took place outside the embalming workshop, then the body was being either dropped off or picked up.[1] The following study is divided into two sections, namely, sources referencing the actual funerary ritual, and those referencing the mythologized ritual.

The first section deals with sources from private funerary contexts. The sources that are devoid of mythological allusion include the tomb scenes from the Old Kingdom, the Funerary Liturgy, and the tomb of Amenemhet (TT 82). TT 82 is a noteworthy case in that it dates to the New Kingdom, when the mythological allusions in it (which began in a royal context) have already spread to the private realm. However, events depicted in tomb scenes do not necessarily reflect the sequence of the events of an actual funeral even in the Old Kingdom. Frandsen points out that the scenes do not supply a "reliable source for a simple reconstruction of a ritual process."[2] Frandsen, citing Settgast's 1963 work,

asserts that in the New Kingdom and later, the scenes "cannot be regarded as trustworthy evidence of what actually took place at the particular time,"[3] since the scenes tend to depict only excerpts from a funeral program. Assmann also discusses the themes in New Kingdom funerary scenes and asserts that in the early New Kingdom many anachronistic scenes appear where ancient rituals are performed but which have fallen out of use by this time.[4] Tombs like Pepiankh's from the Old Kingdom, and Rekhmire's from the New Kingdom, illustrate more lengthy and involved funerary programs, and it is tombs like these that help scholars make sense of the more meager displays of funerary events.

The second section examines the royal sources — the ones with a clear royal origin. In these sources the rite of *ḥ3i* occurs in the mythological realm. These sources include the Pyramid Texts, Coffin Texts, Book of the Dead, Amduat, Book of Gates, and Louvre Stela C 286 (BD 185A). Although the Coffin Texts and the Book of the Dead were mostly used by private individuals, these texts originated from a corpus related to the Pyramid Texts of the Old Kingdom. Louvre Stela C 286 is included in the second section despite its private status because it displays a hymn to Osiris — Chapter 185A of the Book of the Dead.[5] The sources that describe the ritual of *ḥ3i* in the mythological realm are more perplexing. Their settings do not display parallels for the events presented in the private sources that depict genuine funerals listed above.

The early sources are of crucial importance for understanding the original location of the ritual of *ḥ3i* and the time it was performed. There is abundant evidence to show that the rite originated in the Old Kingdom or earlier. Although the rite continued to be performed after the Old Kingdom, its significance diminished. Its inclusion in later ceremonies resulted from its importance as an historic, anachronistic ritual. When there is a concrete location given in the later mythologized sources it corresponds to the rite's placement in the earlier sources.

There is a marked difference between the two groups of sources under discussion. In general, it is clear what is depicted in the private sources of the first section. These excerpts of ritual are identifiable and can be placed in a logical sequence. This contrasts with the sources from the second group that illustrate the rite of *ḥ3i* in unusual and mythological settings. The most direct connection between the two groups is the transmission of the Osiris myth from the second group to the first group, which is clear by the New Kingdom. This transference is first visible in the tomb of Amenemhet (TT 82). Even though the Coffin Texts are usually found in a private context, the texts are laden with myth; and in actuality they reflect a royal tradition. The phenomenon of the mythologization of ritual affects this investigation, in that the later sources are steeped in mythical references, which prevents them from being analyzed using the same criteria which were applied to the early sources.

Private Sources

In the private sources the word *ḥ3i* appears in scenes illustrating a real funeral. The word occurs in the account of an actual event, not in a mythological setting. In the tomb of Debehni and in the service described in the Funerary Liturgy, the rite occurs at the tomb on the day of interment.

In the case of Debehni, there are three different interpretations offered by several scholars as to where the ritual is being held. J. Wilson simply describes the scene as taking place "at the tomb, on either side of a

[1] If the body was being dropped off then one might assume this time corresponds to the time of death, as opposed to the time of burial. Differentiating between these two scenarios can be difficult, if not impossible. New Kingdom sources indicate that the body would spend seventy days at the embalmers' workshop.

[2] Frandsen 1992, 57.

[3] Frandsen 1992, 57.

[4] Assmann 2005, 299-301.

[5] T. G. Allen 1974, 203.

table of food offerings."[6] Hassan posits that the women are "performing a ceremonial dance in front of the embalming-house," citing Schäfer, "*Die Frauen des Toten führen vor dem Grabe einen jener Tänze auf, die immer einen wesentlichen Ziel der Trauer gebildet zu haben scheinen. Hier stehen vier Tänzerinnen nebeneinander und ihnen gegenüber die drei, Sängerinnen hinter einen männlichen Anverwandten des Verstorbenen.*"[7] There is no evidence in this scene in the tomb of Debehni to indicate that the rite is taking place specifically in front of the embalming house. It is possible that when he was drawing his conclusion S. Hassan was considering the scenes in the tombs of Qar and Pepiankh where this ritual does take place in conjunction with the *wꜥbt* (see below.) Therefore, he assumes that this scene provides a parallel. Bolshakov explains this same scene as illustrating the procession approaching the tomb, and ending in dancing and making offerings on the roof of the mastaba, near the opening of the shaft.[8] Wilson and Bolshakov are correct in that it is the tomb that is depicted in this scene, not the embalming house (although the *wꜥbt* is presumably nearby). However, one cannot discern where in relation to the tomb the rite of *ḥꜣi* is taking place. There is no logical reason to believe that the dancing is on top of the mastaba, especially since the offerings are being brought to the deceased's statue on top of the mastaba, while the dance scene is depicted below. It would seem that a more appropriate location might be in front of the mastaba, especially since this can be paralleled in other sources.[9] The offerings are significant since they also appear in close proximity to the ritual of *ḥꜣi* in the Old Kingdom tomb scenes of Hetepherakhti, Qar and Pepiankh.

In Gardiner's discussion of the Funerary Liturgy, he notes Grdseloff's assertion that there are two possible occasions when a ceremony, such as the one described, could take place: the day of the removal of the corpse from the home to the place where it would be mummified, and the day when the prepared body was brought to its final resting spot.[10] Because of the references in the Liturgy to circulating around the mastaba, Gardiner rightly suggests that it may be the latter occasion that is described. Unfortunately, because of the fragmentary nature of the papyrus, not much more can be derived from this description. It should now be reiterated that Gardiner suggests an Old Kingdom origin for the Funerary Liturgy, supporting Černy's proposal of a possible Third Dynasty date. Consequently, it is fitting to compare this text with the reliefs presented in the Old Kingdom tombs.

Therefore, the scene in the tomb of Debehni and the Funerary Liturgy corroborate each other concerning the location for the ritual of *ḥꜣi*. In turn, these two sources are also consistent with the suggestion that the rite is performed on the day of interment.

The tomb of Hetepherakhti shows the *ḥꜣi* ritual performed on the way to the tomb, also on the day of interment. In the register above the procession there is a row of offerings. According to Eaton-Krauss, the statue "has assumed the identity of the tomb owner and is capable of functioning in the cult."[11] This transformation was the result of the Opening of the Mouth ritual.[12] In the case of Hetepherakhti, the statue replaces the coffin and is considered an appropriate substitute (see Chapter Two.)[13] This situation is reminiscent of the statue appearing in the final rites of the burial of Debehni, mentioned above.[14] Eaton-Krauss states that Debehni's statue was the object of the funerary ceremony, and she points out that Settgast has noted that there is no archaeological evidence for the deposition of statues of the deceased in the burial chamber until the later Old Kingdom.[15] Bolshakov refutes this statement and translates the accompanying inscription in the tomb of Debehni as, "[Bringing the statue] which was made for him in the *wꜥb.t* to the tomb. [Esc]orting [the statue by] the crew of the house of *mrḥ.t*." He uses this text to confirm that on the last day of the funeral a statue could accompany the deceased in his procession, at least in some cases.[16] Therefore, the procession illustrated in the tomb of Hetepherakhti that includes the women performing the ritual of *ḥꜣi* takes place on the day of interment, after the collection of the mummy from the embalmers' workshop, but before the arrival at the tomb.

Another recurrent location for the performance of the rite of *ḥꜣi* is the embalmers' workshop. In the tomb scene of Qar the procession begins at the home of the deceased. From there the body is taken to the *ibw* and then, by boat, to the *wꜥbt,* where the women and the friends of the *šnḏt* approach the entrance of the *wꜥbt* of attending (*wꜥbt ꜥḥꜥw*).[17] Inside the *wꜥbt* the *ḫry-ḥbt* is shown advancing toward the inner room. There is also a stack of offerings present. It can be understood that the

[6] J. Wilson 1944, 212.
[7] S. Hassan 1943, 178, n. 1.
[8] Bolshakov 1991, 40.
[9] The Story of Sinuhe describes the proceedings of a funeral in the following manner: "A night is made for you with ointments and wrappings from the hand of Tait. A funeral procession is made for you on the day of burial; the mummy case is of gold, its head of lapis lazuli. The sky is above you as you lie in the hearse, oxen drawing you, musicians going before you. The dance of the *mww*-dancers is done at the door of your tomb" (Lichtheim 1975, 1:229).
[10] Gardiner 1955, 17.

[11] Eaton-Krauss 1984, 75.
[12] Eaton-Krauss 1984, 75-76.
[13] Eaton-Krauss 1984, 65.
[14] This part of the scene does not appear in Lepsius' publication because of its damaged state. It is included in S. Hassan's work (1943).
[15] Eaton-Krauss 1984, 70, n. 348.
[16] Bolshakov 1991, 45-46.
[17] Simpson 1976, 6; Edel 1969, 5-6. See also Lehner 1997, 25-26.

scene depicts the rituals that take place before the body is embalmed. The dancing and clapping is similar to what takes place for Debehni and Hetepherakhti; however, in this picture the women raise only one arm. Unlike the scenes in the tomb of Pepiankh, there is no scene in this tomb that depicts the collection of the embalmed corpse.[18]

In the tomb of Pepiankh there are two scenes where the rite of *ḥ3i* is performed in front of, or inside, the embalming workshop (*wʿbt*). These two scenes correspond to the body being dropped off at the workshop, and the body being picked up at the workshop. As has been stated previously, this scene of fetching the body is unusual.[19] Inevitably, the embalmed corpse would have had to be picked up before every burial despite the fact that this scene is regularly excluded from tomb decoration. Because the tomb of Pepiankh at Meir displays a remarkable number of scenes, it is particularly useful in reassembling the funerary program. In this case, it suggests that the rite of *ḥ3i* may have been performed both before and after the corpse's sojourn in the embalmers' workshop, simply because the embalming process was a necessary step in the journey to the Afterlife.

The inscription of Sabni provides a further link between the performance of *ḥ3i* and the embalmers' workshop.[20] This source describes the *ḥ3itiw* as originating from the *pr-nfr*. They were sent south from the Residence for the burial of the official Mekhu.[21] As Shore points out, the structure from which the embalming necessities were brought is the *pr-nfr* and the two *wʿbt* structures.[22] The *pr-nfr* is referred to as if it is related to, but not equal to the *wʿbt*. According to Frandsen, "a *pr-nfr*, at this time at least, was not connected with the process of embalming as such...but may be seen as some sort of department of funerary storehouses, which later came to incorporate also the function of the *wʿbt*."[23] At any rate, for the purpose of this study, suffice it to say, the *ḥ3itiw* were associated with the *wʿbt*.

As one can see from the sources discussed above, there are two names that are connected with the location for embalming: the *wʿbt*[24] and the *pr-nfr*.[25] Some texts indicate that the two locations are synonymous, while others suggest that they are two separate locations.[26] *wʿbt* literally means "pure place," but generally connotes a workshop.[27] Often the *wʿbt* is followed by *n(y)t wty*, "belonging to the embalmer," and this is where Shore believes the body underwent the natron treatment.[28]

According to Frandsen, *pr-nfr* means "funerary workshop."[29] Shore believes the term refers to the structure where the mystery of Osiris was performed,[30] while Frandsen thinks that the embalming could take place in either the *wʿbt* or the *pr-nfr*.[31] Donohue references CT Spell 45 (CT I 195) to show that the deceased will be restored to life in the *pr-nfr*.[32] The depiction of the *pr-n*fr in TT C4 shows the funeral procession approaching this structure (Figure 24).[33] Shore uses the inscription of Sabni, where the *sšt3w* came from the *pr-nfr* and the two *wʿbt* structures, to confirm that the *pr-nfr* refers to at least a particular part of the *wʿbt*, or possibly a separate structure.[34]

The term *pr-nfr* suggests the place of making perfect.[35] Frandsen proposes that the *pr-nfr* may originally have belonged to the Residence. But once the *wʿbt* and the *pr-nfr* merged, the structure was erected when needed.[36] Frandsen also postulates that the word *nfrw* designates the most private part of a structure; and because of the sacred purpose of these innermost rooms, he suggests that the term implies "creation," "rejuvenation," or "end and beginning."[37] Donohue suggests "*nfr* must have possessed a more dynamic sense than is suggested by its translation as 'good' or 'beautiful'" and posits the idea that its qualities may have been peculiar to Osiris.[38] Donohue furthers this notion by stating that the meaning of the title *pr-nfr* is "house of rejuvenation."[39] By the New Kingdom the embalming structure was called the *wʿbt n(y)t pr-nfr*.[40] The *wʿbt* appears to be the older designation,[41] while the term *pr-nfr* seems not to have been used until the end of the Old Kingdom.[42] In the Middle Kingdom the

[18] I am curious about whether the A 28 pose is intentionally omitted here simply because the deceased is not quite ready to travel to the Hereafter.
[19] Blackman 1953, 54.
[20] *Urk.* I 138,3.
[21] Breasted 2001, 1:164-165.
[22] Shore 1992, 232.
[23] Frandsen 1992, 59. See also Lehner 1997, 236.
[24] *Wb* I 284; Faulkner 1991, 57.
[25] *Wb* I 517; Faulkner 1991, 89.
[26] See Shore (1992, 232) for an overview of the sources.
[27] Shore 1992, 232.
[28] Shore 1992, 232.
[29] Frandsen 1992, 52.
[30] Shore 1992, 232.
[31] Frandsen 1992, 56.
[32] Donohue 1978, 145, n. 4.
[33] Manniche 1988, 111. Frandsen (1992, 58) points out that tomb scenes are not necessarily reliable and accurate for the reconstructing of funerary ceremonies. As he rightly notes in his article, "Egyptian scenes combine the actual and the symbolic." He also remarks that pictorial representations were subject to rules of decorum and genre, and that illustrated practices should not be generalized regardless of changing circumstances (1992, 57).
[34] Shore 1992, 232.
[35] Shore 1992, 232.
[36] Frandsen 1992, 60.
[37] Frandsen 1992, 53.
[38] Donohue 1978, 146-7.
[39] Donohue 1978, 148; Frandsen 1992, 56.
[40] Frandsen 1992, 56; Davies and Gardiner 1915, 73; Smith and Dawson 2002, 35.
[41] Frandsen 1992, 56.
[42] Donohue 1978, 145.

wˁbt is connected with the *pr-nfr* in the phrase "*wˁbt n(y)t pr-nfr*."[43] This phrase continued to be in use until at least the New Kingdom.[44] Edel notes that both terms appear in the New Kingdom and later.[45] Although there is conflicting evidence for the use of both the *wˁbt* and the *pr-nfr*, the one certainty is that both terms refer to structures that are associated with the process of embalming and its accompanying rituals.

How does one reconcile the two different locations of the tomb and the embalmers' workshop as the setting for the performance of *ḥ3i*? As early as 1927, Dawson reports that nobles and private individuals erected their own embalming booth or kiosk. He also notes that certain texts speak of "your place of embalming" and "his place of embalming."[46] Likewise, he points out that the use of such names as "tent of the god" or "god's booth" (*sḥ nṯr*) illustrates the temporary nature of the structure.[47] Frandsen posits that the structure was collapsible and was erected near the tomb when it was needed.[48] According to Brovarski, there is ample archaeological and textual evidence to show that the embalming workshop was attached to private Old Kingdom tombs.[49] Again, Frandsen proposes that the first room of a tomb may have been the actual place of embalming, especially for the lower classes.[50] Nevertheless, these collapsible booths would have been erected in the necropolis. This fact corroborates the scenes in the tombs of Debehni and Hetepherakhti, and the Funerary Liturgy, which point to the tomb as the location for the ritual. Therefore, all Old Kingdom sources and the Funerary Liturgy (which may possibly date to the Old Kingdom, or earlier), show the ritual taking place at the tomb, sometimes in conjunction with a temporary embalmers' workshop, which would have been set up near the entrance to the tomb.

The connection between the ritual of *ḥ3i* and the embalmers' workshop lies in the physical preservation and magical ceremonies that took place within said workshop. This preservation allowed the deceased to utilize his body in the Afterlife. In a royal context, this ceremony equated the deceased with the god Osiris.[51] There is archaeological evidence suggesting that private individuals were attempting to imitate royal burials as early as the Fourth Dynasty.[52] The god himself was actually conceived of as a mummy.[53] There were many rites that contributed to the resurrection of the deceased. In fact, it was inside the embalmers' workshop that the mystery[54] of resurrection was performed.[55] The priests performed the embalming rituals, and it was they who possessed the secret knowledge of the mysteries of Osiris. Dawson notes "the embalmers and their assistants impersonated the gods who figured in the mythological embalming of Osiris. The embalmer's chamber was consequently not a mere workshop. But in a sense a kind of shrine in which certain prescribed rites were performed."[56]

Notwithstanding any magical rites that may have been employed for rejuvenation, the purpose of the embalmment itself was to enable the deceased to retain his living form and continue to thrive in the Hereafter, like Osiris.[57] To demonstrate the connection between embalming and the cult of Osiris, it is necessary to recount the history of the burial of the dead. Originally the ancient Egyptian was buried in the ground. The body had to be above the subsoil water level but deep enough that it would not be dug up by scavenging animals. Due to the hot dry climate of Egypt the moisture in the body evaporated and left the corpse permanently dry. In the Predynastic period the bodies were wrapped in an animal skin or linen and placed in a shallow grave. By the end of the Early Dynastic period royal graves were deeper and lined with materials like sun-dried mud bricks or wood; sometimes there was even a superstructure. According to Lucas and Harris, the royal bodies had close fitting wrappings, sometimes exhibiting separate wrappings for each limb. This took place before artificial mummification was introduced. The coffin was an additional measure of protection. All of these protective measures eventually prevented the body from drying in the same manner as before, and therefore its preservation was imperfect.[58] Lucas and Harris demonstrate that these supposed improved measures of protection eventually led to a new manufactured method of preservation, owing to the need for an eternal body, according to Egyptian religious beliefs.[59] Thus, the procedure of embalming, or mummification, was invented. The ritual of preservation was later interpreted as imitation of the rejuvenation of Osiris.

After the wrapping was finished the new mummy was roused to life.[60] The speech of the women in the tomb of Debehni can attest to this idea by their ritual

[43] Frandsen 1992, 56.
[44] Davies and Gardiner 1915, 73.
[45] Edel 1969, 6.
[46] Dawson 1927, 41; Frandsen 1992, 58.
[47] Dawson 1927, 41.
[48] Frandsen 1992, 58.
[49] See Brovarski (1977, 110) for a description of this evidence.
[50] Frandsen 1992, 60.
[51] Griffiths 1980, 56, 86.
[52] Griffiths 1980, 55-56.
[53] Griffiths 1980, 86.

[54] The ancient Egyptians used the word StAw to refer to this concept (Shore 1992, 226).
[55] Vos 1993, 34.
[56] Dawson 1927, 40-41.
[57] As Shore (1992, 227) notes, not much is know about the secrets of Osiris. However, he remarks that the process of mummification may perhaps shed some light on the subject.
[58] Lucas and Harris 1962, 271.
[59] Lucas and Harris 1962, 271.
[60] Vos 1993, 36.

exclamation, "His flesh is complete!"[61] This notion is confirmed by Shore, who cites Vercoutter, and draws attention to the later stelae erected in the Memphite Serapeum that mention the people who wait outside until the god comes out of the *wꜥbt*.[62] It is thought that the only people who were allowed inside the embalmers' workshop would have been those initiated to the mysteries of Osiris. Everything that went into the *wꜥbt* had to be pure.

The advent of mummification and evidence for the cult of Osiris appear more or less simultaneously. As Griffiths points out, "the iconography of the god confirms the association of mummification with his cult, for he is always portrayed in a mummified form."[63] The earliest evidence for the process of mummification is from the early Fourth Dynasty.[64] The viscera of Queen Hetepheres were found wrapped in linen and lying in natron in a canopic box. Unfortunately, the Queen's body has not been preserved, but it has been assumed that the body was also artificially maintained.[65] The Museum of the Royal College of Surgeons, London, had a Fifth Dynasty mummy; however, it was destroyed during an air raid in 1941.[66] Junker and Reisner also found other mummies from the same time period at Giza.[67] Originally, mummification was reserved for royalty and the more privileged classes.[68] Mummification continued to be employed until the Christian Period.

In the sources under discussion here, the myth of Osiris does not yet appear to have penetrated the ritual. The scenes in the tomb of Pepiankh at Meir show that the *ḥ3(i)w* is allowed into the *wꜥbt*; this may confirm that the *ḥ3(i)w* was considered to be pure. The inscription of Sabni indicates that the *ḥ3(i)tiw*, who came from the *pr-nfr*, were also part of the essentials needed for resurrection. Regardless of who was allowed inside the workshop during the rites of embalming in Old Kingdom private funerals, there were other equally essential rituals that took place outside. It appears that the rite of *ḥ3i* occurred in conjunction with the embalming process, perhaps to encourage the outcome, and that the performers of the *ḥ3i* rite were ritually symbolic of the end goal of resurrection.

[61] See comparable exclamations in the tomb of Djehuty-hotep from el-Bersheh (Newberry 1893:16) and the tomb of Amenhotepsise, TT 75 (Davies and Davies 1923, pl. XV). In these examples the deceased is being ritually purified, a "prior condition to all blessing" (Davies and Davies 1923, 16).
[62] Shore 1992, 228, n. 22.
[63] Griffiths 1970, 35.
[64] Smith and Dawson 2002, 72-8; Lucas and Harris 1962, 271.
[65] Lucas and Harris 1962, 271.
[66] Lucas and Harris 1962, 271.
[67] Smith and Dawson 2002, 76; Lucas and Harris 1962, 271.
[68] Lucas and Harris 1962, 272.

In the New Kingdom tomb of Amenemhet (TT 82), the rite of *ḥ3i* is performed on a skiff during the sacred voyage to Abydos. In this example the location is clearly discernible, as is the time when the ritual occurs. This is the only example of the *ḥ3i* ritual taking place on the water. The crossing to Abydos has its origin in the voyage to the sacred Delta localities performed in the Butic ceremony. It is probable that this scene is labeled as *ḥ3i*-ing because it depicts the ritual transportation to the Hereafter. The deceased is actually traveling there and rite of *ḥ3i* was performed to encourage the deceased, as an Osiris, to resurrect in time for the skiff's arrival at the west bank. Abydos may have been considered to be the world of the Hereafter, or the Kingdom of Osiris, according to Brunner-Traut.[69] If this were the case, then the ritual of *ḥ3i* would have needed to be performed before the deceased, as Osiris, reached the necropolis. In the tomb scene depicted, the ritual is saturated with mythological interpretation, making it difficult to compare the funerary rites with those of the Old Kingdom. The one thing that does provide a parallel for the Old Kingdom scenes is the fact that in both cases the deceased is on route to rebirth (compare with the scenes in the tombs of Hetepherakhti and Amenemhet – TT 82). Unfortunately there is no additional New Kingdom source where the rite of *ḥ3i* is performed on earth for a deceased individual. Table 8 presents the location and the time of the ritual of *ḥ3i* in the private sources.

Mythologized Sources

This section will briefly discuss the remaining sources, which originated in a royal context (see Table 9). As noted above, some of these sources do not present tangible locations or times for the ritual of *ḥ3i*. Some Pyramid Texts reference locations, such as the heavens or Nedit, which cannot be physically located. At the same time, PT §§2112 and 2117 specifically state that the rite takes place at the tomb, which is clearly in line with what the contemporary private sources reveal. PT §§550 and 1585 suggest that the ritual is performed simultaneously with the deceased's ascension to the sky. This, in other words, would indicate that the rite was performed in conjunction with the deceased's attempt at life in the Hereafter and during transport or during the voyage. Theoretically, there is a connection between the tomb and ascension to the sky, in that after death the deceased's body will spend eternity at the tomb while his spirit will ascend to heaven. The gravesite is the last place where relatives and friends of the deceased can contribute to the deceased's spiritual success for the future. Furthermore, PT §1255 recounts an excerpt from the myth of Osiris, and states that the mythological Nedit is the location for the rite, which is thought to be a place near Abydos where Osiris was murdered. In the myth, it is in this location that the acts

[69] Brunner-Traut 1938, 57; Reeder 1995, 70.

of rejuvenation and spiritualization occur. Accordingly, this would parallel PT §1585, which indicates that the rite was necessary before life could be achieved after death.

The next series of texts to explore are the Coffin Texts. Some of the Coffin Texts describe locations that cannot be fathomed here on earth, while other texts seem to replicate earthy scenarios.

CT III 297i clearly indicated that the ritual of *ḥ3i* is performed in the Pure Place, or the *wʿbt*. The passage also shows that the goal is the spiritualization of the deceased as an Osiris. Likewise, a passage in CT III 310-311 alludes to the funerary workshop, the secret portals of Anubis, and the Pure Place. These references would seem to confirm that the ritual of *ḥ3i* is associated with this location.

Also paralleling the conclusions from the private sources is Coffin Text III 308d that specifically states that the ritual of *ḥ3i* is performed on the day of interment, presumably at the gravesite. This locality is mirrored in CT IV 373a as well.

Almost all of the Coffin Texts speak of the transformation of the deceased into an Osiris. This is when the rite of *ḥ3i* is said to occur.

As concerns the New Kingdom mythological sources, it can be taken for granted that the location of the enactment of the ritual of *ḥ3i* is the realm of the dead. Chapter 172 of the Book of the Dead explains that this passage presents the beginning of the spells for praising performed in the god's domain. Likewise, the Amduat and the Book of Gates feature scenes set in the god's domain, or the realm of the dead.

The hymn to Osiris featured on Louvre stela C 286 parallels Pyramid Text §1255[70] and shows the rite being performed in Nedit.[71] This hymn confirms that the rite was performed before Osiris was fully resurrected, that it was an essential prerequisite for resurrection, and that the acceptable emotion surrounding the rebirth was joy.

Chapter One of the Book of the Dead speaks of the *ḥ3yw* performing in Busiris on the Shores of the Washerman. Busiris was located in the ninth nome of Lower Egypt,[72] in the middle of the Nile Delta on the west bank of the Damietta branch.[73] According to Faulkner, Washerman's Shore refers to the extreme north of Egypt. It is generally thought that the cult of Osiris originated in Busiris.[74] Again, the text says, "I was born in Busiris when I was with the men who *ḥ3i*-ed."[75]

These mythological examples cannot be compared to examples of authentic rituals taking place.

Conclusion

In summation, the scene from the tomb of Debehni and the description of the rite in the Funerary Liturgy establish the fact that the ritual of *ḥ3i* can occur at the tomb on the day of burial. The scene from the tomb of Hetepherakhti substantiates this point. However, in this case the rite occurs before the arrival of the corpse at the tomb, during transportation. The tomb scenes of Qar and Pepiankh show that the rite of *ḥ3i* can also occur when the corpse is left at the embalmer's workshop (*wʿbt*). Likewise, another scene in the tomb of Pepiankh shows that the rite occurs on the day of burial when the corpse is picked up from this same location. In both cases the participants are inside the *wʿbt*. The inscription of Sabni corroborates the connection between the rite of *ḥ3i* and the embalming workshop in that the *ḥ3itiw*, along with other embalming essentials, originate from the *pr-nfr*, a building connected to the *wʿbt*. In the private examples from the Old and Middle Kingdoms[76] the ritual of *ḥ3i* appears to have been performed between the commencement of the embalming process and the deposition of the body in the tomb, and in all cases the ritual was performed in the cemetery. Most likely this was a continuous ritual that lasted for some time during the transportation from the embalming workshop to the tomb and probably for some time at the tomb as well. When the mythologized sources refer to a recognizable location they corroborate the places and times presented in the private sources. Thus the rite of *ḥ3i* was included in the funeral ceremonies that were performed to prepare the deceased for eternal life, namely the voyage to the Hereafter.

[70] Griffiths 1980, 9.
[71] Faulkner 1994, 174.
[72] Baines and Málek 1994, 15.
[73] Baines and Málek 1994, 167.
[74] Griffiths 1980, 3, 136-137.
[75] Faulkner 1994, plate 5.
[76] If we take the 13th Dynasty date for the Funerary Liturgy.

TABLE 8: LOCATION AND TIME OF THE RITE OF *ḥ3i* IN THE PRIVATE SOURCES

	Source	Location	Time
1	Tomb of Debehni	In front of the embalming house;[77] at the tomb;[78] on roof of mastaba[79]	During funeral procession[80]
2	Tomb of Hetepherakhti	En route to the tomb[81]	Nearing the end of the funeral procession
3	Tomb of Qar	In front of the embalming house	During funeral procession, before embalmment
4	Inscription of Sabni	The *ḥ3itiw* arrive in Wawat from the Embalming House[82]	Before burial
5	Tomb of Pepiankh First Scene	Inside the embalmers' workshop	During funeral procession after the delivery of the body[83]
	Second Scene	Inside the embalmers' workshop	During funeral procession just before procession leaves *wꜥbt* with mummified body
6	Funerary Liturgy col. 16	At the mastaba	Day of Interment
7	F.L. col. 44-45	At the mastaba	Day of Interment
8	F.L. col. 64	At the mastaba	Day of Interment
9	F.L. col. 84	At the mastaba	Day of Interment
10	Tomb of Amenemhet	In a skiff on Water	Day of Interment

TABLE 9: LOCATION AND TIME OF THE RITE OF *ḥ3i* IN THE MYTHOLOGIZED SOURCES[84]

	Source	Location In Mythological Realm	Time
1	PT §550	During king's ascension to sky	?
2	PT §744	While king is inducted into pavilion by Isis	?
3	PT §1255	Coming from the west and arriving in Nedit	During the search for Osiris
4	PT §1280	?	During the search for Osiris
5	PT §1585	During king's ascension to sky (on a ladder which Khnum made)	?
6	PT §1791	?	?
7	PT §2112	At the tomb	?
8	PT §2117	At the tomb[85]	?
9	CT I 73d	In the presence of the gods	?
10	CT I 74e	In the presence of the gods	?
11	CT I 303g	?	During the prevention of

[77] S. Hassan 1943, 178.
[78] J. Wilson 1944, 212.
[79] Bolshakov 1991, 40.
[80] If we are to follow S. Hassan's opinion that the performance is taking place outside the embalming hut, then the time may be just before or just after the embalming. If we follow either of the other two suggestions, then the performance is taking place at the end of the procession before the body is deposited in the tomb.
[81] Mohr 1943, 38; Bolshakov 1991, 40.
[82] The passage in the inscription makes it clear that the "*ḥ3tiw*" are associated with the *wꜥbt* and the *pr nfr*.
[83] Blackman notes in his publication that the procession to the Embalmers' Workshop to fetch the embalmed body occurs only at Meir (1953, 54).
[84] When I insert a question mark it means that there is no place name available in the text that clearly identifies a location; likewise, a question mark will be placed in the "time" column if no particular time in the funeral ceremony can be discerned. It can be assumed that all of these passages deal with the mythological realm. It is also assumed that the Pyramid Texts were recited only at a royal funeral. It is also assumed that all of these mythologized spells are funerary related and were intended to function in such a capacity.
[85] It can be supposed that this same action is taking place in the same location and in the same time frame as that of the last example since they are both a part of the same text.

			putrefaction of deceased as Osiris
12	CT II 177h	Realm of the dead	?
13	CT II 238b	Realm of the dead	When a man is made into a spirit by becoming a human falcon
14	CT II 239a	Realm of the dead	When a man is made into a spirit by becoming a human falcon
15	CT III 22a	?	?
16	CT III 297i	*Wꜥbt*	During rejuvenation of deceased as an Osiris
17	CT III 307a	?	During rejuvenation of deceased as an Osiris
18	CT III 307b	?	During rejuvenation of deceased as an Osiris
19	CT III 308d (x2)	At the interment	During rejuvenation of deceased as an Osiris
20	CT III 311h	Connection with *wꜥbt*?	During rejuvenation of deceased as an Osiris
21	CT III 317e	?	During rejuvenation of deceased as an Osiris
22	CT III 317l	Behind Anubis	During rejuvenation of deceased as an Osiris
23	CT IV 373a	Realm of the dead; at the burial of Osiris	Day of Interment; "on that day of the sixth-day festival in which the gods swooned."
24	CT IV 373a	Realm of the dead; at the burial of Osiris	Day of interment; "on that day of the sixth-day festival in which the gods swooned."
25	CT V 332c	Netherworld/Realm of the dead	?
26	CT VI 360j	?	?
27	CT VI 385o	Realm of the dead?	?
28	CT VII 28o	?	?
29	CT VII 51s	Island of fire?	?
30	BD 1	Busiris – on the Shores of the Washerman[86]	When deceased was born and Osiris vindicated (rebirth?)
31	BD 172 (incl. Flor 1594)	In the necropolis[87]	Day of interment?
32	Book of Gates	Realm of the dead	?
33	Louvre Stela C 286	In Nedit	During search for and rejuvenation of Osiris
34	Amduat IV 34	Waters of Osiris in the realm of the dead	?

[86] According to Faulkner (1994, 175) this is a place in the extreme north of Egypt.
[87] Manniche 1988, 119.

Chapter Seven

Introduction

The A 28 gesture (Figure 25) has been repeatedly utilized throughout the aforementioned sources that deal with the rite of *ḥ3i*. From the earliest source, which dates to the Fourth Dynasty, until the Ptolemaic Period, this gesture was employed by the ancient Egyptians to symbolize the voyage of spiritualization and rebirth that transformed the deceased in preparation for his entry into the Hereafter. Van Lepp corroborates this notion in his work on the Old Kingdom dance scene in the tomb of Wa'tetkhethor, where he suggests that there is an intense interrelationship between text and visual image. He postulates that the dance movements signify what is taking place in the mortuary rituals.[1] This phenomenon is paralleled in the relationship between the A 28 pose and the spiritualizing rituals that take place in conjunction with the embalming workshop and as a part of the funeral procession on the day of burial. This pose appears regularly in Egyptian art and as a determinative in hieroglyphic writing. The A 28 gesture has two distinct associations, which appear to be in conflict with one another – to mourn and to rejoice.[2] Upon further investigation I discovered that the gesture was, in certain cases, being used in a more specific manner and was intimately related to the word *ḥ3i*.

First, I will summarize the past research conducted on this topic. Then I will restate my research with regard to the A 28 determinative appearing in Egyptian texts. Lastly, I will discuss how this gesture appears in art, beginning with Predynastic objects and finishing with paintings and reliefs from the New Kingdom. I will also make brief mention of an isolated Ptolemaic example. My intention is to document the usage of this pose throughout the Pharaonic period in an attempt to clarify the relationship between the A 28 pose and the word *ḥ3i*.

Past Research

Gardiner calls the A 28 sign "man with both arms raised." He lists this as a determinative for *ḳ3i* "to be high," for *ḥꜥi* "rejoice," and in *sw3š* "extol." Subsequently, he adds that the sign appears in *ḥ3i* "mourn" and, for unknown reasons, in *i3s* "bald."[3]

In 1938 Marcelle Werbrouck published a book, entitled *Les Pleureuses dans l'Égypte ancienne*; in it she discusses the pose in question.[4] She notes that this gesture can signify jubilation, supplication or grief. She also concludes that this gesture is rarely found in the Old Kingdom; but in the Middle Kingdom and the New Kingdom, one finds the gesture most frequently being performed by the common folk, especially females, and by mourners. In her figures, Werbrouck presents six variants of the A 28 pose, ranging from right angles at the elbows, to the hands touching the head.[5] It is doubtful that all six gestures are indeed variants of the same pose. This gesture seems more reminiscent of the mourning gesture where either one or two arms cover the face.[6] Buurman shows six variants of the A 28 pose as well, all of which are relatively similar.[7]

In 1955, in his article entitled "A Unique Funerary Liturgy," Gardiner further mentions his confusion about the signification of this sign. He writes:

> But apart from the fact that the hieroglyph of the man raising his arms above his head is well known as the determinative of *ḥꜥi* 'to rejoice,' there are Old Kingdom reliefs which associate the verb *ḥ3i* with dancing – in fact with what, one would think, was an essentially joyous occupation.[8]

Elaborating on Gardiner's observation, it is noteworthy that there are three instances where the individuals connected with these captions hold their arms in the A 28 pose, namely the funerary scenes in the tombs of Debehni at Giza, Hetepherakhti at Sakkara, and Pepiankh at Meir.

Fekri Hassan also studied this pose as it appears on Predynastic female figurines and on Naqada II pottery, coming to the conclusion that the raised arms were in imitation of cow horns. He suggests that these female figures may represent an early deity, perhaps the goddess Hathor or Bat.[9]

Richard Wilkinson has also considered this gesture.[10] He classifies this pose as one of rejoicing, remarking that "a man with both arms raised high in jubilation formed the determinative used for the writing of *ḥꜥi*: 'rejoice,' and several other related words."[11] He notes that this same gesture is featured in many scenes of the deceased appearing in triumph after being found innocent at the weighing of the heart. Wilkinson further explains that this gesture can appear in secular contexts, such as victory or investiture scenes (see below). But he also points out that not all raised-arm figures suggest joy, noting this gesture's connection with one word — although he does not state which one — meaning "to mourn" and with some representations of mourning. He

[1] Van Lepp 1987, 5.
[2] Dominicus 1994, 58-61.
[3] Gardiner 1994, 445.
[4] Werbrouck 1938, 145.

[5] See Figures 97-102 in Werbrouck 1938.
[66] For examples of this pose see Figures 172-175 in Werbrouck 1938.
[7] Buurman, *et al.* 1988, 54.
[8] Gardiner 1955, 10.
[9] F. Hassan 1992, 312-315. See also Hornblower 1929.
[10] Wilkinson 1992, 27; 1994, 206.
[11] Wilkinson 1992, 27. See also Hermann 1963.

states that the two uses are clearly discernible in context.

The question then arises: Are the rejoicing gesture and the mourning gesture the same? It appears that the illustrated pose is the same in both contexts. However, the evidence seems to show that the symbolism of the gesture evolved over time.

A 28 Gesture as a Hieroglyphic Determinative

In Chapter One it was demonstrated that the A 28 gesture is associated with the rite of *ḥ3i*. It is assumed that *ḥ3i* is the mourning word that Wilkinson refers to in his book (see above). This determinative does not occur in the more common mourning words. In fact, this determinative is generally absent from the corpus of mourning words, except for the three examples discussed in Chapter One. To account for these three instances one can acknowledge that the rite of *ḥ3i*, and thus the A 28 gesture, is not connected to mourning but is part of the funerary ritual. Wishing and encouraging someone to be reborn in the Hereafter does not replace the sense of loss felt by a loved one.

Pictorial Evidence

Predynastic Period

One way to understand religion, rites, and rituals in ancient Egypt is to utilize visual culture.[12] For the Predynastic period one has only the pictorial evidence for the A 28 pose. For these artifacts the archaeological context is significant for understanding the temporal, spatial, and depositional elements.[13] In this case, a contextual study should include the burials in which these artifacts functioned.[14] However, relatively speaking, there are very few artifacts that have been discovered in a controlled archaeological context, making this a difficult task.[15]

The earliest examples we have of the A 28 pose date to the Naqada II/Gerzean period, where the pose is illustrated on linen[16] and pottery,[17] exhibited in female figurines[18] and rock art,[19] and displayed in Tomb 100 at Hierakonpolis.[20]

One of the most intriguing examples comes from the Upper Egyptian site of Gebelein. Several portions of linen were discovered in a tomb in 1930 by the Italian Egyptological Expedition.[21] Apparently these fragments were part of a long canvas that was folded beside a mummy.[22] Otherwise, the excavation report by Farina is rather vague as to the particulars. The women are portrayed in red and they wear long skirts worn from the waist down that hide the feet. The composition shows the female figures taller than the males, which is reminiscent of the figures portrayed on the D-Ware pots. There are a total of eight fragments that have been reconstituted to create a scene thought to represent a funeral dance. Scamuzzi describes the recreation as follows:

> The space between the two women is occupied by male figures arranged in three parallel rows: those on the first row, beginning from the top, are wearing white loin-clothes, as we can see from the remnants around the waist of the first figure from the left, and have both arms raised; those on the second row have only one arm raised, while those on the third stand hand in hand with their arms down.[23]

The women in the top row have their arms raised and curved inward very much like the other predynastic examples.

D-Ware pottery is another medium through which one can observe depictions of women with upraised arms. On one Middle Naqada II pot from el-Adaima (no. 21) there are three boats with a palm branch at each prow, and a pole with streamers bearing a standard. Each boat has a different standard. It has been suggested that these standards designate the locality from which the boats originated.[24] On each boat stands an oversized female figure with raised arms, who is attended by smaller male figures. This pot is now in the Brooklyn Museum.[25] This female also appears in the same pose on other examples of D- Ware.[26] Because of her size in

[12] Hendrickx, *et al.*, 2010, 24.

[13] Wengrow 2006, 108; Hendrickx, *et al.*, 2010, 24.

[14] Hendrickx, *et al.* 2010, 26; Ucko 1968.

[15] Ucko 1968, 66, 165-167; Wengrow 2006, 93, note 21.

[16] A fragment of painted linen from Gebelein is one example of pictorial images on perishable material. It is dated to either Naqada I or early Naqada II (Scamuzzi 1965, pls. 1-5; Donadoni Roveri 1990; 23-25; Wengrow 2006, 109).

[17] D-Ware (Decorated Ware) has a pale background allowing for painted designs in a dull red, ochre pigment. The earlier C-Ware (White Cross-Lined) offered white-on-dark painting. Marl clay was used for D-Ware and Nile silt for C-Ware (Wengrow 2006, 92-93).

[18] Anthropomorphic figures with upraised arms are found painted on C-Ware bowls and beakers, and become more common in the later D-Ware (Wengrow 2006, 104).

[19] Carved images of human figures with upraised arms standing on boats are common in the Eastern Desert. One intriguing rock carving from Wadi Abu Wasil in the Eastern Desert features five people dragging a boat that carries a figure with upraised arms (Wengrow 2006, 113, Figure 5.7).

[20] Tomb 100 presents the most extensive pictorial composition from Predynastic Egypt. This tomb is now dated to Naqada II C. The decoration differs from that of the pottery in that the painting is polychrome (red, black, and white). There are many commonalities between the mural in Tomb 100 and D-Ware. What is of importance for this study are the depictions of human figures with upraised arms. However, the humans in the mural are more angular and their arms do not round like the humans on D-Ware.

[21] Donadoni Roveri 1990, 25.

[22] Scamuzzi 1965, see Foreword to Plates I-V.

[23] Scamuzzi 1965, Plate I.

[24] Needler 1984, 205; Vandier 1952, 340-341.

[25] Brooklyn 09.889.400. This piece was found during H. de Morgan's excavations in 1907-08 (Needler 1984, 205-206, pl. 16).

[26] Needler 1984, 206. For an accessible publication of three additional D-Ware pots see Wengrove 2006, Figure 4.6).

relation to the adjacent figures, it has been suggested by a number of scholars that she represents a deity,[27] since in Egyptian art size is directly related to importance. Another example is Berlin 20304 where a similar scene is depicted.[28] It is not a coincidence that the A 28 pose appears in a traveling context. These are the earliest examples to provide evidence for the link between the A 28 pose and ritual transportation.

The female figure is prolific in clay figurines from the Predynastic period as well.[29] Cyril Aldred suggests that she represented either the mother goddess or a symbol connected with magical practices.[30] The clay figurines with raised arms, dating to approximately the same time as the pots mentioned above (Naqada II period), are reminiscent of the other painted illustrations. The figures depicted on the pottery unquestionably possess human heads, while many of the figurines have bird-like heads.[31] One particular terracotta figurine comes from Burial Two at el-Ma'mariya and is 11 ½ inches high.[32] It has a small bird-like head devoid of facial features. The arms curve upward and slightly back with the hands turned inward.[33] The paint remnants indicate a white full-length skirt, and resin shows that the figurine may have worn a wig. Aside from two similar figurines found in Burial Two at el-Ma'mariya, sixteen comparable, but smaller, figures were found in Burial 186 from the same site.[34] Again, as illustrated earlier, birds represented the one logical means to reaching the heavens or the Afterlife – a primary mode of ritual transport richly attested in ancient Egyptian texts (see above).

As mentioned above, Fekri Hassan, in his article "Primeval Goddess to Divine King," discusses the pose's relevance to early goddess cults and its association with the cow. F. Hassan suggests that the A 28 stance depicted on the pots and in the female figurines is paralleled in the iconography of the Predynastic cow goddess.[35] He compares a palette illustrating a cow's head and horns with these figures with upraised arms, suggesting that they are mimicking cow horns.[36] Hendrickx, in a 2002 article makes a similar presentation and compares the arms of the figurines to bovine horns.[37] M. A. Murray actually postulated this theory back in 1952, where she remarks that there are two possible interpretations for the slate palette — the image may represent the head of a cow, or it may depict a giant goddess with upraised arms.[38] Murray suggests Hathor or Nut.[39] With regard to this palette and the cow goddess that appears on the Narmer palette, Hornung remarks that these images are iconographically closer to Bat, although he acknowledges that prehistoric evidence pertaining to the gods is sparse and ambiguous.[40]

Their symbolism is not certain;[41] it has been suggested that they may represent servants,[42] dancers,[43] mourners,[44] protectors,[45] or that they might be symbolic of sexuality, fertility[46] or rebirth.[47] A more recent study concludes that this particular attitude is assumed by victors in violent scenes and that the upraised arms are to be considered a symbol of power, referring to bulls horns.[48] It is not stated if this conclusion applies only to male figures. Needler suggests that the image is a "representation of an abstract idea familiar to its contemporaries."[49] When presenting the social circumstances of predynastic Egypt, F. Hassan speaks of ritual duties divided between male and female spheres.[50] Noting the preponderance of female figures in Naqada II iconography, he remarks that, "the potency of a female deity was primarily a result of her association with birth, death, and resurrection."[51] Due to the continued use of this gesture in contexts of rejuvenation and rebirth, this pose symbolizes the regenerative, spiritualizing energy, originally embodied in the female life-force. Additionally, considering the avian character of the figurines one cannot help but equate them with later images of Isis, for example, as a *ḥ3(i)t* bird aiding the deceased in reaching the Hereafter.[52] It is also appropriate to connect these predynastic images of figures on boats with the later scene illustrated in TT 82 (Figure 22). In all cases the image depicts the ritual transportation of the deceased, which is synonymous with his arrival in the Hereafter.

---

[27] F. Hassan 1992, 315.
[28] See F. Hassan 1992, 314.
[29] Dreyer, *et al.* 1998, 114, Fig. 12:4; pl. 6:c; Ucko 1968, 44-48, 53, 99-100, 105, cat. 69-73, 83; Needler 1984, 336-343, cat. 267-273.
[30] Aldred 1965, 29.
[31] Graff 2008, Figure 4.
[32] Brooklyn 07.447.505. See Needler 1984, 336. A similar figurine (07.447.502) was found with the aforementioned object in Burial Two.
[33] Needler 1984, 336-337.
[34] Needler 1984, 340.
[35] F. Hassan 1992, 314-315.
[36] F. Hassan 1992, 314-315.
[37] Hendrickx 2002; Hendrickx, *et al.* 2010.
[38] Murray 1956, 95-96.
[39] Murray 1956, 96.
[40] Hornung 1982, 103. See also Fischer 1962.
[41] Needler 1984, 336.
[42] Needler 1984, 336.
[43] Needler 1984, 206.
[44] Lacovara 1988, 70.
[45] Hornblower 1929, 35.
[46] Needler 1984, 337.
[47] Needler 1984, 337; H.-W. Mueller 1970, no. 4.
[48] Hendrickx, *et al.* 2010, 27.
[49] Needler 1984, 336. Van Lepp (1987, 52) comments in his publication of the dance scene of Wa'tetkhethor in the mastaba of Mereruka that, "symbolism has inherent cultural associations which enable the members of society easily to comprehend the presented message."
[50] See F. Hassan (1988 and 1992, 312) for his work on the importance of women in divine kingship.
[51] F. Hassan 1992, 312.
[52] Note PT §1255 and Louvre Stela C 286.

Old Kingdom

In the Old Kingdom, evidence for the A 28 pose exists primarily in tomb scenes. There appear to be three contexts in which this gesture occurs: in dance scenes pertaining to funerary ritual, in scenes where the coffin or statue is dragged during the funeral procession, and in scenes where a man stands before an offering table.

In dance scenes, the gesture is depicted with the arms raised, the elbows bent at ear level, and the palms facing outward (or inward in the case of Iy-Mery[53]) (Figure 26).[54] Irena Lexová, in her book *Ancient Egyptian Dances*,[55] remarks that the A 28 pose was the most common movement depicted in ritual dance scenes,[56] and each example of the A 28 pose presented in her book is classified as a ritual dance. In some tomb scenes it looks as though the dancers are proceeding in a straight line without much movement. The A 28 pose does not seem to occur in acrobatic dances. Lexová suggests that the A 28 gesture originally belonged to the funerary dance, and was later adapted by mourners and executed rhythmically.[57] The gesture was performed to a beat in the Old Kingdom in a funeral context for the purpose of rebirth. Looking ahead, in the New Kingdom the gesture was used by mourners in a funerary context, possibly without the knowledge of the gesture's previous connection with *ḥ3i* and its symbolism of rebirth.

The second context featuring the A 28 pose is the dragging scene of the funeral procession, as exhibited in the tombs of Hetepherakhti, Ptahhotep, and a tomb at Barnûgi (see Chapter Two above). Some of the poses represented in these tombs are rather solemn while some show a slightly livelier version where the dancers are accompanied by clappers (Figures 8-10). In the Old Kingdom, women perform this gesture in the dragging scenes.

The third and last context, as evidenced in the tomb of Pepiankh at Meir,[58] shows a man standing in the A 28 pose before an offering table. An offering table is also present in scenes in the tombs of Debehni (Figure 4) and Mereruka[59] in conjunction with the appearance of the A 28 gesture; those examples, however, also exhibit clappers, which is why they are allocated to the first category.

As is shown in Werbrouck's[60] and Buurman's[61] collection of the forms of A 28 gesture, the actual positioning of the arms varies from scene to scene in the Old Kingdom. Within the same type of scene actors sometimes have their palms facing outward, and other times have their palms facing inward; likewise their elbows are bent at different angles. This latter fact can easily be seen in two scenes in the tomb of Pepiankh at Meir, where the *ḥ3(i)w* is shown with both arms at a different angle in each scene.[62] The same pose is depicted in all cases. It may simply be a matter of illustrating different stages of a continuous movement, possibly even a dance; or people may hold the pose in slightly different ways. The fact that the A 28 sign is used in hieroglyphic writing to determine the word *ḥꜤi* "rejoice" confirms that this rhythmic arm movement may be construed as a joyful act, or dance. In her book on gestures in the Old and Middle Kingdoms, Brigitte Dominicus notes the variation in the writings of the A 28 sign in both the words *ḥ3i* and *ḥꜤi*.[63] She compares the palms facing inward (PT §§744b, 2117) with those facing outward (PT §550b), and she remarks on the different angle of the elbow.[64] In Dominicus' *Abb.* 13 three examples of the A 28 gesture are superimposed to show their inconsistency.[65] So it may be assumed that different artists rendered the pose in their own way but that all the images actually represent the same gesture.

Middle Kingdom

Although the evidence is scarce, the A 28 gesture continues into the Middle Kingdom. Most likely this is due to the accident of preservation in the sources rather than to a decreased use of the pose. Dance scenes involving the A 28 pose can be found twice in the tomb of Khety at Beni Hasan (Figures 27-28),[66] and in the tomb of Ahanakht at el-Bersha (Figure 29).[67]

Additionally, a variation of the traditional dragging scene can be found in the tomb of Senet, where six people — three men and three women with their arms in the A 28 pose — precede six men hauling the coffin and barque on a sledge (Figure 11).[68] The individuals depicted represent the sacred localities of the Delta region;[69] they are an early example of a New Kingdom trend which can be seen in numerous private tombs on the west bank of Thebes and at Elkab (see Chapter Two).[70] However, it is fascinating that an analogous scene of a barque being hauled (without a caption) is found as early as the predynastic period carved in rock at Wadi Abu Wasil.[71]

---

53 *LD* II, 52.
54 See Altenmüller 1978, *Abb.* 1 for Nebkauhor from Sakkara.
55 Lexová 2000.
56 Lexová 2000, 36, figs. 4, 5, 8.
57 Lexová 2000, 39.
58 See funeral procession of Pepiankh in Blackman 1953, plates 42-43.
59 See J. Wilson 1944, plate XV.
60 Werbrouck 1938, 145, plates 97-102.
61 Buurman, *et al.* 1988, 54.
62 See funeral procession of Pepiankh in Blackman 1953, plates 42-43.
63 Dominicus 1994, 58.
64 Dominicus 1994, 58.
65 Dominicus 1994, 59.
66 Newberry 1893, 2: pl. XIII.
67 Griffith and Newberry 1894, 2: pl. XIV.
68 Davies 1920, 20, pl. XIX.
69 Werbrouck 1938, 145.
70 Settgast 1963, *Taf.* 2.
71 Wengrow 2006, 113, Figure 5.7.

New Kingdom

In the New Kingdom, the A 28 pose no longer occurs in dance scenes, although it is revived in the Saite Period.[72] Dragging scenes including the A 28 pose do continue into the New Kingdom and are discussed in detail in Chapter Two. In a separate dragging scene from the tomb of Ramose (not mentioned above), an inscription occurs between the two groups of four men who walk with their arms in the A 28 pose. Davies translates the inscriptions as follows: *ḳ3 b3w.k mi pt mn mnw.k*, "thy fame is exalted like heaven; thy monuments are secure."[73] Instead the text may read: *ḳ3(i) n b3w.k mi mnw(y) mnw(w).k*, "Exalted is your mystical power, just as your monuments are monumental."[74] This exaltation, or uplifting, of the deceased's mystical power (*b3w*) is synonymous with his spirit prospering in the Hereafter. Some also interpret this passage inconjunction with the gesture to mean that the men are rejoicing at Ramose's eternal existence.[75]

It is in the New Kingdom that the A 28 gesture becomes common amongst mourners during funerals,[76] amongst those who surrender in combat scenes,[77] or are otherwise submitting to the king.[78] There is also New Kingdom evidence to show that this pose can symbolize joy: for example, a relief from the tomb of Khai at Sakkara.[79] In addition, this pose appears in victory celebrations,[80] and ceremonial investitures.[81] Furthermore, at least as early as the Twenty-First Dynasty, the deceased can hold this pose after having been vindicated at the weighing of the heart in the Book of the Dead.[82] This latter context can in fact be interpreted as being synonymous with revivification or rebirth, in that the deceased will not die another death and be eaten by the devourer, but instead will live in the Hereafter.

Conclusion

The most intriguing and significant evidence for the connection between *ḥ3i* and the A 28 pose comes from the predynastic period. At this time, female figurines posed in the A 28 gesture were being produced, along with illustrations of comparable figures painted on pottery vessels, tomb walls, and linen, and carved in rock. The pictures painted on the pottery vessels, in Tomb 100 and in rock art support the proposition that the A 28 gesture was performed in transit, and the representations on the linen from Gebelein in particular suggest a funerary context.

This tradition was continued into the Old Kingdom and beyond as evidenced by the scenes in the Old Kingdom tomb of Hetephherakhti, the Middle Kingdom tomb of Senet, and the New Kingdom tomb of Ramose, to name only a few. Moreover, the connection between the gesture itself and its avian origin also continued into the Pharaonic era, where Isis can appear as a bird in her capacity to resurrect Osiris and have him live eternally in the Hereafter (PT §1255 and Louvre Stela C 286). Graff demonstrates that that the A 28 gesture as seen in the predynastic figurines can be compared to the wings of a bird.[83]

The A 28 pose had a very specific usage in the Old Kingdom, appearing in funerary dances, dragging scenes, and in a funerary ritual before an offering table.[84] In the Middle Kingdom, it is difficult to document thoroughly the use of the A 28 pose due to scanty evidence, although there are examples of the gesture appearing in dance scenes and during the funeral procession. By the time of the New Kingdom, this gesture has expanded in its symbolism,[85] and appears in a variety of new contexts: contexts of mourning, submission, and joy. It also continues to feature in the traditional dragging scenes. It is now apparent that the symbolism of the A 28 pose is quite complex and that its significance has evolved over time.

There is a clear connection between the word *ḥ3i* and the A 28 pose in Egyptian writing—meaning it is repeatedly used as a determinative for this word. This link is also apparent during only the Old Kingdom in the pictorial evidence, namely, in the tomb scenes of Debehni and Hetepherakhti where the pose of the women doubles as a hieroglyphic determinative for the accompanying caption – *ḥ3it*.[86]

The connection, however, becomes attenuated through time, and the association between the word *ḥ3i* and the A 28 gesture is more ambiguous in the New Kingdom,

[72] Lexová 2000, 37.

[73] Davies 1941, plate XXVI and page 23, n. 2.

[74] I would like to thank Lanny Bell for helping with a new translation of this passage.

[75] www.osirisnet.net/tombes/nobles/ramose/e_ramose.htm. The author of this site is Thierry Benderitter.

[76] Tomb of Neferhotep (TT 49), Davies 1973, plate XXIII; Tomb of Nebamun and Apuki (TT 181), Davies 1971, plate 19; Tomb of Ramose (TT 55), Davies 1941, plate XXVI.

[77] Combat scenes from the temple of Ramesses III at Medinet Habu, Donohue 1992, figures 20-21.

[78] Foreign delegates submitting to the king in the tomb of Horemheb at Sakkara, Martin 1991, figure 49.

[79] R. Wilkinson 1994, 206.

[80] For example, the Temple of Ramesses III at Medinet Habu, R. Wilkinson 1992, 26.

[81] For a ceremonial investiture from reign of Ramesses IX from the Temple of Amun-Re at Karnak see R. Wilkinson 1992, 26.

[82] See R. Wilkinson (1992, 26) for scene of the weighing of the heart from Papyrus Konsumes, 21st Dynasty; Seebers 1976, 98-101.

[83] Graff 2008, figure 4.

[84] The expression of mourning is rare in Old Kingdom tomb scenes so it is not known if the A 28 pose was used as a mourning gesture. However, there is currently no evidence to confirm this association. Mourning scenes are depicted only in the tombs of Mereruka, Ankhmahor and Idw (Harpur 1987, 113).

[85] As noted earlier, Hendrickx, *et al* has suggested that the upraised arms signified victory in the predynastic period (2010, 27).

[86] See Mohr 1943, figure 3.

Third Intermediate Period, and Late Period where they rarely occur in conjunction with one another in representations.[87] Even the A 28 sign in hieroglyphic writing appears less frequently than earlier, that is, until the Ptolemaic Period where it is again ubiquitous. The relationship is clearly reestablished in the Ptolemaic temple inscriptions where there are a multitude of examples of the writing of *ḥꜣi* with the A 28 determinative.

[87] The A 28 determinative is used in the example from TT 82 and in BD 172 in Pap. Nebseni. Little can be determined about the A 28 gesture in either the Third Intermediate Period or the Late Period simply because evidence is sparse or altogether lacking.

Chapter Eight

Introduction

The goal of this chapter is to introduce systematically all of the citations of the word *ḥ3i* in the various forms in which it appears in the ancient Egyptian sources, in order to illustrate how the word *ḥ3i* was utilized. This chapter will focus on the examples of *ḥ3i* that date from the Old Kingdom to the end of the Late Period, the latest reference before the Ptolemaic Period dating to Dynasty Twenty-five or Twenty-six. These references will be organized chronologically on the basis of Old, Middle or New Kingdom, or Late Period date, with a brief summary of the Ptolemaic sources at the end. Within each of these categories the examples are grouped either by context – for example, those occurring in the Pyramid Texts – or by grammatical form. For a better understanding of how *ḥ3i* occurs in the sources, different methods of organization were necessary.

As has been noted, all of the sources where *ḥ3i* appears are of a religious nature except for those examples that refer to the *ḥ3(i)t*-bird itself. When necessary, the translations cited are from the most recent published sources. However, the word *ḥ3it* (and its variants) is translated as "ritually transport" with the express purpose of rebirth, in light of the research conducted for this work. The word in question appears in bold print when found in a longer text. To reiterate, *ḥ3i* means to ritually transport the deceased to the Hereafter with the explicit intention of achieving rejuvenation or rebirth in the Next World. As this is quite a cumbersome translation I have limited the definition in most instances to "transport" or "ritually transport."

In some cases, such as in the Old Kingdom tomb inscription of Hetepherakhti, *ḥ3i* focuses on the physical movement or transference of the deceased, but his spiritual journey to the Hereafter is implicit. While in CT III 297i *ḥ3i* is more suggestive of the deceased's assimilation with Osiris and his physical transformation into a spiritual being. The emphasis in the latter case is not on a physical journey but a spiritual one, however, the destination in each case is the same – the Hereafter. Because of the apparent emphasis on the physical transportation of the deceased in some of the sources any definition of *ḥ3i* necessarily needs to include this sense. While the word "rejuvenation" applies only to the spiritual journey and denotes nothing of a physical voyage – which in most cases is intimately linked with the avian motif.

Likewise, the term *ḥ3(i)t*-bird in employed in this work instead of the word Kite, simply because there is not enough evidence to prove that this was indeed the bird being referred to in the sources, and there is some scholarly disagreement over the bird's identification.

Old Kingdom

The earliest example of *ḥ3i* appears in a caption in the Fourth Dynasty tomb of Debehni at Giza (Figure 4).[1] In the bottom right-hand corner of Figure 4, the caption that reads: ***ḥ3(i)t*** *i(w)f.f tmi*,[2] "**The ritual transport**: His flesh is complete,"[3] runs horizontally from right to left above the dancers. Below the caption are four women dancers with their arms in the air and their right leg lifted, wearing long transparent dresses with straps over the shoulders. They appear to be dancing in front of an offering table filled with food. Behind these dancers stands the Embalming Priest who carries a long staff in his left hand and holds his right hand on his left shoulder. There is a vertical inscription in front of him that reads: *3w(i)t n(yt) sš ḏ3ḏ3t*, "Offering gifts of the scribe of the *ḏ3ḏ3t*." Across from the first group of women are three more women who are clapping, and who wear similar dresses. All women have their hair cut short. The caption over this second group of women reads: *ḥs(i)t n(yt)* ***ḥ3(i)t*** *in [šnḏt(y)t]*,[4] "The singing of the **ritual transport** by the women of the Acacia House,"[5] and runs at first vertically and then horizontally from left to right. Both groups of women face inward toward the offering table which is labeled *w3ḥ(wt) ḥr ḏ3ḏ3t*, "Setting down (offerings) upon the *ḏ3ḏ3t*."[6] Behind the clapping women stand two men, each carrying a stave in his right hand, and each placing his left hand on his right shoulder. The caption above them has been reconstructed by Edel to read *ḫnmsw n šnḏt*, "Friends of the Acacia House."[7] S. Hassan[8] suggests that this action is taking place in front of the embalming house, while

---

[1] Lepsius 1897, 111-112; 1972, 35; S. Hassan 1943, 176-178, pl. 50; J. Wilson 1944, pl. 18.

[2] The *tmi* is stative (Edel 1955, §573 aa).

[3] J. Wilson guesses that this is the beginning of Pyramid Text §1298, the mourning song, "Your entire flesh is that of Atum" (J. Wilson 1944, 212).

[4] This last word is a *nisbe*-adjective used substantively. The word is not written in its entirety in S. Hassan's copy; however, there is enough there to be able to distinguish the word.

[5] This is my translation. There has been much discussion regarding this passage. J. Wilson (1944, 212) states with regard to this last group of signs, "I cannot transliterate or translate X, but I believe that the evidence points to a place rather than the title of a person, that the place is the women's quarters, and that this section of the community had a special part to play in the ritual at the door of the tomb, particularly in the singing and dancing. Although I toy with the idea of reading X as 'the sycamore-house' (*nht*) and connecting it with Hathor, goddess of music and dance, it probably should be rendered *im3t*, "the gracious place." Edel (1970, 9-10) restores this group of signs as *šnḏt*t, *"die šnḏtt-Mädchen."* However, Nord (1981, 140-141) points out that most scholars have restored the group as *ḫnrt*, meaning musical troupe. See also Grdseloff 1941 and Fischer 1960.

[6] This is my translation. J. Wilson (1944, 212) suggests the following transliteration: *ḏ3ḏ3t ḥr n im3t*. And Edel (1970, 11) transliterates and translates as follows: *w3ḥ (j)ḫt ḥr ḏ3ḏ3t*, *"Niederlegen der Speisen auf den ḏ3ḏ3t-Tisch."*

[7] Edel 1970, 16.

[8] S. Hassan 1943, 176.

Wilson[9] guesses the location to be the tomb (see Chapter Six above).[10] This is particular scene it is impossible to confirm the exact location for the ritual. In any case, the scene is representing the rituals at or near the tomb on the day of burial, whether this is closer to the *wꜥbt* or the tomb itself, as both are located in the cemetery.

The second example of *ḥꜣi* occurs twice in the scenes depicted in the covered corridor running between the south side of Niuserre's Sun Temple at Abu Ghurob and the obelisk.[11] This caption contains a derivative of *ḥꜣi* and refers to the *ḥꜣ(i)t*-bird itself on both occasions. The caption is used in nature scenes depicting animal behavior in conjunction with seasonal activities such as netting fish and trapping birds.[12] Here *ḥꜣ(i)t* is being used as a label to specify a particular bird (see Chapter Five above).

The third example of *ḥꜣi* appears in the Fifth Dynasty tomb of Hetepherakhti at Sakkara (D 60), now in Leiden (Figure 8).[13] In the first corridor on the north wall in the third register, the word *ḥꜣ(i)t* appears as a caption in a scene. Here there are four women facing left leading a procession, clearly referring to the transportation of the deceased en route to rebirth; the first three have their arms in the air in the same manner as the women from the tomb of Debehni, and the fourth woman is clapping her hands. These women also have short hair. It appears that the first three women are topless and wear a short skirt with a sash. The fourth woman is wearing a dress identical to the one worn by the women in the tomb of Debehni — ankle length and transparent with shoulder straps. *ḥꜣ(i)t*, "**transporting**" is the only word written above the women. Mohr translates this as "Mourning-dance."[14] Brunner-Traut[15] also mentions this scene in her study on dance in ancient Egypt; she states that the women are performing the *ibꜣ* dance and translates the caption as *"Klagelieder."*[16] Behind the women, a shrine with a statue is being dragged towards the tomb by two oxen. The inscription above them reads: *šms(i) in*[17] *ng(ꜣw)*: "Following by the red oxen."[18] In front of the shrine are two priests, one with the caption *ẖr(y)-ḥb(t)*, "lector priest." Above the women and the oxen is a row of food offerings. This scene is the earliest example of a funerary event that is to become commonly depicted in the future. Later, however, men regularly replace the women.

The fourth, fifth and sixth examples all appear to date to around the time of Pepy II, although there is some debate as to when the official Qar held office. These three sources are described in no particular order.

The first reference appears in the tomb of Qar at Giza (G 7101).[19] The chapel of Qar can be dated *at the earliest* to the reign of Pepy I based on certain titles that appear in the structure.[20] In this example *ḥꜣ(i)t* appears in the caption: ***ḥꜣ(i)t*** *in šnḏty*, "**transporting** by the two acacias."[21] Below the caption there are three women facing left, each with her right arm raised in the air and her left arm hanging at her side. Following them is a fourth woman clapping. The caption *ibꜣ*, "dancing," is written before each of the first three women, and the caption *mꜣḥ*, "beating time," is written before the fourth woman. The first three women are topless and have their shoulder straps hanging down from their waist. The fourth woman is wearing a dress with one strap. They appear on the upper register of a two-level scene. In the bottom register there are three more figures.[22] The first woman faces in the same direction as the women in the register above her, and has both of her arms outstretched in front of her. She is accompanied by the caption *bbit;* Simpson suggests the meaning "leader."[23] She is followed by two men bowing, each with his left hand on his right shoulder. Each carries a whip in his right hand. Above these two men is found: *ẖnmsw šnḏt*, "friends of the acacia house."[24] To the left of these two groups of figures there is a schematic plan of the embalming house that encompasses both registers. At the top of the plan is a pile of offerings and in the bottom right corner is an angled entrance. In the outer room of the house there is a man holding out a jar; above him is the caption *iw ẖr(y)-ḥb(t) ḥr pr*, "the lector priest attends to the house."[25] In the vestibule an identical figure appears. In the inner room appears the caption *ḥr(y)t-ib n(y)t wꜥbt ꜥḥꜥw*, "central hall of (the) *wꜥbt*[26] of attending."[27]

[9] J. Wilson 1944, 212.

[10] This example of *ḥꜣi* is classified as *"von tanzenden und singenden Frauen beim Leichenbegängnis"* in the Berlin Dictionary (*Wb* III 6, 10).

[11] Edel 1961, *Abb.* 11; *PM* III,i, 319-324.

[12] Gay Robins (1997, 62-63) suggests that these scenes did not come from traditional royal funerary decoration but possibly relate to scenes in the temple of Re at Heliopolis. From the surviving fragments it appears that the reliefs illustrate two seasons: *ꜣḫt*, "inundation" and *šmw*, "summer" or "low water."

[13] Rijksmuseum van Oudheden I 1905, pl. IX; Mariette 1889, 343; Mohr 1943, 38-39; J. Wilson 1944, 211, pl. 17.

[14] Mohr 1943, 39.

[15] Brunner-Traut 1992.

[16] Brunner-Traut 1992, 20.

[17] Edel 1964, §756.

[18] Mohr (1943, 38) translates this passage, "The red oxen forming a procession."

[19] Grdseloff 1941, 36-37; Simpson 1976, 5-6, fig. 24; Badawy 1978, 41, fig. 57; Strudwick 2005, 413-414.

[20] Simpson 1976, 1-2; Baer, in *Rank and Title* (288, 294) dates Qar to years 15-35 of Pepy II. There is some discussion as to who is the father of the other: Idu (G 7102) or Qar.

[21] This scene appears in court C on the lower half of the north wall. See Simpson (1976, 6) for this translation. Edel (1970, 12) translates as follows: *Das Klagen vonseiten der SnDt-Mädchen.*

[22] Gardiner (1955, 10-11, n. 7) considers them to be male.

[23] Simpson 1976, 6.

[24] Simpson 1976, 6. See also Edel 1970, 16.

[25] For translation see Simpson (1976, 6).

[26] Faulkner 1991, 57 gives both "place of embalmment" and "tomb" among his translations for *wꜥbt*.

The next Sixth Dynasty example comes from an inscription on the façade of Sabni and Mekhu's tomb (no. 26) at Qubbet el-Hawa on the west bank at Aswan (Figure 17).[28] Sabni was a noble living during the time of Pepy II. The passage below comes from a text found in his tomb describing how Sabni dealt with the death of his father in Nubia. The passage reads:

> When this Iry returned from the Residence, he brought a decree to confer (the offices of) *haty-a*, seal-bearer of the king of Lower Egypt, sole companion and lector priest (on) this Mekhu. He (also) brought...two embalmers, a senior lector priest, one who is on annual duty, the inspector of the *wabet*, **ritual transporters**, and the whole of the equipment from the *per-nefer*. He brought *setj-heb* oil from the *per-nefer*, the secrets of the two *wabets*, ...from the house of weapons, linens (from) the treasury, and all the needs of burial which come from the Residence...[29]

In this example, the relevant word is *ḥ3(i)tiw*.[30] This is the earliest example of this derivative of *ḥ3i*. Since it appears in the masculine plural form, we can assume that the people that were summoned were men, or at least that the group contained at least one male. These men are associated with the embalming place, the *pr-nfr*, as it is termed in this context,[31] and were considered a necessity for a burial. The *ḥ3(i)tiw* were important enough in the burial ceremony to be sent to Nubia, whereas ordinary mourners could have been found locally.

The last example dating to the reign of Pepy II comes from Pepiankh's[32] tomb chapel at Meir.[33] The tomb chapel has six rooms with only one undecorated. Room F, where the examples of the word *ḥ3i* are located, originally functioned as a *serdab* for the tomb owner's statues.[34] When the chamber was enlarged, its function was changed, and the east and west walls were decorated with ink drawings. These illustrations depict two funeral ceremonies.[35]

The first ceremony commences with the coffin being carried from the house of the deceased to the river. Here it is taken by boat to the west bank where the *ibw* is set up. The *ibw* is a purification tent where the deceased is purified before entering the cemetery. Next the cortege takes the coffin to the embalmers' workshop and the first ritual ends. The bearers take the coffin with them when they leave.

After some time has elapsed, namely, the time it takes to mummify the corpse, the second ceremony begins with the cortege crossing over to the west bank again. On the west bank they go to the embalming house with the coffin to pick up the mummified body. After this, the cortege proceeds back to the *ibw* to conduct the Opening of the Mouth ceremony. The second ritual ends with the procession through the cemetery to deposit the body in the tomb.[36]

The depiction of the first ceremony appears on the east wall, and the second on the west wall. In the first ceremony, after the body is delivered to the embalming workshop, there is a presentation of food and drink offerings. A frieze to the right of the embalming house displays a pile of offerings accompanied by a lector on the right who is summoning the deceased to the meal. Another lector behind him is making an oblation and carrying a papyrus scroll. The latter is followed by an embalmer and a "kite" (*ḏryt*). To the left of the pile of offerings there are three figures: a male ***ḥ3(i)w***, a "kite" and a scribe. There is a door behind the scribe through which the procession will leave carrying the empty coffin. The *ḥ3(i)w*[37] has both arms raised in the air in a gesture identical to that portrayed in sign A 28 of Gardiner's sign list. Blackman determines that this man is a mourner based on this inscription and the fact that his arms are upraised; he further cites Winifred Blackman's book, *The Fellahin of Upper Egypt*, and states that this gesture is still used in modern times as a sign of mourning. This can quite certainly be accounted for through the use of this gesture in mourning contexts beginning in the New Kingdom. This man has short hair and wears a short kilt with a sash around his waist, identical to those worn by the friends of the Acacia House in the tomb of Qar.

As mentioned above, the second ceremony consists of the procession back to the embalmers' workshop after the embalmment is complete. Blackman notes that the retrieval of the body from the embalming house and the activities held therein appear only at Meir.[38] Seven members of the funeral procession are depicted inside the workshop on either side of a pile of offerings. To the right there is a lector reading from a papyrus-roll. Another lector stands behind him holding an unopened book. He is accompanied by the inscription, "Making an oblation." Behind him stands the master embalmer, and the last of the four figures is a "kite." To the left of the

[27] Simpson 1976, 6. See Edel (1969, 5) where he explains this as the chamber of provisions.
[28] *Urk.* I, 137-139; Strudwick 2005, 335-339.
[29] This translation appears in Strudwick 2005, 337. See also J. Wilson 1944, 202; Breasted 2001, 164-169; Roccati 1982, 218.
[30] This is a masculine, plural form. See Edel 1955, §§247 and 274.
[31] Frandsen 1992, 49-62.
[32] Also known as Heny the Black (Blackman 1953, 24).
[33] Blackman 1953, 53, pls. 42 and 43.
[34] Blackman 1953, 45.
[35] Blackman 1953, 50.
[36] Blackman 1953, 50-51.
[37] Blackman calls him a male mourner (1953, 53).
[38] Blackman 1953, 54.

offerings, stand a *ḥ3(i)w*, a "kite," and an embalmer.[39] The *ḥ3(i)w* and his label appear as they do on the east wall; the only difference is that his elbows are slightly lower in this scene, thus illustrating that the specifics of the pose are not identical from example to example even within the same context. The reason for this anomaly appears to be the lack of space in the scene on the west wall.

In addition to the instances mentioned above, the word *ḥ3i* appears seven times in the Pyramid Texts, a collection of utterances first inscribed on the walls of the burial chamber of the pyramid of Unas at the end of the Fifth Dynasty. These examples will be listed numerically beginning with the lowest numbered utterance. The first example (Figure 30) occurs in Utterance 337 (PT §550) which Faulkner terms an 'ascension' text:[40]

> T: *rmii sw iki(i) sw* ***ḥ3(ii)*** *sw*
> P: *rmii sw ikii sw* ***ḥ3ii*** *sw*
>
> [The sky thunders, the earth quakes, because of the dread of you, O Osiris, when you ascend. O you milch-cows who are here, you nursing cows who are here, go round about him,] beweep him, lament him, **(ritually) transport** him [as he ascends and goes to the sky among his brethren the gods.]

This spell is short and can be presented here in its entirety. The cows are the subject of the verb *ḥ3i*. This utterance unmistakably describes the deceased king's journey to the Afterlife, in which the cows, who symbolize rebirth and fertility, encourage ascension to the sky. It is intriguing that in the later citation (P) the word *ḥ3ii* uses a determinative depicting the head and upraised arms of a person.[41] The word *ikii*, appearing before *ḥ3ii*, uses a similar sign; but instead of two upraised arms, the left arm is in the air and the right arm is across the chest (or where the chest would be).[42] This further illustrates the connection between the word *ḥ3i* and two upraised arms, adding to the evidence from the tombs of Debehni, Hetepherakhti, and Pepiankh.

The second example occurs in Utterance 419 (PT §744) where the king is addressed by his son on the occasion of his funeral (Figure 31). It reads:[43]

> T: ***ḥ3i*** *wršiw.k*
> M: ***ḥ3(i)*** *wršiw.k*
>
> [Arms are linked for you, feet dance for you, hands are waved for you. Isis has grasped your hand and she inducts you into the baldachin. The land is covered,[44]] your[45] watchers[46] **(ritually) transport**... Stand up, repel your earth, clear away your dust, raise yourself, and you will course amongst the *3khs*, with your wings of a falcon and your range of a star.[47]

Again, we have another unambiguous example where the deceased is traveling to the Hereafter and needs support from Isis. Furthermore, his form of a falcon reinforces the avian motif that is ever present in the sources referencing *ḥ3i*. It is curious that the first sentence talks about arms linking, feet dancing and hands waving; it gives the sense of a dance in progress. Faulkner notes similar passages in Utterances 553 (PT §1366) and 676 (PT §§2013-2014) which do not include the word *ḥ3i*, and respectively state:

> The sky weeps for you, the earth quakes at you, the Mourning-Woman[48] calls to you, the Great Mooring-Post[49] cries out to you; your feet stamp, your arms wave, and you ascend to the sky as a star, as the Morning star.[50]
>
> The Mourning-Woman[51] cries out to you, the Great Mooring-post calls to you, hands are clapped for you, feet are stamped for you, you ascend here as a star, as the Morning star.[52]

Also note Coffin Text I 272 (Spell 63):

> Here comes the Great Despoiler(?); guard yourself, guard yourself, go down to...,[53] wave

[39] Blackman 1953, plate 43.

[40] See Sethe (1908, 281) for hieroglyphs and Faulkner (1998, 109) for translation. For many of the citations of the Pyramid Texts and the Coffin Texts I have included extra text in the transliteration and/or translation to convey the context in which the relevant passage appears. The parts of the texts which do not occur in hieroglyphs in the accompanying figures will be enclosed in square brackets.

[41] It resembles the top portion of sign A 28.

[42] This sign resembles the top portion of A 32, which is a dancing man. Gardiner states that this is a common determinative for words like *ḥbi* dance and *hy-hnw* jubilate (Gardiner 1957, 445).

[43] See Sethe 1908, 407 for hieroglyphs and Faulkner 1998, 138 for translation.

[44] At this point in the translation Faulkner (1998, 138) suggests an allusion to funeral garb and points out that this word should be translated literally as 'adorned' or 'clad.'

[45] Faulkner (1998, 138) translates "the mourners" where I read the pronoun "your."

[46] Gardiner (1955, 12) translates *wršiw* "the watchers" which I have employed here.

[47] For the latter part of this translation see Allen 2005, 86.

[48] *smnt(y)t*.

[49] *mni(w)t wrt*.

[50] Faulkner 1998, 213.

[51] *smnt(y)t*.

[52] Faulkner 1998, 290. Note the reference to the Great Mooring Post in this spell and the last. This can be seen again in the Hymn to Osiris from the New Kingdom discussed below.

[53] Faulkner reads the hieroglyphic texts as *h3 r wrwty*.

the hands. Be put together, be put together, O you who should be put together(?). Your limbs are released, your bonds are loosed like Seth who is in *ḫnt*. Isis has summoned you, Nephthys has called to you,...[54]

The only difference between the two Pyramid Text examples (Utterances 553 and 676) is that in the first one it is the King who is dancing, while in the second example the performer is not named. In all three Pyramid Texts (PT §§744, 1366, 2013-2014) there is a sense of resurrection and a connection with Osiris.

The next example comes from an Osirian text, Utterance 532 (PT §1255),[55] where the goddess Isis is directly equated with a *ḥ3(i)t* (Figure 32). The following is a reconstruction of the two versions of the Utterance, namely P and N:[56]

[ii 3st ii nbt-ḥwt wᶜ(i)t.sn(i) m imn{t} wᶜ(i)t.sn(i) m i3b{t}] wᶜ(i)t.sn(i) m ***ḥ3(i)t*** *{ii nbt-ḥwt} wᶜ(i)t.sn(i) m ḏr(y)t*

[Isis comes and Nephthys comes, one of them from the west, one of them from the east,] one of them as a ***'ḥ3(i)t,'***[57](Nephthys comes), one of them as a *ḏr(y)t* [they have found Osiris, his brother Seth having laid him low in Nedit... They prevent you from rotting in accordance with this your name of Anubis; they prevent your putrefaction from dripping to the ground...]

If parallelism were applied to this text, it would appear that Isis comes from the west and is a *ḥ3(i)t*, while Nephthys comes from the east and is a *ḏr(y)t*. A *ḏr(y)t* is a "mourning bird" and is a well-known title from the Old Kingdom onward.[58] It can then be assumed that a *ḥ3(i)t* was also used as a title. It is curious that in a previous example, Utterance 419, Isis is also linked to the action of *ḥ3i*, but is not called a *ḥ3(i)t*. Utterance 532 explains that these two goddesses prevent the body of Osiris from putrefying. In this case *ḥ3(i)t* is written with a bird determinative; however, *ḥ3(i)t* without a bird determinative can be the feminine singular noun deriving from the verb *ḥ3i*. Both variations have an association with Isis and a funeral context.

The next utterance containing an example of *ḥ3i* is Utterance 535 (PT §1280), an Osirian text adapted for the king (Figure 33). It reads:[59]

P: *ii* ***ḥ3(i)t*** *ii ḏr(y)t 3st ḥnᶜ nbt-ḥwt*

[Thus said Isis and Nephthys:] The ***'ḥ3(i)t'*** comes, the kite comes.
Isis together with Nephthys;
[they have come seeking their brother Osiris, seeking their brother the King...
Weep for your brother, O Isis;
weep for your brother, O Nephthys;
weep for your brother!
Isis sits down with her hands on her head,
Nephthys has grasped the tips of her breasts because of their brother the King, who crouches on his belly, an Osiris in his danger (?)...
You shall have no putrefaction, O King...]

Again, if parallelism were maintained, it can be assumed that Isis is the *ḥ3(i)t* and Nephthys the *ḏr(y)t*.[60] It is important to note here that the two goddesses (in bird form) are searching for their brother Osiris (the King). There is no disparity between the actions associated with Isis and Nephthys above, namely, dancing (PT §744) and revivification (PT §1255) and those expressed in PT §1280. The searching they are doing in this spell is for the purpose of revivification and prevention of putrefaction, which is a joyful event. All of this is done for the end result of the arrival of the deceased in the Hereafter with his body intact. It is also essential that the goddess perform this act in bird-form, as it is through flight that the result will be achieved.

Another example occurs in Utterance 586A (PT §1585), "The king is a star" (Figures 34 and 35). *ḥ3i* appears only in Queen Neith's Pyramid (Nt 16). It reads:[61]

N *is pw* ***ḥ3i*** *ṯw*[62]

[O Great One of Atum, son of a great one of Atum, the King is a star in the sky among the gods. Tell your mother, O *šs3*, that it is the King

[54] De Buck 1935, 272 and Faulkner 2004, 1:59.
[55] See below for version preserved in CT Spell 73.
[56] See Sethe 1908, 210 for hieroglyphs and Faulkner 1998, 200 for translation.
[57] Faulkner translates *ḥ3(i)t* as 'screecher.' He also notes, "A falcon or similar raptor...."
[58] See Fischer 1976.

[59] See Sethe (1908, 219) for hieroglyphs and Faulkner (1998, 203) for translation.
[60] Later on in this utterance (PT §1284) a word *ḥ3(i)t(y)* is used, but it has an obscure sense, "O *ḥ3t(y)* son of *ḥ3t(y)*." Faulkner suggests the translation, "he of the tomb" (Faulkner 1998, 203).
[61] Faulkner 1998, 238 and Supplement, pages 11-12.
[62] In P the word *i3t* appears as a hieratic error: P *is pw i3t ṯw*. The confusion seems to lie in the fact that the wick of twisted flax, Gardiner's V 25 and Möller's 525, was accidentally read as the reed leaf, M 17/282, when transferring the hieratic text into hieroglyphs. Likewise, the abbreviated A 28/4 was misconstrued for N 30/326 *bis*, the mound of earth with shrubs. Therefore the sentence should read: P *is pw ḥ3(i)t ṯw* like that in the tomb of Neith. See Möller 1965 and Goedicke 1988.

who weeps for you,] it is the King who **transports** you [... give a hand to the King when he comes].

In this context it appears that the king has already reached the Afterlife and is now shining as a star in the sky among the gods. The latter part of the utterance is elusive and the reason the king is weeping for *šs3* is unknown to the author.

The next spell we are concerned with is the very short Utterance 633 (PT §1791) (Figure 36). It reads:[63]

N: *ḏ(d) mdw ṯmt* ***ḥ3(i)t*** *ḥr.f*

To be said: It is you who have **ritually transported** because of him.[64]

Unfortunately, this is the only line in the utterance, so it is impossible to infer more about the meaning of *ḥ3(i)t* from its context. And there is no doubt that the presence of the preposition *ḥr* after *ḥ3i* makes the translation difficult. In his translation, Faulkner notes that the feminine pronoun probably refers to Isis and that the use of this obsolete pronoun points to the great age of the utterance.

Another utterance that contains two examples of *ḥ3i* is number 690 (PT §§2112 and 2117-18). This utterance is actually a miscellany of short utterances (Figures 37 and 38). The first section (Figure 37) in question reads:[65]

N: *ḥ3(i).n(.i) ṯw ḥr* ***ḥ3t***

[O Osiris, the inundation comes, the flood hastens, Geb engenders.] I have **(ritually) transported** you to the tomb, [I have smitten him who harmed you with scourges (?). May you come to life, may you raise yourself because of your strength. O King, the inundation comes, the flood hastens, Geb engenders(?); provide the efflux of the god which is in you, that your heart may live, that your body may be revived(?),...]

This spell is another example that deals with the revivification of the deceased as Osiris.[66] Another item to note is the determinative used with this example; there is a human head with the arms apart and down in front, possibly indicating an act to be done with the arms.[67]

The second example of *ḥ3i* (Figure 38) that appears in this spell reads:[68]

N: *iw* ***ḥ3(i)****.n(.i) ṯw*

[O King, (I have) wept (for you),] I have **transported** you, [and I will not forget you...]

Old Kingdom Summary

To conclude, there are both private and royal sources that include the word *ḥ3i*, with the earliest example appearing in a private context in the Fourth Dynasty tomb of Debehni. The earliest royal attestation appears in the Pyramid Texts; however some of the grammatical elements in the relevant passages suggest an older date for the ritual. There is a clear association between the word *ḥ3i*, the revivification of the deceased, and his arrival in the Next World. It is at this time that the contexts presented in the sources are the most homogeneous.

Middle Kingdom

Turning to the Middle Kingdom, there are only two sources for *ḥ3i* that date to this period: the Coffin Texts and a unique Funerary Liturgy from a Thirteenth Dynasty tomb.[69] As has been noted in previous chapters, the contextual settings of the term *ḥ3i* in the Coffin Texts are numerous, and the varied spellings suggests that the term may have been very antiquated by this time.

Coffin Texts

To begin, the examples from the Coffin Texts are described, beginning with the lowest numbered spell (see Table 10 below for a complete list of citations).

There are two occurrences of the word *ḥ3i* in Spell 24 (CT I 73d, 74e).[70] In reconstructing the original text that the others are derived from, two versions were discovered for the first clause and three versions for the second clause. They read as follows:[71]

First Clause:

1 – *iw* ***ḥ3(i)****.{n} n.k/ṯ bik*
2 – *iw* ***ḥ3(iw)*** *n.k/ṯ in bik*

[63] See Sethe (1908, 436) for hieroglyphs and Faulkner (1998, 262) for translation.
[64] A special thank you to Leo Depuydt who helped make some sense of this passage.
[65] See Sethe (1908, 514) for hieroglyphs and Faulkner (1998, 299) for translation.
[66] Faulkner 1998, 299 (see PT § 2114).
[67] See Hannig 1995, 1133. It also must be noted that Hannig (754) quotes this word as an example of the word "to search for" (#19274).
[68] See Sethe (1908, 515) for hieroglyphs and Faulkner (1998, 299) for translation.
[69] Gardiner 1955.
[70] Coffin Texts Spells 20-25 correlate to Chapter 169 of the Book of the Dead.
[71] See de Buck (1935, 73-74) for hieroglyphs and Faulkner (2004, 1:15-16) for translation.

Second Clause:

1 – *iw ng{g}{.n} n.k smn*
2 – *iw ng(gw) <n> n.k/ṯ in smn*
3 – *iw ng(g).n(.i) n.ṯ m smn*

The following three versions continue the spell into CT I 74c-f.

iw ḏ3(iw) n.k ꜥ in ḏḥwty iw sḫ(w) n.k ḫpš n(y) ḫft(y).k/ṯ

B1P: *iw* ***ḥ3i*** *n.k in*
B6C/B4C: *iw* ***ḥ3(i)***{.*n*}[72] *n.k/ṯ*

ḏr(y)ty 3st pw ḥnꜥ nb(t)-ḥwt

[Ho N!] The Falcon has ***ḥ3i*-ed** for you, the Goose has cackled for you. A hand is extended to you by Thoth, the arm of your foe is chopped off for you, the Two Kites, who are Isis and Nephthys, ***ḥ3i*** for you,...

This is one of those intriguing examples where the word *ḥ3i* is used in its authentic capacity with reference to bird activity and in its ritual capacity as an action performed by the goddesses Isis and Nephthys. In his translation Faulkner has chosen to translate *ḥ3i* as "scream" and *ngg* as "cackle."[73] Most likely he is making a comparison between the sound the falcon makes and the sound of mourners. There is no doubt that Isis and Nephthys appear in their bird-form in this context for the purpose of the salvation and rejuvenation of the deceased; however, they are labeled as *ḏr(y)ty*, not *ḥ3(y)ty* which confuses the matter further. This context implies that the birds will perform the transportation of the deceased to the Hereafter. Perhaps the cackle of the goose is meant to be a call, or summons of sorts to the deceased.

Faulkner notes the many variations in the spelling of the word *ḥ3i* in this passage.[74] This may suggest that by this time the word was out of fashion and not familiar to the scribes, or that there was some confusion as to its ritual meaning.

The next example appears in Spell 73 (CT I 303g). This is a copy of Pyramid Text Utterance 532 listed above, "Isis comes and Nephthys comes, one of them from the west and one of them from the east, one of them as a kite and one of them as a ***ḥ3yt*-bird**."[75] No other comment is necessary, as it is described above, except that the birds are reversed[76] (see Chapter Two).

In Spell 143 (CT II 177h) there is another reference to *ḥ3(i)*. This word is the same as the example that appears in the inscription of Sabni, written *ḥ3(i)tiw*, except the spelling is different (compare with Figure 17). The passage reads:[77]

in ***ḥ3(i)tiw*** *ꜥḫm.s[n] s(y)*

[you shall go up <in> fire, to those who are in the Abyss, and] it is the ***ḥ3(i)tiw*** who will quench it.

This label describes a group of beings (involving at least one male) who play a role in a mythological setting. The significance of this passage may lie in the fact that the *ḥ3itiw* can rejuvenate the deceased, and bring him back to life by transporting him out of the fiery Abyss; the fire having the potential to permanently destroy the deceased's body. This assumes that *s(y)* refers to the fire. According to Leahy, based on an inscription from a stela at Abydos, death by burning was well known to the Egyptians.[78] Punishment by fire was reserved for the worst offences and this meant that the criminal was not allowed to enter the Afterlife because of the complete destruction of his body.[79] There is only one version of this spell.

The next example comes from Spell 149 (CT II 238b) and is particularly intriguing because it exhibits the form *ḥ3(i)w* like that occurring in Pepiankh's tomb at Meir. It reads:[80]

First Part:

1 - *ḏnḥwy.i {(i)r.f} m*

Second Part:

1 - ***ḥ3(i)w***
2 - *i33{w}*

[I have appeared as a great falcon, I have grasped him with my talons, my lips are on him as a gleaming knife, my talons are on him like the arrows of Sakhmet, my horns are on him as the Great Wild Bull,] my wings are on him as a ***ḥ3w*-bird**, [my tail is on him as a living soul...]

---

[72] In de Buck's copy of Coffin Texts I 74, version B4C, note 2 states that a sign at the end of *ḥ3i lqqks like Gꜥrdiner's ḏ 2 sign. Mqst likely this is the hierꜥtiś fqrm qf ḥꜥnnig*'s D 81 (1995, 1133).
[73] In Faulkner (1991, 142) *ngg is trꜥnslꜥted ꜥs* "cackle, of goose" and "screech, of falcon."
[74] Faulkner 2004, 15, n. 1.
[75] Faulkner 2004, 68, n. 4.
[76] In the Coffin Texts the birds are written in a fuller form.
[77] See de Buck (1938, 177) for hieroglyphs and Faulkner (2004, 1:122) for translation.
[78] Leahy 1984, 200-201 and 1989; Zandee 1960, 14-16; Willems 1990.
[79] Leahy 1984, 201.
[80] See de Buck (1938, 238) for hieroglyphs and Faulkner (2004, 1:127-128) for translation.

In at least four of the versions the word *i33{w}* replaces the word *ḥ3(i)w*. Once again,[81] it is likely that during the conversion from hieratic to hieroglyphs the wick of twisted flax was confused with the reed leaf.[82] There also seems to be a bird called *i33w*.[83]

There is another example of *ḥ3i* appearing in this same spell (CT II 239a). Faulkner does not provide a translation for this portion of the spell in his edition of the Coffin Texts:[84]

> *gb3wy.i (i)r.f m* ***ḥ3ywy***
>
> My pinions are on him as two **ḥ3(i)w(-birds).**[85]

There are also two other possible examples of *ḥ3i* in the Coffin Texts (CT II 239b and 254p). Faulkner does not translate either of them. The example present in CT II 239b is awkward and is only a possible reference. For the second citation (CT II 254p) he transliterates the word in note 11 as *ḥ3tyw*, and states that the meaning is unknown.[86]

The next example comes from Spell 167 (CT III 22a) and reads:[87]

> ***ḥ3(i)wt*** *ir(i) n.i sm3.ṯ*[88]
>
> **Transporter**, do your scalp for me (for "this Osiris" in the case of B4Bo).

In texts S2C, S1C, B4Bo the quail chick hieroglyph (G 43) was inserted after the clump of papyrus, thus rendering the word *ḥ3(i)wt* (the *Wb* identifies it as *ḥ3j.tj* [*Wb.* III, 7,7] and Meeks [1978] as *ḥ3jt*). Texts S1C, M22C, B4Bo, B3C and B2L use the god determinative. Likewise, M22C writes Gardiner's throw-stick (T 14) instead of the papyrus clump (M 16), which was probably because the papyrus clump in hieratic (Möller's 279) resembled the throw-stick. The last four entries appear to substitute the word *wḏt* for *ḥ3(i)wt*; however, in the hieratic Möller's 279 (the papyrus clump) also resembles his sign 474, or Gardiner's V 24, the cord wound on a stick. At this point the scribes of B17C and B1C added the D as a phonetic complement, for what they assumed was the sake of clarity. B3C writes S 35/36, the sunshade, which in hieratic is similar to the cord wound on a stick (V 24). Therefore, this spell exhibits a number of variants in the spelling of the word *ḥ3i* due to hieratic errors. Faulkner notes that the word must have puzzled the copyists.[89]

The fact that the divine determinative is repeatedly used is intriguing. This coincides with the divine nature, or other worldliness connected with the appellation *ḥ3it*, which is used by Isis and Nephthys in the Pyramid Texts, among other sources.

The subsequent example of *ḥ3i* occurs in Spell 229 (CT III 297i). There are two versions of this spell and they both read as follows:[90]

> ***ḥ3(i)t*** *ḥr.f/n ḥr.f m-ẖnw wꜥbt*
>
> [Hail to you, Lady of Goodness who raised up the head of Osiris and] who **ritually transported** him in the Pure Place [in this your name of 'Headrest(?) which is under the head.']

This spell is clear about who carries out the action of *ḥ3i* and where the action is performed. The Pure Place refers to the mortuary workshop where the embalming takes place. This spell maintains the notion of rejuvenation that is so prominent in the Pyramid Texts.

Spell 237 contains five examples of the word *ḥ3i*. Both examples from CT III 307a-b are presented in the following transliteration:[91]

> *inḏ-ḥr.ṯ* ***ḥ3(i)t***[92] *Wsir ḥ3(i)t wr ib3g(i)w*[93]
>
> Hail to you, **Transporter** of Osiris who **transports** the limp Great One...

Version T2L exhibits the D 36 determinative that indicates an action. Version T1Be includes the sign *tp* in the spelling of *ḥ3i*, indicating some confusion with the word *ḥ3*, "back, behind, around."[94] The text between the aforementioned passage and the next two examples in Spell 237 reads:

> who makes a spirit of the Bull of the West; <at> seeing whom the Westerners rejoice; Lady of All in the secret place; to whom Osiris turns his back in these his moments of inertness; who is in front of the Lord of Abydos; whose place on the paths of the Netherworld is hidden...

[81] Compare with Utterance 586A (PT §1585), where *ḥ3i* becomes *i3t*.
[82] See de Buck (1938, 238, n. 2).
[83] Van der Molen 2000, 12, 307.
[84] See de Buck (1938, 239) for hieroglyphs.
[85] For the translation, "pinion," see van der Molen 2000, 684-5.
[86] See de Buck (1938, 254) for hieroglyphs and Faulkner (2004, 1:130) for translation.
[87] See de Buck (1947, 22) for hieroglyphs and Faulkner (2004, 1:144) for translation.
[88] B4Bo renders: *ḥ3(i)wt ir(i) n N [tn sm3.ṯ]*.
[89] Faulkner 2004 1:144.
[90] See de Buck (1947, 297) for hieroglyphs and Faulkner (2004 1:183) for translation.
[91] See de Buck (1947, 306) for hieroglyphs and Faulkner (2004 1:185) for translation.
[92] Version G1T writes *ṯ* instead of *t*.
[93] Edel 1955, §630 ff.
[94] Faulkner 1991, 161.

The passage then continues in CT III 308d:[95]

> ***ḥ3(i)t*** *nb.s m sm3-t3 m rn.s pw{y} n(y) ḥ3(i)t nb.s*
>
> who **transports** her lord at the interment in this her name of 'She who transports her lord.'

A1C and T3l use the F 4 sign (*ḥ3t*, front) in rendering the first example of *ḥ3i*. Version T1Be employs the reed leaf (M 17) as the determinative instead of the seated god (A 40). Lastly, A1C tried to convert *pn* into *pw* but neglected to cancel the *pn*. There is one further mention of *ḥ3i* in this spell (CT III 311h), which is identical to the first example. It reads:

> *ind-ḥr.ṯ* ***ḥ3(i)t*** *Wsir*
>
> Hail to you, **Transporter** of Osiris...

In this spell the word *ḥ3i* is functioning specifically in relation to Osiris and his spiritualization at the time of burial. The word, in its various forms, is applied to both the action and the title of the person who performs the action. The passage is specifically concerned with Osiris being born again in the Hereafter and the fact that this is to be done at his interment.

The following Spell 238 has three examples of the word *ḥ3i* (CT III 317e and l). Faulkner renders only the first two examples that appear in CT III 317e as examples of *ḥ3i*. Faulkner guesses that the citation that occurs in CT III 317l may be a corruption for *ʿḥʿ* and thus renders the passage as follows:[96]

> *ind-ḥr.ṯ imyt tp nb.s* ***ḥ3(i)[t]*** *Wsir wrt* ***[ḥ]3(i)t*** *nbt pr-nw* [...] *b3w imntiw di.ṯ n.i w3t n(y)t tp(y)w-t3 r bw 3ḫ mr.n* [...] *iw m ḥtp k3(i).tw (i)r.i ḥtp.n.i dit wr 3ḫ.i ir(i)t.snpw*[97] *ḥ3(y)t* [...] *m ʿnḫ nb rḫ* [...] [*di.ṯ n*].*i 3ḫ mi Inpw* ***ḥ3(i).n*** *snty ḥ3.f*
>
> Hail to you, you who are in attendance on your lord, **Transporter** of Osiris, the Great One, the **Transporter**, Mistress of *Pr-nw*(?) [...] the souls of the Westerners; grant me the path of those who are on earth at the place of power(?) which [I(?)] have desired: 'Come in peace' shall be said to me. I am content, for the causing that my power be great is what *šnpw* does. O [my] champion in life, lord of knowledge (?), [... give] me power like Anubis, behind whom the Two sisters **transported** (?)...

I see no reason to assume that *ḥ3(i)t* is a corruption of *ʿḥʿ*, since the text makes sense as it is.[98] In this spell and the last, the deceased is speaking to the same entity. In both cases the addressee is referred to in the same way; among the common epithets are, "you who split open my mouth for me and who gathered together for me what issued from my flesh."[99] It is plainly stated that the addressee is a single female who revivifies the deceased Osiris by raising him up, gathering his body parts and pulling his flesh together. The addressee is described as the helper of Anubis and the mother of the deceased. Faulkner states that the deceased is equating himself with Horus, son of Isis.[100] This would imply that the addressee is the goddess Isis.

CT III 317 provides yet another context where a ritual transport is explicit. In this case, "grant me the path of those who are on earth at the place of power(?)... 'Come in peace' shall be said to me...".

Another example of *ḥ3i* occurs in Spell 337 (CT IV 331g). There are three versions of this part of the Osirian spell, which can be reconstructed as follows:[101]

> *ḏ3ḏ3t ʿ3(i)t im(y)t idbwy* ***ḥ3(i)t*** *grḥ pf/pw n(y) mḥ(i)t nṯr ʿ3(i) m ʿnḏt*
>
> The great tribunal which is in the Two Banks of the ***ḥ3(i)t*(?)** on that night of the drowning of the great god in 'Andjet.

A similar passage occurs in Spell 338 (CT IV 336d),[102] "The tribunal which is in the Islands of the ***ḥ3(i)ty***(?) on that night of Isis making mourning for her brother Osiris." The Egyptian word used for "mourning" in this context is *i3kb*. The writing of "***ḥ3(i)ty***" is different in each copy of this passage. Faulkner assumes that the "two Kites" is the proper rendering,[103] in which case it would provide a parallel for CT IV 331g. Therefore, we have two examples that cite a location for the tribunal that has the word *ḥ3)i)t* in the name. The reference seems to be avian in nature.

Next we have another spell containing two examples of the word *ḥ3i*. Spell 345 (CT IV 373a) reads as follows:[104]

[95] See de Buck (1947, 308) for hieroglyphs and Faulkner (2004 1:186) for translation.

[96] See de Buck (1947, 317) for hieroglyphs and Faulkner (2004 1:187) for translation.

[97] This should read *Inpw* for the god Anubis.

[98] For Faulkner's second *ʿ* of *ʿḥʿ*, see the determinative D 36 in the word *ḥ3i* in CT III 307b above. Note also the three examples (S5C, B15C and B9C) in CT IV 373a where the striking arm is used as a determinative. These variants may indicate some sort of action, one specifically related to the arms.

[99] CT III 309e and 312g in Spell 237 and CT III 316a-b.

[100] Faulkner 2004, 188, n. 17.

[101] See de Buck (1951, 331) for hieroglyphs and Faulkner (2004, 1:272) for translation.

[102] See de Buck (1951, 336) for hieroglyphs and Faulkner (2004, 1:273-274, n. 3) for translation.

[103] Faulkner 2004, 1:274, n. 3.

[104] See de Buck (1951, 373) for hieroglyphs and Faulkner (2004, 1:280) for translation.

ḫ3(i) *ṯw/ṯn* **ḫ3(i)w** *Wsir*

Those who **ritually transported** Osiris will **ritually transport** you [on that day of the sixth-day festival in which the gods swooned].

There appears to be only one original version of this text from which all the others are derived. In fact, in these texts the spelling of the word *ḫ3i* is more uniform. However, there are expectable variations, and small anomalies exist in some versions. For example, S5C contains an odd spelling of *ḫ3i*, rendered *ḫiw*.[105] Likewise, B15C includes an archaic version of the dependent pronoun: *[ḫ]3y kw ḫ3(iw) Wsir*. Finally, B9C uses the first person dependent pronoun *wi* with a seated god. In this spell *ḫ3i* occurs parallel to *rmi*, which appears in the preceding section: "Those who wept for Osiris will weep for you on that day of the fourth-day festival."[106] This is an Osirian spell that refers to the mysteries performed for the god. The divine nature of the ritual is apparent by the usage of the god determinative.

Spell 458 (CT V 332c) offers a remarkable context for the word *ḫ3i* not seen in the other examples. The purpose of the spell is to not die a second time in the realm of the dead. Here *ḫ3i* is an action done by fowl over the deceased. The action is portrayed as something negative and something the deceased king does not want done to him. The text concerns the fowl of the dwellers of the Netherworld and reads as follows:[107]

n **ḫ3(i)** *3pdw{.sn} ḥr-tp.i*

[I will not die a second time, and the dwellers in the netherworld have no power over me. I will not eat their fish,] their fowl shall not **ḫ3i** over me, [for I am Horus, son of Osiris.]

This word *ḫ3i* is written with a bird determinative in both copies of this spell, each using a different bird. Most likely the word here is being employed for its original meaning – *ḫ3i* refers to a specific avian activity. This passage should be contrasted with the aforementioned text where the term *ḫ3i* is of a ritual nature. Could this mean to carry off the deceased to an undesirable location? Or maybe the birds will pick and gnaw at his corpse and render his body obsolete for the Afterlife? This is one of the few examples where *ḫ3i* is used in a negative context.

The next example of *ḫ3i* comes from Spell 728 (CT VI 360j). The one copy of this text is badly preserved and difficult to understand. In fact, the word *ḫ3i* itself is not quite extant. It reads:[108]

ḫ[3(i)].*n.sn Wsir im.f m sfḫt.f n(y)t sndw*

They **transported(?)** Osiris in it in his robe[109] of the *sndw*-garment[110]...

The conditions of preservation do not allow this spell to be analyzed further. Suffice it to say, this is an Osirian spell.

The next relevant passage occurs in Spell 755 (CT VI 385o). The significant part reads:[111]

m pr(i)t.sn rm{i}.sn **ḫ3(i)**.*sn*

[There is put together for me the worm of Him who approaches his father(?). Weep! I do wish that the Great One who weeps were one {who weeps for} them, the two Sisterly Companions, West and East – and *vice versa* -] when they go out weeping and **ritually transporting** [– and vice versa – for the Great One and for their father and their son...]

Again, this spell contains Osirian allusions and is intended to prevent putrefaction, as the title and the last line of the spell respectively state, "A MAN IS NOT TO PUTREFY IN THE REALM OF THE DEAD," and "[May the putrefaction] of Osiris [be stopped(?)]." It is assumed that the "two Sisterly Companions, West and East," are Isis and Nephthys, and they are the ones who are weeping and then revivifying Osiris by magically transferring him away from putrefaction to the Hereafter. The spell first describes Osiris' dead body, and then proceeds to address someone who comes from the acacia-tree of the Double Lion and will prevent the corpse from rotting, "O you who come from the [acacia-tree] of the Double Lion [to Horus in the midst of] his corruption... ." The Double Lion is a form of the sun-god as two lions back-to-back, whose Egyptian name is Ruty.[112] The acacia tree is relevant in that it is linked to *ḫ3i* in the Old Kingdom tomb scenes and is a symbol of regeneration and resurrection (see Chapter Two above for a discussion on the significance of the acacia tree). The latter part of the spell describes who Isis and Nephthys are crying for (i.e. Osiris) as they go out searching for him.

---

[105] *ḫ3ii* may have been the word used here in a semi-phonetic spelling. "A" shifts to "*i*" at the end of a syllable: *ḫ(3)iw* or *ḫ(i)iw*.

[106] CT IV 372a-b.

[107] See de Buck (1954, 332) for hieroglyphs and Faulkner (2004, 2:88) for translation.

[108] See de Buck (1956, 360) for hieroglyphs and Faulkner (2004, 2:278) for translation.

[109] See van der Molen (2000, 487).

[110] See van der Molen (2000, 516).

[111] See de Buck (1956, 385) for hieroglyphs and Faulkner (2004, 2:289) for translation.

[112] Faulkner 1994, 173.

The penultimate example of *ḥ3i* in the Coffin Texts appears in CT VII 28o, in Spell 828, entitled "[...] OF THE BACK OF THE HEAD [...]." This spell is similar to Spells 237 and 238, mentioned above, and reads:[113]

> ***ḥ3(i)t*** *Wsir ḥ3pt* [*wr*] (*i*)*r 3gb*(*i*)*w*
>
> ...you **Transporter** of Osiris, who conceals [the Great One] from the flood of ill.

The Westerners appear in Spells 237, 238 and 828, and in the first and last spells they are rejoicing. This point is intriguing because as shown in Chapter Seven the action associated with *ḥ3i* looks very much like rejoicing. As noted above, the words *ḥ3i* and *ḥꜥi* ("to rejoice") both have the same A 28 determinative.

The last example of *ḥ3i* in the Coffin Texts appears in CT VII 51s, Spell 847. This is a rather enigmatic spell and reads as follows:[114]

> *sꜥḥ N pn m nb wr.ṯn pw* ***ḥ3(i)*** *iꜥnw*
>
> This N is ennobled as a lord, and it is your Great One who ***ḥ3i*'s** "Woe!"

Unfortunately, there is no determinative to designate the type of action to which this word is referring. It is unlike the other passages where *ḥ3*i occurs in that it is the only example that might introduce speech.

Funerary Liturgy

The other Middle Kingdom source where the word *ḥ3i* can be found is a fragmentary funerary liturgy that was discovered by Quibell in a Thirteenth Dynasty tomb beneath the Ramesseum.[115] It is on one of the Ramesseum papyri and was written retrograde in cursive hieroglyphs. The scroll was unrolled in 1927 and is now over two and a half meters in length. Paul Smither was the first to transcribe the text; and Gunn, and later Gardiner, continued the work. Originally the text was termed the Processional Papyrus; but then, due to a better understanding of the text, it was thought to be a funerary liturgy. There were four reasons for this conclusion. First of all, the phrase, *dbn ḥ3 iꜥ sp* 4, "circulating round the mastaba four times" appears regularly. Second, *ḥ3i* occurs in columns 7(?), 16, 44, 64, 84, which at the time was thought to mean "mourn" and thus constituted an appropriate action for a funeral – a point which is now moot. Third, the *imy-ḫnt* priest and lector priest are mentioned. And fourth, the person for whom the rites are performed is *Wsir mn pn*. It is not known for certain whether the text is royal or private (see below). There are 118 columns that fit into four categories: ritual action, address to the deceased, procession, and food or drink offerings.

The first clear example of *ḥ3i* occurs in column 16: *sp 2-nw* [*n*(*y*) *dbn ḥ3*] *iꜥ*; *nis ḫft dmḏt* ***ḥ3(i)***[*.sn?*] "Second time [of circulating around] the mastaba; a summoning in the presence of the *dmḏ*(*y*)*t*, [they] **ritually transporting**".[116] Here the *dm*(*y*)*ḏt* is doing the *ḥ3i*-ing[117] (see Chapter Three above). The ritual circulating is occurring and just prior to the action by the *dmḏ*(*y*)*t* a recitation is taking place.

Another significant point is the presence of the word *wršiw* in the Liturgy. Gardiner believes that the beginning of column 22 should read: *wršiw*, "the watchers." This is the same word that appears in PT §744 as the subject of *ḥ3i* (see above), thus providing further evidence to support a connection between the *wršiw* and *ḥ3i*.

The next example appears in columns 44-45, which describes a ritual act. It reads: *ꜥḥꜥ* ***ḥ3(i)*** *dbn ḥ3 ḏ3ḏ3t*, "Arises **transporting**; circulation around the *ḏ3ḏ3t*."[118] A *ḏ3ḏ3t* also appears in the Fourth Dynasty Tomb scene of Debehni in the same context as the ritual of *ḥ3i*.

Although columns 64-65 have been largely destroyed, it seems that column 64 began with *ḥ3i*; and column 65 makes mention of the *dmḏ*(*y*)*t* again, the women who ritually collect and unite the limbs of the deceased (in anticipation of rebirth).[119] At this point the procession was apparently halted to welcome some newcomers.

The last example appears in column 84: *rḫyt nbt* ***ḥ3(i)****.sn* "All the common folk **transporting**" or ***ḥ3(i)****.sn ḫr*(*y*)*w dḥr*[120] "**transporting** the bearer of skins."[121] Following, in column 87 we see again the *imy-ḫnt* priest and the lector priest along with the bearers of unguents and the bearers of linen-cloth. Gardiner suggests that this section concludes with the mention of the place of embalmment (*wꜥbt)*, although the house determinative is absent.[122] This reference is important for discerning the location of these rituals (see Chapter Six above).

---

[113] See de Buck (1961, 28) for hieroglyphs and Faulkner (2004, 3:17) for translation.

[114] See de Buck (1961, 51) for hieroglyphs and Faulkner (2004, 3:32) for translation.

[115] Gardiner 1955.

[116] Gardiner 1955, 12.

[117] There is an associated masculine word in CT Spell 345 (CT IV 371a): *dmḏw r Krs Wsir* "The crowd at the burial of Osiris" (Gardiner 1955, 12).

[118] Gardiner 1955, 13. This is the same word that appears twice in the tomb of Debehni, apparently used in association with a pile of offerings. To the best of my knowledge it does not appear in any dictionary.

[119] Diamond 2008a.

[120] Other words such as *msk3*, *inm* or *ḥnt* are also possible.

[121] The latter is an option only if column 85 is a continuation of column 84 (Gardiner 1955, 14).

[122] Gardiner 1955, 14-15.

Although the rituals are discussed in more detail above, it is useful to mention briefly some information about the age of the ceremony recorded here. Due to the presence of the word *iʿ* "mastaba" instead of the word *mr* "pyramid," Černý believes that the text dates back to the Third Dynasty.[123] He also notes that the King's children would not have attended anything but a royal funeral, which is what is described in this liturgy. Likewise, due to the numerous actors in the funerary ritual, the deceased must have been a person of high rank. The fact that the term *mn* "so-and-so" is employed has been used to demonstrate that this is a private source. However, J. Allen notes that *mn* appears in Pyramid Text §147a in the pyramid of Unas instead of the deceased's name.[124] Additionally, the literary style of the phrasing suggests a high antiquity. Because of these reasons Gardiner was hesitant to place this text as late as the First Intermediate Period.[125]

Gardiner was one of the few scholars to write in some depth about the word *ḥ3i*. He believed that *ḥ3i* means "to mourn" in the context of the funerary liturgy. He also states that it occurs parallel to *rmi* "weep" (which we have seen above), and he notes that there is a bird *ḥ3(i)t*, which the Pyramid Texts equate with Isis. He further associates the hieroglyph of the man raising his arms above his head (A 28) with the word *ḥʿi* "rejoice," and acknowledges that certain Old Kingdom reliefs (those mentioned above) connect *ḥ3i* with dancing. Gardiner specifically notes that the word *ḥ3i* does not refer solely to the movement of dancing, since the word *ib3* is present in front of each woman[126] in the tomb of Qar.[127] Moreover, he notes that the dancing people described by the caption *ḥ3(i)t* (infinitive) are found only in scenes of funerary rites. Gardiner suggests that the verb derives from the mournful cry of the bird[128] and renders the word as "wail" or "bewail" in his translation of the liturgy.

It is, however, important to bring into the discussion additional sources that reference *ḥ3i* to understand the broader context in which it was employed. It is now apparent that another meaning, namely to ritually transport for the purpose of rejuvenation in the Afterlife, is a preferable option that not only fits the context of the Funerary Liturgy but also conforms to the word's usage in other contexts.

Another possible example of *ḥ3i* occurs in Berlin Papyrus No. 3024.[129] Most likely, though, this is an occurrence of *nḥ3t* and not *ḥ3(i)t*.[130]

Middle Kingdom Summary

Overall, when *ḥ3i* was employed in the Middle Kingdom it was usually misspelled, possibly due to its infrequent use. Or, it may be that the ritual was rather antiquated by this time which may be evidenced by the archaic pronouns employed in some versions of the spells. Unfortunately, there are no examples that date to the Middle Kingdom that appear as a caption for a representation, so we have even less information about the ritual for this period than we do for the Old Kingdom. What is intriguing is that the word in its original sense seems to be reappearing as various spells use the word *ḥ3i* to characterize the action of a bird. Although the avian motif appears in the Old Kingdom (for example, to label a bird, Isis appearing as a bird), the word is not describing a bird doing bird pursuits. It should also be noted that the source supplying possible Thirteenth Dynasty examples appears to date back to an earlier time, possibly as early as the Third Dynasty. It therefore makes sense that the word *ḥ3i* would be spelled correctly and appear in a funerary context consistent with our Old Kingdom examples.

New Kingdom

The New Kingdom sources offer a variety of contexts featuring the ritual of *ḥ3i*. There are ten[131] references to

[123] Gardiner 1955, 17.
[124] J. Allen 1988, n. 4.
[125] Gardiner 1955, 17.
[126] Gardiner refers to them as men (1955, 11).
[127] Gardiner 1955, 11.
[128] See also Griffiths (1980, 50) and Frankfort (1958, 40-41).

[129] This source is referenced as containing an example of *ḥ3i* in *Wb* III 7 (*Beleg*. III, 2) meaning *Kummer, Leid.*

[130] This papyrus dates to the Twelfth Dynasty and contains the only version of a literary work about a discussion between a man and his *b3*-soul, modernly entitled "The Man Who Was Tired of Life" (Faulkner 1956). The beginning of the text is missing, but what is preserved appears in 155 vertical columns. The possible occurrence of the word *ḥ3(i)t* is to be found in column 57: *iw wp(i).n n.i b3.i r.f wšb.f ḏdt.n.i ir sẖ3.k ḳrs nḥ3t-ib pw*; "My *b3* opened its mouth to me that he might answer that which I had said: if you think of burial it is a sad matter" (Faulkner 1991, 136). Although the circumstances of this example refer to burial and funerary preparations, it appears that this is not an example of the word under discussion (*Beleg.*III 7, 10). From this point on, this example will be discarded.

[131] Two other examples display the form *ḥ3(y)t*, which has a related meaning of "sadness or grief." Bull 1932, 130; TT 76 <32> = *Wb* III 7, 11: *ohne Kummer, ohne Leid*. Both examples appear in funerary contexts. The first example of *ḥ3i* occurs on a green slate funerary model of a scribe's writing palette from the Eighteenth or Nineteenth Dynasty. There is an offering formula in the middle columns invoking Amun-Re. This piece was acquired by the Metropolitan Museum of Art through the gift of an anonymous donor (MMA 30.7.1). The text reads: *ḥtp di nswt imn-rʿ nswt nṯrw diw.f ʿḥʿw nfr šwi m* ***ḥ3(y)t-ib*** *ḳrst nfrt m-ḫt i3w(it) n k3 n(y) sš iḳr n wn-m3ʿ ḥs(i) n(y) nswt ḥr s3rt.f ḥm-nṯr nḥmʿy* "A boon which the king gives to Amun-Re, king of the gods, that he may grant a lifetime devoid of **sadness**, and a goodly burial after old age, to the *k3* of the truly excellent scribe, favored of the king by reason of his wisdom, the priest *Nehemay*." This is the author's translation. Here *ḥ3(y)t-ib* is used in an offering formula associated with the funerary cult. The second example included in this category appears in Theban Tomb 76, the tomb of Thenuna, dating to the time of Thutmose IV (PM I.i, 149-150; *Wb* III 7, 11). The inscription is presented as an unpublished example in the *Beleg*. It reads as follows: *di(w).f n.k ʿḥʿw*

this word and its variants. These include three examples of the verb *ḥ3i*, one each found in Theban Tomb 82, Book of the Dead Chapter 172, and the twelfth hour of the Book of Gates.[132] There are four examples that refer to the *ḥ3(i)t*-bird itself (now written *ḥ3yt*), found in Papyrus Sallier IV, Papyrus Chester Beatty III, Gardiner's *Onomastica*, and Thutmose I's Tombos Stela.[133] A further example in Louvre stela C 286 refers to Isis as a *ḥ3yt*-bird.[134] The penultimate example refers to a *ḥ3yt* in the Amduat.[135] The last example occurs in Chapter One of the Book of the Dead and refers to the *ḥ3yw*.[136] The next section will discuss these instances in this sequence, regardless of their chronological order.

The first example comes from the tomb of Amenemhet (TT 82). This official lived during the reign of Thutmose III of the Eighteenth Dynasty.[137] Here *ḥ3i* occurs in the top register on the south wall in the caption of a scene included among the funerary depictions (Figure 22). There is a skiff containing a white naos approaching the hieroglyph for necropolis (*ẖr(y)t-nṯr*). A lector kneels in the bow with a burning lamp behind him. Above the lamp is the inscription:[138]

> ***ḥ3(i)t*** *m ḫsf(w)*
>
> "**Transporting** while faring upstream"

There is a courtier standing at the stern holding a steering oar, and a figure (whose hands alone are seen in the Figure 22) kneeling on land placing the paddle in the water. The title of the scene is, "Going about upstream on the surface of(?) the water by the steward and scribe Amenemhet, the justified, opposite the tomb-shaft. Putting to land at the great city in the Thinite nome."[139] Related to this scene is another illustration of a man running toward a shrine with two steering oars in his hands. The inscription explains that they are being offered to Osiris. Nearby two women kneel and offer bowls of water before four tanks. Gardiner reads the names of these goddesses as *mnknw* and *ḏmd(y)t*, respectively (Figure 18).[140] The appearance of *ḥ3i* under these circumstances is not comparable to any previously mentioned example from the Old or Middle Kingdoms, except for its connection with Osiris, it being a ritual transport scene, and the presence of a *dmḏ(y)t*. It should also be noted that appearing in a related scene[141] are two men, with their arms upraised in the A 28 gesture, who follow the man driving the oxen and who precede those pulling the mummy (Figures 13 and 14). There is no caption relating specifically to the action of these two men but it can be assumed that the men are taking Amenemhet to his final burial spot on the day of interment. Between the groups of men who actually pull on the ropes appears the inscription: "All the patricians and all the common folk are dragging."[142] This scene, along with others like it, has been discussed in Chapters Two and Four.

The second source is Chapter 172 of the Book of the Dead, which appears in the papyrus of Nebseni, in a scene from TT C4, on the linen wrapping of Princess Ahmose of the Seventeenth Dynasty, and in a Ptolemaic Book of the Dead in Turin.[143] In the papyrus of Nebseni, there are at least nine examples of *ḥ3i*, appearing at the beginning, or end, of each of the nine stanzas that comprise the spell. Faulkner places the relevant line at the beginning of each stanza, while T. G. Allen and Hornung place it at the end of each stanza.[144] There is no vignette for this spell in this example; however, in tomb TT C4 the chapter is accompanied by an illustration.[145] There is no need to present all nine examples since the word functions the same in each instance. The following is the end of the first stanza and the beginning of the second, both written in retrograde fashion:[146]

> *[ḥwt sn-nw i mk rm(i).t(w).k mk s3ḫ(w).k mk sk3iw.k mk 3ḫ.k mk wsr.k] i mk* ***ḥ3(i).t****(w).k sp-sn*
>
> [Second stanza. See you are lamented, see you are glorified, see you are exalted, see you are a spirit, see you are mighty.][147] See, you are doubly **transported**.

---

nn ***ḥ3wt-ib*** *i3w(it) nfrt ḫr nswt* "...that he may grant for you a lifetime without **sadness** and good old age with the King." This passage is reminiscent of the previous example cited from the scribe's model palette in that it too comes from a funerary formula.

132 Davies and Gardiner 1915, pl. XI; Naville 1971, pl. CXCIII; Manniche 1988, 119; Lesko, 2007; Hornung 1980, 284.

133 P. Sallier IV, *verso* 4, 8; Gardiner 1947, 2:257; P. Ch. Beatty III, *recto* 8, 9; *Urk*. IV 84,10.

134 This stela contains a Hymn to Osiris (Moret 1931), which is considered by T. G. Allen to be BD 185A (1974, 203-204).

135 Hornung 1987, 289.

136 Faulkner 1994, pl. 5.

137 Davies and Gardiner 1915, pl. XI.

138 The translation that appears in the publication of the tomb by Davies and Gardiner (1915) is: Rejoicing in faring upstream.

139 Davies and Gardiner 1915, 52.

140 Davies and Gardiner 1915, 52. This same scene appears in the tombs of Paheri at Elkab and Rekhmire at Thebes (TT 100). In the tomb of Paheri, on the north end of the west wall, the funeral rites are depicted (Tylor and Griffith 1894, 22). Here two women kneel offering bowls of liquid before four libation tanks. They are identified as Isis and Nephthys by their titles: *ḏrt wrt* and *ḏrt nḏst*. In the tomb of Rekhmire, however, the women have different titles: *dmḏ(y)t* and *knwt* (Davies 1943, pl. LXXIX). These same titles repeat themselves elsewhere in the Rekhmire scenes (see discussion below).

141 Davies and Gardiner 1915, pl. 12, bottom right.

142 Davies and Gardiner 1915, 49.

143 T. G. Allen (1974, 178) notes that this spell is unique to Nebseni but the Florence fragment (Nr. 1594/Inv. 2473) discussed below is another occurrence of this text. See also L. Lesko (2007) for more information on the variants and for additional insight.

144 See Naville (1971, pl. CXCIII) for cursive hieroglyphs and Faulkner (1994, 129), T. G. Allen (1974, 178-181), and Hornung (1979, 351-358) for translation.

145 See Manniche 1988, plate 33.

146 Manniche 1988, 120.

147 Faulkner 1994, 129.

In their method of organization, T. G. Allen and Hornung add the line in question to the end of the previous stanza. This order follows the logical progression within the text, and is consistent with the placement of the *ḥwt* designation. Faulkner describes this chapter as the beginning of the praising that is made in the God's Domain.[148]

Another example of BD 172 occurs in an inscription from a fragment of painted tomb wall in the *Museo Archeologico di Firenze* (Nr. 1594 = Inv. 2473).[149] As Manniche points out, this version of the chapter differs slightly from that of Papyrus Nebseni in the opening passages; but beginning with the second column the texts are closely paralleled.[150] This fragment belongs to TT C4 whose owner was Merymaat, a *wꜥb*-priest of Maat.[151] This tomb owner's title is still extant in the hieroglyphs of the fragment.[152] The fragment measures 30 by 28 cm; it contains 11 columns of text and dates to the late Eighteenth Dynasty, during the time of Amenhotep III. Manniche states that this date is quite certain because of the style of the paintings. Likewise, the name of a wife called Amenhotep has the Amun element erased, which would indicate a pre-Amarna date.[153] The top and right sides are broken, and in the bottom left corner there are two women sitting with their knees pulled up in front of them facing left, with two young girls standing behind them, one holding a *khepesh* haunch over a cup.[154] This example of *ḥꜣi* is written quite distinctively with the determinative of a woman with her hair flung forward (Figure 39). The relevant part in column 10 reads as follows:

> *i mk* ***ḥꜣ(i)***.*t*(*w*).*k*
>
> See, you are **(ritually) transported**.

This fragment is also published in Werbrouck's *Les Pleureuses,* where one can read the following description:

> *Sur l'un d'eux (Inventaire no 1594), deux pleureuses sont assises les genoux relevés. Elles ne font aucun geste de douleur. Peut-être prenaient-elles de la cendre pour se la jeter sur la tête, mais on ne peut l'assurer car le fragment est cassé à cet endroit. Derrière elles se tiennent, debout, deux femmes dont la coiffure et le costume rappellent Isis et Nephthys. L'une croise les bras sur la poitrine (doigts replies); l'autre tient la coupe et le khepesh....Le texte parle de lamentations et emploie un des signes typiques de la pleureuse.*

It is intriguing that the accompanying illustration does not seem to depict any action of mourning. This is also the case with all of the depictions that accompany the term *ḥꜣi* in the Old Kingdom. As Werbrouck notes, it is curious that one girl displays a posture characteristic of the goddess Isis. A similar scene appears in the tomb of Ramose but without the accompanying text.[155]

The next example is from the twelfth hour of the Book of Gates, where the rebirth of the sun god occurs. Hornung believes that this book originated in the Amarna Period since it appears in the tomb of Horemheb for the first time, although this version is incomplete.[156] The earliest complete and continuous version decorates the alabaster sarcophagus of Seti I.[157] The Book of Gates — the original title is not attested[158] — is similar in context to the Amduat. It is also divided into the twelve hours of the night; however, gates are depicted at the end of each hour, each being guarded by a serpent and two anthropomorphic guardians. The relevant section occurs in the lower register of the twelfth hour where one can also see crowns as symbols of power for leaving the Netherworld and nurses for rearing the newborn sun (Figure 40).[159] Hornung records this inscription from the following four locations: the alabaster sarcophagus of Seti I, the Osireion at Abydos, the tomb of Queen Tawosret and Sethnakht, and the tomb of Ramesses VI.[160] It appears in retrograde above four goddesses and reads:

> ***ḥꜣ(i)***.*sn m šnw.sn m-bꜣḥ nṯr pn ꜥꜣ(i) m imnt(y)t*
> *ꜥnn.sn st r sbḫt* [*ṯn*] *n ꜥḳ.sn m ḥr(y)t*[161]

---

[148] Faulkner 1994, 129.
[149] *Wb* III 7, 1; Schiaparelli 1887, 318-19; Werbrouck 1938, 86; Manniche 1988, 100ff. I wish to thank both Gloria Rosati and Maria Cristina Guidotti who provided me with information from the *Museo Archeologico* in Florence.
[150] Manniche 1988, 119.
[151] In *PM* I, 156, the authors attribute this block to the tomb of Horemheb, Royal scribe, Scribe of recruits, TT 78. However, Annelies and Artur Brack (1980, 72-73) deny the association, noting: *"Es paßt nach dem Stil von Bild und Schrift nicht in das Grab 78, auch ist es inhaltlich nicht unterzubringen. Die Darstellung auf dem Fragment paßt stilistisch kaum in die 18. Dynastie, sie ist viel eher ramessidisch. Das Stück gehört damit auch nicht zu den beiden vorhergehenden. Die Zugehörigkeit zum Grab des Haremheb ist auch bei diesem Fragment mit Sicherheit auszuschließen."*
[152] Manniche 1988, 119.
[153] Manniche 1988, 102.
[154] Manniche 1988, plate 33.
[155] Davies 1941, 24-25.
[156] Hornung 1999, 54.
[157] Bonomi and Sharpe 1864.
[158] Hornung 1999, 57.
[159] See Bonomi and Sharpe 1864, pl. 9; Hornung 1979, 400-401; 1980, 284-285; 1999, 65, fig. 41.
[160] Hornung 1979, 400-401.
[161] This is my transliteration of the alabaster coffin of Seti I. After the word *m-bꜣḥ* the scribe wrote a bolt "s" (O 34) in place of the book role determinative (Y 1). This is a hieratic error; see Möller's O 366 and W 538. The passage appearing in the tomb of Ramesses VI shows another hieratic error in which the scribe writes the word *ḥꜣi* as *ḥwꜣḏꜣ*, replacing the clump of papyrus (M 16) with the stem of papyrus (M 13). See Möller's M 279 and M 280.

> They **ritually transport** with their hair before this great god in the West. They return to this gate. They do not enter heaven.[162]

Although the four goddesses depicted are not labeled, Hornung compares them to the gods that appear earlier in the lower register of his scene 93, where they are labeled as *"i3kbiw."*[163] He further explains that this illustration concerns mourning for Osiris, which contrasts with the jubilant theme present in the following scene, the birth of Re.[164] I believe this scene reflects the joyous nature of the deceased/sun god arriving in the west. After all, the passage states that the goddesses return to this gate — assuming that they actually traveled somewhere and then came back. This refers to the ritual transport that leads to rebirth.

The next category of references employs the term *ḥ3yt* to refer to a bird. There are four New Kingdom examples that are comparable to those references found in the Sun Temple of Niuserre; however, the spelling has changed from *ḥ3(i)t* to *ḥ3yt*. The first instance is in Papyrus Sallier IV, *verso* 4, 8 (BM 10184). This papyrus contains the Calendar of Lucky and Unlucky Days on its *recto*, and on its *verso* a miscellany of texts occupying the first meter and a half (the back of *recto* 1-5). The reference to the *ḥ3yt*-bird occurs in the text called "A Letter Concerning the Wonders of Memphis." The copy of the composition possibly dates to the reign of Ramesses II, since year 56 of that king is mentioned in another text on the *verso*.[165] The passage reads:[166]

> ***ḥ3ywt*** *n(ywt) t3-f3yt-ṯ3w n(ywt) mw ḥms n(y) sḫmw*
>
> [(vs. 4,7)...*mst*-geese of the inundated land, quails of the lake of Ptah, *ḥri*-birds of the lord (vs. 4,8)...image of Atum;] ***ḥ3yt*-birds** of the sailing waters and of the reservoir of the Sistra(?).

Caminos states that the bird is unidentifiable. There does not seem to be any sense of mourning or any indication of funerary or ritual activity.

The second New Kingdom reference to a *ḥ3yt*-bird is in Papyrus Chester Beatty III from Deir el-Medina.[167] It appears in the context of a Dream Book and dates to the late Nineteenth Dynasty. Here again there does not seem to be any connection to a funeral or ritual. Gardiner translates the relevant passage as follows:[168]

> *ḥr* ***ḥ3yt*** *m-ʿ.f*
>
> [If a man sees himself in a dream] having the head of a ***ḥ3yt*-bird**...

The third example appears in Gardiner's Supplement to his *Onomastica.* The *Onomastica* consists of three compositions that are concerned with lists of entities: the Ramesseum *Onomasticon*, the *Onomasticon* of Amen(em)ope (of which there are 9 versions), and the University College Writing-board. The word occurs on papyrus fragment C 4 in line 1.[169] The writing on the relevant fragment resembles that of version R (the Ramesseum papyrus fragments) of the *Onomasticon* of Amen(em)ope.[170] However, Gardiner also suggests that the fragment could belong to the Ramesseum *Onomasticon* because this composition has a section that deals with birds.[171] Gardiner compares the entry on this fragment to the same word in Papyrus Sallier IV (*Wb* III 16, 1) mentioned above. Without giving much commentary, he finishes the passage noting the further reference to the same bird in the aforementioned Dream Book.

The fourth example appears in Thutmose I's inscription from Tombos, an island just above the Third Cataract. The text was written in reference to the king's campaign southward in order to extend Egypt's boundaries. The relevant passage speaks of the king's victory over the Nubians. It reads:[172]

> *3sw.sn bʿḥi.f inwt.sn sšw rw.sn mi snmw ḥwyt mw* ***ḥ3yw*** *ḥr.s ʿš3w n3 3pdw ḥr ḫnp iṯit r ky bw*
>
> Their gore inundated their valleys, the mouths of which were worn smooth(?) as with a cloudburst of driving rain. The **carrions** were overhead, a host of birds, picking and carrying away.[173]

It appears here that the *ḥ3yt*-bird was a scavenger, feeding on corpses. This idea of a savage bird is very

---

[162] Zandee 1960, 112. Hornung (1980, 284) translates the whole passage, *"So sind sie beschaffen in dieser Pforte. Sie machen die Totenklage mit ihren Haaren vor diesem großen Gott im Westen. Sie wenden sich um bei dieser Pforte, sie treten nicht den Himmel ein."*
[163] Hornung 1980, 281.
[164] Hornung 1980, 284-285.
[165] Gardiner 1937, XVIII.
[166] For hieroglyphs see Gardiner (1937, 88-92; *LEM* 9,4 v. 8). For translation see Caminos (1954, 335, 349).
[167] Gardiner 1935, 17; Gardiner 1947, 2:257*-258*.
[168] In his 1935 publication of the Dream Book, Gardiner translates the passage, "folding wings around himself(?)." In note 11 he states that *ḥ3yt* is probably the same verb as *Wb* III, 13. This author corrects himself in his later publication of the *Onomastica* where he presents the translation used here (1947, 257*-258*).
[169] Gardiner 1947 2:257*-258*.
[170] Gardiner 1947, 2:256*.
[171] Gardiner 1947, 2:256*.
[172] For hieroglyphs see *Urk* IV 84, 10, and for translation see Grayson and Redford (1973, 25).
[173] Breasted originally translated the passages as follows, "their .... he inundated their valleys. The fragments cut from them are too much for the birds, carrying off the prey to another place" (Breasted 2001, 2:30).

much in line with the bird portrayed in some of the Coffin Texts encountered earlier.

The next example of the word *ḥꜣi* occurs in a hymn to Osiris that dates to the first half of the Eighteenth Dynasty, most likely during the reigns of Amenhotep I and Thutmose I.[174] The word in question appears on Louvre stela C 286 belonging to the official Amenmose and his wife Nefertari. It contains 28 lines and is the fullest surviving account of the Osiris myth extant in Egyptian sources. It reads:[175]

> *[ꜣst ꜣḫt nḏt sn.s*
> *ḥḥ(ỉ)t sw ỉwt(y)t b(ꜣ)gg.s]*
> *pḫrt tꜣ pn m* ***ḥꜣyt***
> *[n ḫn(ỉ).n.s n gm(ỉ)t<w>.s sw*
> *ỉr(ỉ)t šw(y)t m šw(w)t.s*
> *sḫprt ṯꜣw m ḏnḥwy.s(y)*
> *ỉr(ỉ)t hnw mnit*[176] *sn.s]*
>
> Isis, the sorceress, the protector of her brother,
> who searches for him ceaselessly,
> who traverses this land as a ***ḥꜣyt*-bird**,
> she does not stop until she has found him;
> she who makes shade with her feathers,
> who creates air with her wings,
> who does (the rites) of jubilation
> and moors/revives her brother.[177]

This passage is unique when compared to other hymns to Osiris. This version displays a nominal form of *ḥꜣi* that refers to a bird. Alexandre Moret interprets the meaning of *m ḥꜣyt* differently. He translates this line as follows: *"qui parcourt le pays dans (son) deuil."*[178] Moret reads the bird determinative as the "bad" bird, or G 37 (the sparrow), thus indicating that the meaning of *ḥꜣyt* had something to do with illness or the like thereof. However, after taking a closer look at the photograph of the stela presented as Plate 3 of Moret's article it appears that the swallow with the forked tail (G 36) is being depicted, as in PT §§1255, 1280, and in the Abu Ghurob relief.[179] Additionally, the bird determinative usually occurs only when the term is referring to an entity. This is a very valuable example because it shows the goddess Isis in the form of a *ḥꜣyt*-bird, performing the rites of jubilation to revivify Osiris and take him safely to the Next World. Her bird-form is especially important as it is the means of revivification. She needs her wings to ritually transport Osiris to the other realm. It is through Isis's bird-form that he will achieve rebirth.

The penultimate example is from the Theban area and may refer to the goddess Isis[180] (Figure 41).[181] The word appears in the top register of the third hour of the Amduat and is inscribed in seven tombs: Thutmose I (KV 38), Useramun (TT 61), Thutmose III (KV 34, including Thutmose IIIk = *Götterkatalog*), Amenhotep II (KV 35), Amenhotep III (KV 22), Seti I (KV 17) and Ramesses VI (KV 9).[182] Hornung subtitles the section: *Gottheiten des Registers*. The Amduat describes the journey of the sun god through the twelve hours of the night. This is the first religious treatise to consistently insert the king into the daily course of the sun.[183] The third hour takes place in the actual Netherworld and the Waters of Osiris.

According to Trigger,[184] beneath the ground was a realm inhabited by supernatural powers. This area was often associated with moisture and life, but also with death. However, this notion of death was the seed from which new life, or rebirth, would spring.[185] Contact between this world and the others would occur at the *axis mundi* (see Chapter Two above).[186] This concept of the Underworld, prevalent in many early civilizations, is applicable to ancient Egypt as well. It is not a coincidence to find the *ḥꜣyt* appearing in the Waters of Osiris since she was responsible for the ritual voyage of rebirth.

The word *ḥꜣyt* appears as a label accompanying a goddess. There are a total of four labeled goddesses. The captions read as follows:

> ***ḥꜣyt***;[187] *ỉꜣkbyt; mꜣtyt; rmyt*
>
> ***Die sich entblößt****; Die Trauernde; Die Preisend; Die Weinend*[188]

[174] See de Buck (1948, 110-113) for hieroglyphs, Moret (1931) for transcription and Lichtheim (1976, 81-86) for translation. See also Chabas (1857, 65-81, 193-212); Chabas (1899, 95-139); S. Hassan (1928); and Assmann (1975, 1999) for parallel hymns.
[175] This is my transliteration and translation.
[176] In Faulkner (1991, 107) under the entry *mni*, he gives the translation "revive (the dead)" as one of the possibilities and references *RB* 111,15. See Chapter Two and Conclusion for discussion on *mni(w)t wrt*.
[177] Author's translation. For more information on this stela and alternative translations see Moret 1931, 741; de Buck 1948, 111; Assmann 1975, 443-448; 1999, 477-482; Foster 1995, 48-53.
[178] Moret 1931, 741; Assmann 1975, 446; 1999, 479-480; Foster 1995, 51.
[179] There have been two different interpretations published regarding the meaning of *ḥꜣyt* in Louvre Stela C 286. I agree with the manner in which the editors of the *Wb* interpret the meaning of this example. They state the definition as follows: *ein Vogel, als Bez. der klagenden Isis*. They compare this usage to that occurring in PT §§1255 and 1280 and the Abu Ghurob relief (see above). I believe the use of the word xni, "to alight from flight" (Faulkner 1991, 192) in this context strengthens the argument that Isis is acting as a bird.
[180] The *Wörterbuch* may assume the label is referring to the goddess Isis due to her association with the *ḥꜣit* -bird in the Pyramid Texts. Other than that, I am not sure what this assumption is based on.
[181] *Wb* III 7, 6; Budge 1906, 53; Hornung 1984, 85; Hornung 1987, 289.
[182] This list includes only the New Kingdom tombs where the original Amduat text is found.
[183] Horning 1999, 33-34.
[184] Trigger 2003, 444-471.
[185] See also Hornung 1989, 103ff.
[186] Trigger 2003, 447.
[187] There are alternative spellings appearing in other tombs. The following text is collated from the various examples: *rmt rmyt mꜣtiṯ mꜣtyt ỉꜣkbyṯ ỉꜣkbyt ḥꜣyt□ṯ ḥꜣyt*.
[188] This is Hornung's translation (1984, 85).

Scholars have made several suggestions for the meaning of *ḥ3yt* in this case.[189] Budge calls these women professional mourners,[190] while Hornung says, "*Vier Göttinnen, die durch ihre Namen als Klagefrauen gekennzeichnet sind....*"[191]

The appellation should be translated as, "she who ritually transports." Hornung's association with nakedness is not unfounded. As is described above, being naked is intricately coupled with rebirth and fertility. The possible play-on-words associated with these two terms has already been noted above. The hair sign is used as a determinative in this example, which corresponds to the numerous references to hair found in previous examples.[192]

The last example comes from Chapter One of the Book of the Dead. This source refers to the deceased who was with "those who *ḥ3i*" Osiris on the Shores of the Washerman. It reads:[193]

> *msy.i m ḏdw wn.i ḥnᶜ* ***ḥ3yw*** *i3kbywt Wsir*
>
> I was born in Busiris when I was with the men who **ritually transported** and the women who mourned Osiris...

This is a masculine plural participle referring to the men who perform the ritual of *ḥ3i* for Osiris. This text shows that the transport to rebirth occurs as part of the funeral and may be performed at the same time as rituals such as mourning. These actions happen simultaneously but are mutually exclusive of one another.

New Kingdom Summary

The conclusions that can be made about the New Kingdom citations are as follows. The word *ḥ3i* continues to appear in this period but the types of sources are now quite varied. This contrasts with the compendium of Old Kingdom sources, where the contexts are more homogeneous. Moreover, because we are now seeing different contexts where *ḥ3i* is being employed, there are now more variants of the term being used. For example, this is the only period where the *ḥ3yt* bird appears in a truly secular context – Papyrus Sallier, the Dream Book, the *Onomasticon*, and the Tombos Inscription of Thutmose I.[194] The Old Kingdom example in the Sun Temple of Niuserre – the most comparable Old Kingdom reference – appears in a religious context, but displays the *ḥ3(i)t*-bird in a secular situation. Unlike the Old Kingdom and Middle Kingdom, the New Kingdom funerary literature does not employ the term as frequently. Additionally, we now have vignettes to accompany these rare examples. There is also a predominance of goddesses being associated with *ḥ3i*; in addition to Isis, which we have seen earlier, there are now goddesses who take the appellation *ḥ3yt* in their capacity as players in the myth of Osiris.

The term *ḥ3i* no longer appears in captions for the dragging scene in the funeral procession, but the notion of ritual transportation with the express purpose of rebirth is definitely still associated with the word. We can see this in the tomb of Amenemhet (TT 82), BD Chapters 1, 172, and 185A (Louvre Stela C 286), the Book of Gates, and the Amduat. Likewise, the A 28 gesture is still associated with the dragging scene.

There is no doubt that the word *ḥ3i* becomes closely connected with mourning contexts in the New Kingdom as does the A 28 pose. With the popularity of the cult of Osiris in the New Kingdom — and the manner in which it manifests itself — the term *ḥ3i* appears not only in different contexts than in earlier periods but also its usage has changed to reflect the significance of the cult of Osiris.

Late Period

There is one example of the word *ḥ3i* that dates to the Twenty-Fifth/Twenty-Sixth Dynasties, and may be defined as "sadness or grief."[195] The word appears in an inscription on a libation-basin with a Hathor head in relief (BM 1292).[196] The vessel is made of black granite and measures 31.5 cm high with a diameter of 68 cm. The inscription runs around the rim top and around the outside edge of the rim.[197] The owner of this libation basin is Mentuemhet, the second and fourth prophet of Amun. The inscription reads:[198]

> *[ḥtp di nswt...3w(it)-ib] nn* ***ḥ3(yt)-ib*** *n (i)r(y)-pᶜ(t) ḥ3ty-ᶜ sḏ3(w)t(y) bit(y) smr wᶜ(i)t(y) ḥm-nṯr sn-nw ḥm-nṯr ifd-nw (ny) imn ḥ3ty-ᶜ niwt mnṯ(w)mḥ3t*
>
> *[Offrande que donne le roi...la joie,] sans* ***souci****, au noble et prince, chancelier royal, ami unique,*

[189] Hornung (1984, 85) is basing his translation on the word HAi, "to be naked" *Wb* III 13, 13-18; 14, 1-8. See Edel 1969, 13-14. A. Piankoff, in his publication of the tomb of Ramesses VI, translates the same passage as follows: "She who cries," "*m3tyt*," "the mourner," and "the veiled one" (1954, 249).

[190] Budge 1906, 53.

[191] Hornung 1984, 85.

[192] PT §1210; images of cropped hair in Old Kingdom tomb scenes; Book of Gates; images in Queen Nefru's tomb illustrations and coffin; CT III 22a; TT C4; Yusas' tresses noted in PT; PT §1363; A 28 sign and its association with baldness; the use of wigs for eroticism; and hair determinative in Amduat reference.

[193] For hieroglyphs and translation, see Faulkner 1994, pl. 5.

[194] If one could truly say there was anything secular at all.

[195] *Wb* III 7, 11.

[196] *PM* I.ii, 841-2.

[197] Leclant 1957, pls. I-III.

[198] Leclant 1957, 113. Unfortunately, the photographs of the basin are not clear enough to be able to read the hieroglyphs.

> *le deuxième prophète, le quatrième prophète d'Amon, prince de la Ville, Montouemhat.*[199]

As is evident, this example of *ḥ3yt-ib* functions in the same manner as the New Kingdom examples from the scribe's palette and TT 76 presented above (see note 131).

Ptolemaic Period

Although beyond the scope of this study, it may be efficacious to enumerate some of the many Ptolemaic references to *ḥ3i* in order to make clear the earlier meaning of the word. At this time there seems to have been a revival of the term *ḥ3i*. There are at the very least twenty-seven citations from five sources:[200] Papyrus Bremner-Rhind, the Temple of Edfu, the Temple of Dendara, the Temple of Philae, and the Ptolemaic coffin of Khaif from Sakkara.[201] First, each source will be introduced and then a general description of the examples of *ḥ3i* will follow. Subsequently, there is a chart that documents these references, including the source, the form, and the meaning.

The first source is the Papyrus Bremner-Rhind (BM 10188), a Graeco-Roman religious papyrus that provides important information for the understanding of myth and ritual in ancient Egypt. It dates to shortly after the end of the Thirtieth Dynasty, or as a colophon notes, 'the twelfth year, fourth month of the inundation-season, of Pharaoh Alexander, son of Alexander.' The exact provenance of this papyrus is unknown, but some suspect that it may come from the tomb of a Theban priest named Nasmin.[202] The papyrus was originally written for a temple.[203] In total, this papyrus contains four ritualistic texts: *Songs of Isis and Nephthys,* the *Ritual of Bringing in Sokar,* the *Book of Overthrowing 'Apep,* and the *Names of 'Apep, which shall not be.* The reference of import here appears in the text called *Songs of Isis and Nephthys*:[204]

> ***ḥ3y**.n ḥr.k m ḫntiw.k*

There is some debate over the true meaning of this example. The *Wörterbuch* (III 7, 2) states: *um jem. Klagen: alt mit ḥr*, Pyr 1791 and Festges 11, 26;[205] however, the dictionary lists further Ptolemaic examples under *Wb* III 7, 3 that use the preposition *n* instead of *ḥr*. The *Wörterbuch* would have the translation read: "We **mourn** over you in your joy." Faulkner believes that in this context *ḥ3y* means "to illumine" and that the crying eye determinative (D 9) should be emended to the sun casting rays of light (N 8).[206] He translates the whole passage as follows: "[Mayest thou expel the great misery of thy Two Women,] May thy face **illumine** us with thy joy…."[207] It seems that hieratic confusion may be responsible for the misunderstanding, in that Möller's sign 85 (crying eye) is similar to sign 306 (sun with rays). Therefore, this is probably not an example of the word *ḥ3i* and should be disregarded.[208]

The next source is the Temple of Edfu, located in Upper Egypt and dedicated to the god Horus of Behdet.[209] This Ptolemaic temple dates to the period between the reigns of Ptolemy III and Ptolemy XII. The majority of the examples of the word *ḥ3i* from the Temple of Edfu appear in two chambers dedicated to Sokar. Three chapels in the north-west corner of the corridor were devoted to the cult of Osiris. The Sokar Chamber is labeled number XIII,[210] and by the Ptolemaic Period Sokar had become little more than a variant of Osiris.[211] Opening off the Chamber of Sokar is room XIV, the inner room of Sokar. The two rooms were called the Portals of the Pillar-god (Osiris). In Chamber XIII Isis is shown reassembling the pieces of Osiris' body, and in Chamber XIV the Osiris mysteries of the month of Khoiak are recorded in the reliefs.[212] According to Penelope Wilson's *A Ptolemaic Lexicon: A Lexicographical Study of the Texts in the Temple of Edfu,* there are three forms of the word *ḥ3i* appearing in this temple: *ḥ3y* "to mourn," *ḥ3y* "mourner," and *ḥ3yty* "Two Mourners." She states:

> They are Isis and Nephthys who mourn for Osiris their brother. In lists naming Isis and Nephthys together it is a common epithet… *ḥ3ity* comes from the verb *ḥ3y* 'to mourn' and is also connected with the word *ḥ3t*… - a bird, which is the name of Isis while mourning, Nephthys being called *ḏrt*. There is a word *ḥ3j.t* (*Wb* II 7, 6)[213] from Amduat IV 34, which Hornung [Amduat II, n. 216] translates as 'Die Klagende', without specifying any further. The noun then is probably not new to GR texts, but its application to both Isis and Nephthys seems to be

[199] Leclant 1957, 110.
[200] This list is in addition to BD 172 found in the Turin Papyrus mentioned above.
[201] Daressy 1917, 18.
[202] Faulkner 1936, 121.
[203] Faulkner 1936, 121.
[204] *Wb* III 7, 2.
[205] *Wb* III 7, 2.
[206] Faulkner 1933, 21, n. d. For this word see P. Wilson 1997, 610.
[207] Faulkner 1936, 129.
[208] In *An Egyptian Reading Book* Budge leaves the determinative as is, and in his vocabulary list he translates *ḥ3i* as "to weep" without providing a translation of the passage (1976, 475). On page 66 he gives the following transliteration: *ḥ3i.n ḥr.k m ḫnti.k*.
[209] Behdet was the name of a city in the Delta (Tell el-Balamun). This was formerly the northernmost extent of the territory of Horus. The name refers to a special solar manifestation of Horus.
[210] *PM* VI, 130.
[211] Watterson 1998, 72.
[212] Watterson 1998, 72.
[213] This should be emended to *Wb* III, 7, 6.

previously unattested. All of these words form part of the same idea and the original verb *ḥ3y* which seems to give rise to the various nouns, may be onomatopoeic, deriving from the wailing noise made by the mourners of the dead or birds. The GR *ḥ3yty* is an invention to describe the two mourners par excellence and it was also used at Dendera and Philae.[214]

As has been shown earlier, the term *ḥ3it* has been used for both Isis and Nephthys as far back as the Pyramid Texts but on an individual basis. And we know that the noun is definitely not new to the Greek texts. A transliteration of the hieroglyphic versions of the words appearing at Edfu and Dendara are included in the chart below.

The third source for references to *ḥ3i* is the Temple of Dendara, located near modern Qena, in the sixth Upper Egyptian nome. The temple is dedicated to the goddess Hathor and dates to the Ptolemaic and Roman Periods. At Dendara the same three forms of *ḥ3i* occur as at Edfu: *ḥ3i*, *ḥ3yt*, and *ḥ3yty*, (referring to Isis and Nephthys). The majority of these references occur in the symbolic mortuary chapels for Osiris located on the roof of the temple. One of the more significant citations is Dendara 132, 12, which states that in the fifth hour of the night Isis and Nephthys *ḥ3i* for Osiris as he is placed in the embalming workshop.[215] This reminds one of the scenes from the Old Kingdom where the women who are labeled *ḥ3(i)t* are performing this rite outside the embalming workshop, or in the case of Pepiankh at Meir, a male *ḥ3(i)w*. Likewise, the Pyramid Texts also equated Isis with the *ḥ3(i)t*. These examples occur in the scenes that illustrate the Osirian Mysteries.

The fourth Ptolemaic source that includes references to *ḥ3i* is the Temple of Philae. A single reference, which is cited in *Belegstellen*, is the only one available at the time of writing.[216] It reads: ***ḥ3yty*** *pw mdw.sn r pt*, "It is the **two transporters**, as they speak toward heaven."[217] The standing temple dates from the Thirtieth Dynasty to the late Roman period and is dedicated to the goddess Isis.

The last source for this section is the Ptolemaic wooden coffin of Khaif from Sakkara.[218] The references in question, which equal six in total, appear in the scene on the right panel of the coffin (Figure 42) and on the lid (Figures 43 and 44).

The first reference on the coffin itself may read:

> ***ḥ3i(t)*** *p*[219] *nṯr... ḥk3.n(.i) n.k ibw*
>
> **transporting** the god ... 'I have conquered hearts for you.'[220]

In his publication, this phrase is accompanied by Daressy's description, *"Génie semblable au précédent."*[221] It is not clear if *au précédent* refers to the preceding figure, it being the god sitting with two lizards, or the preceding genius that looks like Bes.

The section on the lid where the additional references occur is decorated with several vertical bands. In one of these one sees a female kneeling on a rectangular pedestal with her two arms raised in front in a gesture of mourning (not to be confused with the A 28 pose). The fifth entry on the right (not illustrated) may read: *ʿnḫ... st* ***ḥ3y***; again, this does not make sense.[222] Below the columns of hieroglyphs between the two vertical bands of figures, on both the right and left, the texts read:

> ***ḥ3y.t(y) ḥ3y(t)*** *ḥr Wsir*
>
> The Two **transporters** who **(ritually) transport**[223] (concerning) Osiris.[224]

Table 11 below displays the various Ptolemaic references to *ḥ3i*.

Conclusion

To conclude, there are a number of examples of the word *ḥ3i* dating from the Fourth Dynasty to the Ptolemaic Period. There is continuity in the use of the word in that it consistently appears in contexts dealing with Isis, Nephthys, and Osiris. The texts are all of a funerary nature except for certain references to the *ḥ3(i)t* bird itself, which appear in secular, avian contexts. However, the specific types of sources – for example, tomb scene, temple inscription, or funerary text – differ from period to period. In the previous chapters the connections between these citations were strengthened, and the emerging patterns shed more light on the true nuances of the word *ḥ3i*. Table 12 displays a summary of the citations of *ḥ3i* and its derivatives that have been mentioned throughout the previous chapters.

---

[214] P. Wilson 1997, 611.

[215] Cauville 1997, 72. The word used for the embalmers' workshop is *wabet*.

[216] *Wb* III 7, 7.

[217] This translation is the result of a collaborative effort by the author and Leo Depuydt.

[218] Daressy 1917.

[219] It has been brought to my attention by Leo Depuydt that in Adel Farid's *Die demotischen Inschriften der Strategen* (1993, 2) it states that Daressy misread *ḳ* for *p* in a publication dating to 1916 (one year before the publication of this coffin). If this is the case, then perhaps *p* can represent *p3*, the definite article.

[220] This is my attempt at a transliteration and translation.

[221] Daressy 1917, 11.

[222] Daressy 1917, 17.

[223] Or "perform the rite of *ḥ3i*" over Osiris.

[224] See Daressy (1917, 18) for hieroglyphs. This is my translation. Note the common use of the plural writing for the dual form.

TABLE 10: EXAMPLES OF *ḥ3i* IN THE COFFIN TEXTS

CT	Section
I	73d
I	74e
I	303g
II	177h
II	238b
II	239a
III	22a
III	297i
III	307a
III	307b
III	308d (x2)
III	311h
III	317e
III	317l
IV	331g
IV	373a (x2)
V	332c
VI	360j
VI	385o
VII	28o
VII	51s

TABLE 11: EXAMPLES OF *ḥ3i* IN THE PTOLEMAIC PERIOD

	Source	Word
1	Edfu I 160, 4[225]	*ḥ3y.ty*[226]
2	Edfu I 201, 8	*ḥ3y.ty*[227]
3	Edfu I 201, 11	*ḥ3y*
4	Edfu I 205, 5	*ḥ3(i).ty*
5	Edfu I 205, 5	*ḥ3y*[228]
6	Edfu I 209, 1-2	*ḥ3(i)w*[229]
7	Edfu I 209, 5	*ḥ3(i)*[230]
8	Edfu I 210, 2	*ḥ3(i)*[231]
9	Edfu I 210, 8	*ḥ3(i).ty*[232]
10	Edfu I 211, 13	*ḥ3(i)*[233]
11	Edfu I 211, 14	*ḥ3(i)t*[234]
12	Edfu I 214, 1	*ḥ3(i)*[235]

[225] The Edfu references denote passages in Chassinat's *Le temple d'Edfou* vols. 1-14. *Mémoires de la Mission Français*, vols. 10-11, 20-31. Cairo: Institut Français d'Archéologie Orientale du Caire, 1892 ff.

[226] *Wb* III 7, 7.

[227] *Wb* III 7, 7.

[228] *Wb* III 7, 1.

[229] *Wb* III 7, 1. Junker transliterates and translates the passage as follows: *ḏd mdw in ḏr.tj ḥ3.tj*, *"Es sagen die ḏrtj, die Klageweiber"* (Junker 1910, 70).

[230] In the Greek period the preposition n is used instead of *ḥr*. *Wb* III 7, 3. Junker (1910, 71) transliterates and translates the passage as follows: *ij.ni ḥ3.n.i kw sp Π*, *"Ich komme und beweine dich – zweimal."*

[231] *Wb* III 7, 5. This word occurs only in Greek sources, and the Berlin Dictionary follows the entry with a question mark. Junker (1910, 76) transliterates and translates the passage as follows: *nḏ ḥr.k r ḥ3.t n.t mw.t.k*, *"Heil dir! Zur Klage deiner Mutter."*

[232] This citation is not listed in the *Wb*. Junker (1910, 77) transliterates and translates the passage as follows: *i3kb n.k ḥ3.tj m ḏdw*, *"Dich betrauern die ḥ3t in ḏdw."*

[233] *Wb* III 7, 3; Junker 1910, 85.

[234] This word contains the A 28 determinative. The word is found in the phrase *ḥ3.sn ṯw m nṯr.sn*. The passage is translated *Sie betrauern dich als ihren Gott* (Junker 1910, 86).

13	Edfu I 215, 16	*ḥ3(i)t*[236]
14	Edfu I 215, 16	*ḥ3y(t)*[237]
15	Edfu I 216, 3	*ḥ3(i)*[238]
16	Edfu I 216, 3	*ḥ3(i)*[239]
17	Edfu I 216, 7	*ḥ3(i)*[240]
18	Edfu I 216, 9	*ḥ3y*[241]
19	Edfu I 222, 12	*ḥ3y*[242]
20	Edfu I 222, 16	*ḥ3(i)*[243]
21	Edfu I 223, 7	*ḥ3y*[244]
22	Edfu I 223, 10	*ḥ3(i)*[245]
23	Edfu I 459, 18	*ḥ3w(t)-ib*[246]
24	Edfu VI 101, 9	*ḥ3y*[247]
25	Edfu VI 101, 9	*ḥ3y.ty*[248]
26	Dendara 32,4[249]	*ḥ3y.ty*
27	Dendara 126, 5	*ḥ3y.ty*[250]
28	Dendara 132, 12	*ḥ3y*[251]
29	Dendara 135, 3	*ḥ3y.ty*
30	Dendara 135, 3	*ḥ3(i)t*
31	Dendara 141, 9	*ḥ3y.ty*
32	Dendara 145, 9	*ḥ3y.ty*
33	Dendara 147, 4	*ḥ3y.ty*
34	Dendara 213, 5	*ḥ3y.ty*
35	Dendara 292, 7	*ḥ3ywt*
36	Philae <1621> Phot 217	*ḥ3y.ty*[252]
37	*ASAE* 17, 11	*ḥ3i*
38	*ASAE* 17, 17	*ḥ3y*
39	*ASAE* 17, 18	*ḥ3y.ty* (x2)
40	*ASAE* 17, 18	*ḥ3y* (x2)

[235] Junker (1910, 99) transliterates and translates the passage as follows: *wrš.s m jrw ḥr ḥ3.k*, *"Den Tag verbringt sie, indem sie dich beklagt."*

[236] Junker (1910, 109) transliterates and translates the passage as follows: *imw ib n sn.tj ḥ3tj.k*, *"Bekümmert ist das Herz der Schwestern, die dich beklagen."*

[237] Junker (1910, 109) continues the passage above with the following transliteration and translation: *iw whm.n sn.tj ḥ3 sn.tj...*, *"es wiederholen [?] die Schwestern die Klagen, die Schwestern, die Weinenden."*

[238] The *Wb* lists Edfu I 216 in III 7, 3; however, there are four examples of this word on this page, and I cannot discern which example the dictionary is referring to. Junker transliterates and translates the passage as follows: *mj.n ḥ3.n n.f*, *"kommt, laß uns ihn betrauern"* (Junker 1910, 110).

[239] Junker (1910, 110) transliterates and translates the passage as follows: *iw.j ḥ3.j sp TI nb.j*, *"Ich komme und betrauere, betrauerer meinen Herrn."*

[240] Junker (1910, 111) transliterates and translates the passage as follows: *mj.n ḥ3.n n.f*, *"kommt, wir wollen ihn beklagen."*

[241] Junker (1910, 112) transliterates and translates the passage as follows: *ḥ3 n.f rḫ.tj m ḫ3w*, *"Es betrauern ihn die* rxtj *in der Nacht."*

[242] P. Wilson 1997, 611. Junker (1910, 45) transliterates and translates the passage as follows: *rḥtj ḥ3.sn n m33[.k]*, *"Die rḥtj klagen bei deinem Anblick."*

[243] Junker (1910, 46) transliterates and translates the passage as follows: *ḥ3.kw...imw ib r.j*, *"Dich beklagt...trauernden Herzens...."*

[244] Junker (1910, 49) transliterates and translates the passage as follows: *ḥ3.sn kw m nṯr wʿ*.sn, *"Sie beklagen dich als ihren einzigen Gott."*

[245] Junker (1910, 49) transliterates and translates the passage as follows: *ḥ3.s m ḥr.k*, *"wenn sie klagt vor deinem Angesicht."*

[246] *Wb* III, 7, 11.

[247] This example is listed in P. Wilson's *Ptolemaic Lexicon,* p. 611 under *ḥ3y*, "to mourn."

[248] This example is listed in P. Wilson's *Ptolemaic Lexicon,* p. 611 under *ḥ3yty*, "Two mourners."

[249] The Dendara references denote passages presented in Sylvie Cauville's *Le temple de Dendara, Les chapelles osiriennes: transcription et traduction*. IFAO, Bibliothèque D'Étude 117. 1997.

[250] I think here Cauville decided to alter the meaning of *ḥ3yty* because it directly precedes the word *ḏrty* which she translates as *pleureuses* (Cauville 1997, 69).

[251] Cauville 1997a, 72.

[252] *Wb* III 7, 7.

TABLE 12: SUMMARY OF *ḥꜣi* CITATIONS

	OLD KINGDOM
1	Tomb of Debehni at Giza - 4th Dynasty
2	Sun Temple of Niuserre at Abu Ghurob
3	Tomb of Hetepherakhti at Sakkara D 60 - 5th Dynasty
4	Tomb of Qar at Giza G 7101 - Pepy II
5	Inscription of Sabni from west bank at Aswan - Pepy II
6	Tomb of Pepiankh at Meir - Pepy II
7	PT §550
8	PT §744
9	PT §1255
10	PT §1280
11	PT §1585
12	PT §1791
13	PT §2112
14	PT §2117
	MIDDLE KINGDOM
1	CT I 73d
2	CT I 74e
3	CT I 303g
4	CT II 177h
5	CT II 238b
6	CT II 239a
7	CT III 22a
8	CT III 297i
9	CT III 307a
10	CT III 307b
11	CT III 308d
12	CT III 311h
13	CT III 317e
14	CT III 317l
15	CT IV 331g
16	CT IV 373a
17	CT IV 373a
18	CT V 332c
19	CT VI 360j
20	CT VI 385o
21	CT VII 28o
22	CT VII 51s
23	Funerary Liturgy column 16
24	F.L. col. 44-45
25	F.L. col. 64
26	F.L. col. 84
	NEW KINGDOM
1	Tomb of Amenemhet (TT 82)
2	BD 172
3	Book of Gates, Twelfth Hour
4	Papyrus Sallier IV
5	Papyrus CB III: Dream Book
6	Onomastica
7	*Urk.* IV 84,10
8	Bibl nat 20, 15; RB 111,13 Hymn to Osiris, first half of 18th Dynasty - Louvre Stela C 286
9	*BMMA* 27, 130 Scribe's palette
10	Theb Grab Nr 76 <32>
11	The Amduat, Third Hour
12	BD 1
	LATE PERIOD
1	Lond 1292

	PTOLEMAIC PERIOD
1	Edfu I 160
2	Edfu I 201 (2)
3	Edfu I 205 (2)
4	Edfu I 209 (2)
5	Edfu I 210 (2)
6	Edfu I 211 (2)
7	Edfu I 214
8	Edfu I 215 (2)
9	Edfu I 216 (4)
10	Edfu I 222 (2)
11	Edfu I 223 (2)
12	Edfu I 459
13	Edfu IV 101 (2)
14	Dendara 32
15	Dendara 126
16	Dendara 132
17	Dendara 135 (2)
18	Dendara 141
19	Dendara 145
20	Dendara 147
21	Dendara 213
22	Dendara 292
23	Philae <1621> Phot 217
24	*ASAE* 17, 11
25	*ASAE* 17, 17
26	*ASAE* 17, 18 (4)

Conclusions

Finding one word to define *ḥ3i* is not an easy matter. Many things can be said about the rite of *ḥ3i*, but choosing among the words "rejuvenate," "revivify," or "spiritualize," as the defining translation, is meaningless. The process of rebirth is not made clear in the ancient sources, and there is no preserved manual of instruction on how to resurrect someone after they have passed away. In most cases the moment at which the ritual of *ḥ3i* occurs cannot be isolated in the sources. The rite encompasses many concepts associated with the magical[1] act of physical transformation, namely assembling, protecting, and revivifying the corpse, and the ultimate transfer to the Hereafter.[2]

The ceremony of *ḥ3i* was jubilant in character and celebrated the prospects of the deceased in the Afterlife. The ritual involved such actions as dancing, singing, and clapping, in addition to the dragging of the coffin or statue of the deceased. The evolution of the *ḥ3i* ritual is complex; however, the rite always appears in a funerary context.

The origin of this ritual has been obscured by time, but the earliest clear vestige is found in the Fourth Dynasty tomb of Debehni at Giza, which exhibits a version of the ritual performed at a genuine funeral. The original form of the *ḥ3i* ceremony dates back to prehistoric times, although there is no direct textual evidence indicating as much. The predynastic female figurines with their arms in the A 28 pose support this practice of a comparable rite of rejuvenation, as do the similar depictions of females with upraised arms appearing on D-Ware pots, on the linen from Gebelein, in Tomb 100, and in rock art from the eastern desert.

The ritual of *ḥ3i* is at its purest during the Old Kingdom according to available evidence. The Old Kingdom sources display a clear understanding of the rite by the Egyptians, and consistent patterns are manifest to the modern scholar. These references never contain Osirian allusions.

Originally the *ḥ3i* rite may have belonged to the Butic ceremony, which was practiced by the rulers of Lower Egypt, and originated from the religious Delta capital of Buto. With the democratization of religion, private individuals in the north eventually began to imitate the Butic burial. The advent of Upper Egyptian supremacy in Lower Egypt brought with it changes to the royal funerary program, namely the practice of the cult of Osiris. Thus the royal funerary trends changed to reflect this new tradition, and the private funerary program remained focused on the Butic ceremony until around the Fifth Dynasty when the sources suggest the use of the cult of Osiris by the private individual.

Beginning in the Old Kingdom, it was the Acacia House, with its purifying and rejuvenating qualities, that was primarily responsible for the *ḥ3i* ritual. Ptolemaic sources reveal that the Acacia House and Osiris may have been closely related in the Pharaonic Period, thus accounting for the fact that both the Acacia House and the myth of Osiris have the ritual of *ḥ3i* in common. If we take into account Eliade's theory of the *axis mundi* then the acacia tree may symbolize the point on earth where communication between the realm of the living and the realm of the dead can occur. This may explain the common depiction of a tree appearing on top of the burial mound of Osiris.

Early allusions to the rite of *ḥ3i* are also seen in the Pyramid Texts; however, these versions are infused with the myth of Osiris.[3] Beginning with the emergence of the Pyramid Texts, barring the questionably dated Funerary Liturgy, the Osirian overtones abound and the ritual consistently occurs on a different plane – not the land of the living. The most feasible solution for the dichotomy apparent in the Old Kingdom sources lies in the idea of sacred knowledge, that is the cult of Osiris requiring initiation; and thus, until a certain point, it remained inaccessible to the private person, as mentioned above. The privilege of becoming an Osiris was initially reserved only for a king, and the objective of this assimilation was eternal life, with the final event being the revivification of the Osiris/king.[4] The goal of the cult of Osiris coincided with the aim of the *ḥ3i* rite in that both supported the rebirth of the deceased in the Hereafter. It was through magic that Isis resurrected Osiris in the

[1] "Funerary texts are often called magical texts. But the distinction between the magical and the religious is one of definition. The word *magic* is often used simply to label actions, sayings, and ideas that do not seem reasonable from a Western positivistic or Christian point of view" (te Velde 1988, 29). Ritner (1993, 4-5) addresses the issue of differentiating between magic and religion with the following statement: "In any discussion of magical spells and techniques, one is at once confronted by the complete absence of any shared criteria for what constitutes 'magic.' All too often, the religious and medical practices of one culture or era become 'magic' when viewed from the perspective of another...The designation of any given text as 'magical' as opposed to 'religious' or 'medical' is often highly problematic and subjective." See also Pinch (1995, 12) for a discussion on magic and religion.

[2] Lloyd (1989, 130) shows that the Egyptians believed in the ability of ritual activity to restore the dead to life.

[3] Osiris is first mentioned in private funerary inscriptions during the time of Niuserre (Griffiths 1980, 44), and then is mentioned for the first time in a royal context in the Pyramid Texts of Unas (Griffiths 1980, 41). Because Osiris occupied such a prominent position in the Pyramid Texts, it has been assumed that the myth of Osiris had been around for some time (Griffiths 1980, 7). According to Griffiths, the "Osirian System" (Griffiths uses this term in his book *The Cult of Osiris* 1980, 18) is thought to have been contrived by the Heliopolitan theologians and put into practice sometime during the first half of the Old Kingdom (Griffiths 1980, 18-19). See Griffiths (1980, 41-84) for a discussion of the antiquity of the cult of Osiris.

[4] Breasted 1972, 141; Griffiths 1980, 230-231. Griffiths explains that even though it was the king who first assimilated with Osiris, this phenomenon actually involved the whole population because of the idea that the king represented the entire group.

myth.[5] On the human plane, the funeral ceremony and mummification made this result possible. According to Griffiths, the Osiris myth merged with the already existing ceremony used for royalty.[6]

Beginning in the Fifth Dynasty, the bird theme permeates the *ḥ3i* ritual and reveals a complex relationship between the two. The royal ritual clearly involves the characters of the myth of Osiris, and this is where the avian motif emerges. It surfaces in the Old Kingdom royal sources and continues in the Coffin Texts, with the bird determinative becoming quite common. Likewise, beginning in the Coffin Texts, *ḥ3i* can also be written with a divine determinative. The use of this latter determinative reinforces the connection between the Osirian characters and the avian motif, as well as its appearance in a royal context.

The rite of *ḥ3i* originated much earlier than the advent of the Osirian character Isis who is the first to appear as a *ḥ3it*-bird in the Pyramid Texts. Her mythological figure was superimposed on an ordinary funeral attendant who performed this ritual. This returns one to the predynastic figurines that have bird heads and hold their arms in the A 28 pose. Although the bird qualities are not seen in the depictions in the rest of the predynastic evidence, many of these illustrations may be representing a funeral scene where the deceased is being transferred to the cemetery by boat accompanied by the attendant with upraised arms (A 28 pose). There are no superimpositions of mythological characters in these early predynastic examples.

The fact that Isis rejuvenates Osiris in her bird form is not coincidental — flying on a bird to heaven was the deceased's mode of ascension. Likewise, the bird as a symbol of female sexuality is suggested by Manniche.[7] She references a wall-painting in the tomb of Inherkhau (TT 359) at Deir el-Medina where a young girl holds a duckling or a goose. Sexuality and fertility are clear precursors to birth, and therefore, rebirth in the Afterlife. And it is strictly "new life" that is being accomplished by such an ascension. Isis is known from other sources — namely, the Myth of Osiris — to be the one responsible for the resurrection of the deceased.[8]

Even before an ordinary funerary attendant had taken on the role of *ḥ3(i)t* in the funeral, the origin of the term came from the avian realm. As discussed in Chapter Five, many theories have been put forth to account for Isis as a *ḥ3(i)t*-bird. The true identity of the *ḥ3(i)t*-bird is unknown which makes it difficult to discuss the characteristics of this bird. The Coffin Texts definitely suggest the *ḥ3(i)t*-bird had a predatory nature. One of the main theories suggests that the *ḥ3(i)t*-bird was a predatory bird that fed on rotting corpses, and with the bodies' consumption, new life was being sustained out of old. To the contrary, CT V 332c recounts that if the birds *ḥ3i* over the deceased he will die a second time—which is something the dead did not want to happen.

Likewise, it may have been the birds' subsequent flight that functioned as the ascension to the heavens for the deceased. There is no lack of examples of a bird being the method of revivification in that a bird carries the deceased to the sky (see Introduction and Chapter Five), or the deceased turns into a bird in order to reach the sky. It may be a matter of turning a negative or destructive activity into something productive—along the same lines as a *captatio benevolentiae*. Therefore by changing the attitude toward the desecration of the corpses by these birds of prey, the ancient Egyptians imagined the birds as transporting the deceased to the Hereafter. It was a way to seemingly control this natural instinct of the predators while at the same time fulfilling a need, namely to have the individual live forever in the Afterlife. The natural bird activity was then explained through the creation of a ritual which appears in the Fifth Dynasty. This mythologized version includes the Osirian characters and appears in a royal context.

Through the use of the arm determinative employed in the writing of *ḥ3i* in the Coffin Texts it is clear that arm movement was also somehow linked to the ritual. If the predynastic depictions of women with upraised arms do indeed mimic the wings of birds, this may supply the correlation suggested in the Coffin Texts. Also, it is probably not coincidental that the ancient Egyptian word *ḳ3i* is also written with the A 28 determinative, which means to be high or exalted.

As is mentioned in the introduction to this chapter, the exact process of rebirth is not made clear in the sources and the precise point of resurrection is vague. There is a connection between the summoning rite described in the Pyramid Texts and the Old Kingdom tomb scenes that display the rite of *ḥ3i*. In fact, all portrayals depict one and the same event. PT §744 is an account of the rite: "Arms are linked for you, feet dance for you, hands are waved for you. Isis has grasped your hand and she inducts you into the pavilion. The land is covered(?), the *wršiw ḥ3i*."[9] Isis and the *wršiw* are both present, and a dance is performed before the transfer, as is the case in many of the Pyramid Texts listed below. The summons is often preceded by a dance (PT §§1366, 2014; CT I 272d,

[5] Wilkinson 2003, 147.

[6] Griffiths 1980, 35.

[7] Manniche 1987, 40.

[8] In his article te Velde remarks on a coffin in the Metropolitan Museum of Art where the goddess Isis is directed "to free the mummy from its wrappings at the moment of resurrection: 'Ho my mother Isis, come that you may remove the bindings which are on me'" (te Velde 1988, 34). See Hayes 1959, 71.

[9] See Faulkner (1998, 138) for one version of this utterance.

VI 106d). These accounts are reminiscent of the Old Kingdom dance scenes in the tombs of Debehni, Hetepherakhti, Qar, and Ptahhotep described above, and also in others. In the first three scenes the action is clearly labeled as *ḥ3(i)t*.

The fact that the *wršiw* are present for the summoning, which occurs prior to the transportation/ascension to the Hereafter, corresponds to their association with the Souls, or People of Pe made by other scholars. Numerous Pyramid Texts (PT §§478, 624, 725, 795, 942, 1004-1005, 1013, 1089, 1253, 1973-1974) demonstrate that summoning, guiding, and welcoming were some of the functions of the Souls of Pe. The *wršiw* also call the deceased and ritually transport him to eternal life.

In the Pyramid Texts the *mniwt wrt* (feminine active participle) calls, or summons, the deceased to the Afterlife (PT §§726, 863, 1366, 1927, 2013, 2239). As Osiris is sometimes called *mniw wr* (masculine passive participle) "the one who is moored," the *mniwt wrt* guided the deceased toward his eternal destiny and secured his life in the Hereafter by summoning him and helping him "land." Sometimes this call is made by the *mniwt wrt* as Isis or Nephthys, by the *wršiw*, by the *smntyt*,[10] or any combination of the aforementioned. The lack of a coherent, universal religious system, or mythic doctrine, may account for this multiplicity.

On earth, the rite always takes place at the tomb, or more frequently, in conjunction with the embalming workshop, both of which are located in the cemetery. When concrete locations are specified in the mythological sources, they corroborate this local as the spot for the rite of *ḥ3i*. The New Kingdom presents additional contexts, all of which are in the realm of the dead. By the end of the New Kingdom the consistency of the setting has ceased to exist.

One word that may reveal its connection to the rite of *ḥ3i* is *ḥ3(i)t* "tomb," a shelter which safeguards the corpse from maltreatment prior to resurrection. The sense of collection and protection for the express purpose of rebirth can be comprehended in this associated word. Additionally, the tomb itself is the place of transition between this world and the next. The deceased arrives at the tomb alive and will soon be "let loose."[11] The core concepts reflected in the word *ḥ3i* are protection, rejuvenation, and ritual transportation of the deceased's corpse in order to ensure the body's effectiveness in the next life.

Another word that may have a link with *ḥ3i* is *ḥ3y*, to be naked (or the naked one).[12] Nudity can symbolize innocence and rebirth and was the standard costume for children.[13] As we all enter the world naked it is not coincidental that the ancient Egyptians imagined that they would enter the Next World naked. Osiris is often given the epithet *ḥ3y* "the naked one."[14] Likewise, Goelet points out that nude statues were frequently part of the burial goods in Old Kingdom funerals.[15] This connection can be further cemented by the fact that the predynastic figurines mentioned above are also nude.

The appellation *dmḏyt* has also been clarified in this work. The term *dmḏyt* does not refer to a crowd of females, but instead is a title that can be used in the singular or the plural. She is the one who collects and assembles the deceased's limbs in the way that Isis searched for Osiris' body parts and put them back together. She appears in the funeral ceremony to perform this particular function. The *dmḏyt* is logically associated with the rite of *ḥ3i* since the collection and assembling of limbs is one step in the course of rebirth; *ḥ3i* encompasses the various stages of this resurrection.

The consistencies that appeared in the Old Kingdom sources no longer exist in the Coffin Texts. The antiquated status of the *ḥ3i* rite in the Coffin Texts may be seen in the many misspellings and awkward usages of the word. The characteristics of the rite that remained constant throughout the Pharaonic Period and into the Ptolemaic Period were the A 28 gesture, the image of Isis as a *ḥ3yt*-bird, the notion of transportation, and the jubilant nature of the ritual. This last trait can still be seen in one Ptolemaic example of the word *ḥ3i* from Dendera, where the dancing man determinative is employed (Figure 45).

Lastly, there is an observable connection between the rite of *ḥ3i* and hair. However, the evidence is contradictory – in some cases the women performing *ḥ3i* are depicted with a lack of hair (note the Old Kingdom tomb scenes), and in others the fact that they have hair is crucial to the execution of the rite (note the twelfth hour of the Book of Gates). Extensive studies have been done on hair, namely Gay Robins 1995 work, entitled "Hair and the Construction of Identity in Ancient Egypt, c. 1480-1350 B.C." Robins notes in her article that hair

[10] The *smntyt* is found in similar contexts to the *mniwt wrt*. The feminine form, *smntyt*, is usually defined as "mourning woman." See *Wb* IV 136, 1; Hannig 1995, 707; 2003, 1127; and PT §§ 726a, 1366a, 1928, 1997. Judging from the definition "prospector" given to *smnty* (m.s.), the *smntyt* may have a similar function. Possibly, the *smntyt* searches for Osiris' limbs in order to reassemble them. The *smntyt* serves in the final stages of the preparation for the deceased's resurrection, calling to the deceased immediately before the doors of the sky open, or before the deceased ascends as a star, or as the deceased meets the Westerners. This series of events is also accompanied by encircling and dance.

[11] Dodson and Ikram 2008, 13.

[12] *WB* III, 13; Faulkner 1991, 161.

[13] Goelet 1993, 21.

[14] Goelet 1993, 22.

[15] Goelet 1993, 22; see also Eaton-Krauss 1984, 33.

had an erotic significance which aided in recognizing women as icons of sexuality and fertility.[16] Green, in her work on hair, references a passage in the *Story of the Two Brothers* to demonstrate the role of hair in sexual attraction.[17]

The same short hairstyle is present on women in the Old Kingdom tomb scenes as well as in the New Kingdom tomb scenes. Robins suggests that a short black wig may have been worn or that the women's hair was cut for the cultic occasion. There is no evidence to confirm this one way or the other. The continuation of the hair style does demonstrate that it was purposeful and religiously important; however, the meaning is elusive.

As a final note, this study offers a new definition for *ḥ3i*: "to ritually transport, or transfer the deceased with the express purpose of rebirth and renewal in the Hereafter." In redefining the word *ḥ3i* one is confronted with the fact that ritual action is part of a process to revive a memory, thus linking the present with the past. The study of *ḥ3i* offers the opportunity to look at the development of myth and ritual in ancient Egypt as early evidence for this ritual dates to the predynastic period. It is clear that the ritual of *ḥ3i* was used to enforce the power of the elite in early Dynastic Egypt and that the ritual existed in its mythologized form in a royal setting. Mythical knowledge was reserved for the elite, which accounts for the stark contrast between the nature of the ritualistic private sources and the mythologized royal sources, especially in the Old Kingdom. The superimposition of Osirian characters occurs within this context. With the democratization of religion and the spread of restricted knowledge the ritual of *ḥ3i* becomes more visible in the historical record and thus appears in more heterogeneous contexts.

---

[16] Robins 1995, 63.
[17] Green 2001. See Hollis 1990.

Figures

Figure 1: PT §1973.

Figure 2: Second hour of the night from Edfu (Junker 1910, 86).

Figure 3: John Rylands IX 19/16.

*Figure 4: Funeral Procession of Debehni. Fourth Dynasty, Giza (*LD *II 35).*

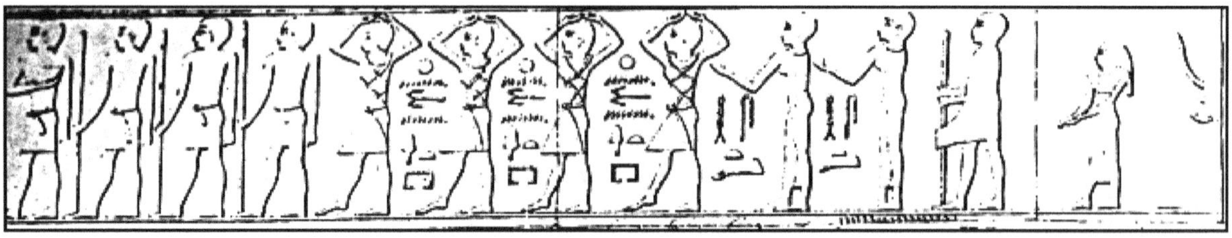

*Figure 5: From the Tomb of Ptahhotep (*LD *II 101b).*

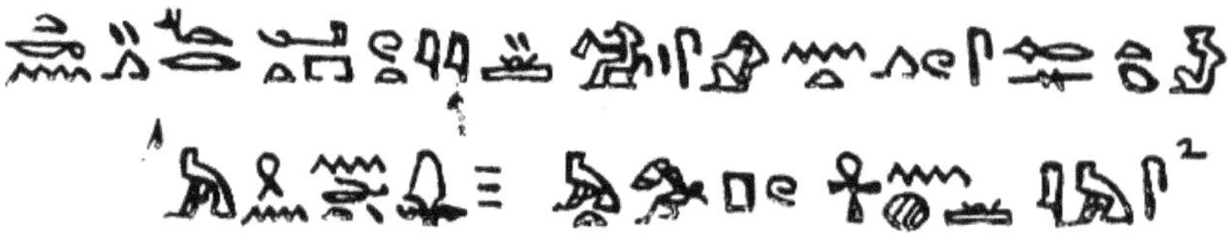

Figure 6: Urk. *VI 20, 15.*

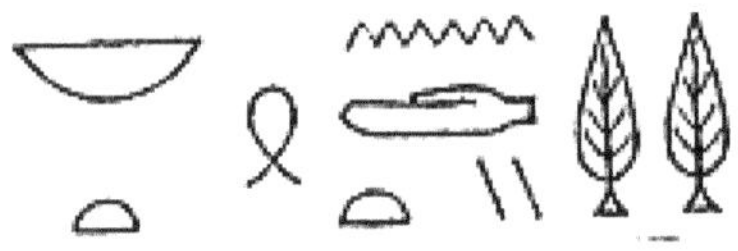

Figure 7: Title of goddess Sakhmet, "Lady of the Two Acacias" (Budge 1909:114).

Figure 8: Funeral Procession of Hetepherakhti. Fifth Dynasty, Sakkara (Adapted from Mohr 1943, figure 3).

Figure 9: Drawing of the dragging scene from the tomb of Ptahhotep (Adapted from Settgast 1963: Tafel *I).*

Figure 10: Drawing of the dragging scene from a tomb in Barnûgi (Adapted from Settgast 1963: Tafel *I).*

Figure 11: From the tomb of Senet (TT 60) (Adapted from Davies and Gardiner 1920: plate XIX).

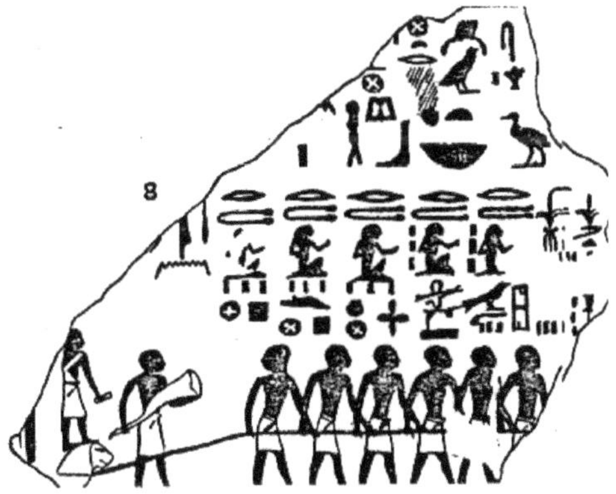

Figure 12: Inscription from the tomb of Djehuty-Nakht at El-Bersheh (no. 1) (Griffith and Newberry 1890: plate IX, no. 8).

Figure 13: Dragging scene in funeral procession of Amenemhet, TT 82 (Davies and Gardiner 1915, plate XI).

Figure 14: Continuation of dragging scene in funeral procession of Amenemhet, TT 82 (Davies and Gardiner 1915, plate XII).

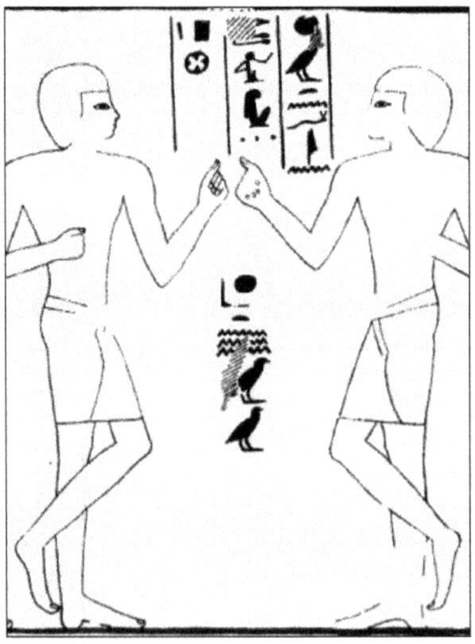

Figure 15: Dance of the mww from the tomb of Amenemhet, TT 82 (Davies and Gardiner 1915, plate XI).

Figure 16: Dragging scene from the tomb of Paheri (Tylor and Griffith 1894, plate V).

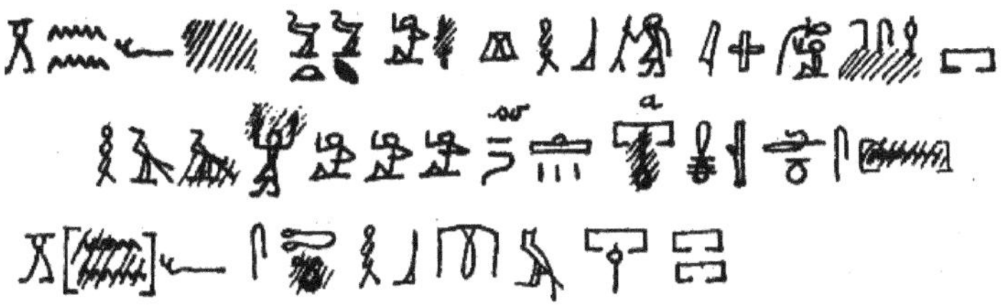

Figure 17: Excerpt from the inscription of Sabni. Urkunden *I 138.*

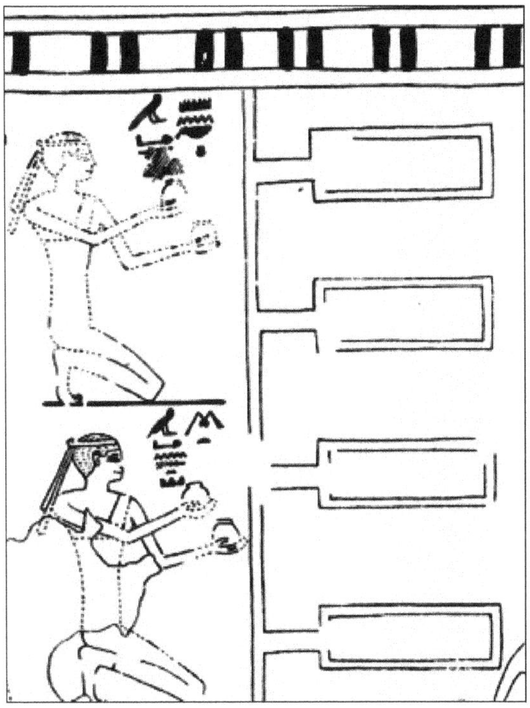

Figure 18: The (mn)knwt and dmḏ(y)t in the tomb of Amenemhet, TT 82 (Davies and Gardiner 1915, plate X).

Figure 19: From the tomb of Paheri at Elkab (Tylor and Griffith 1894, plate V).

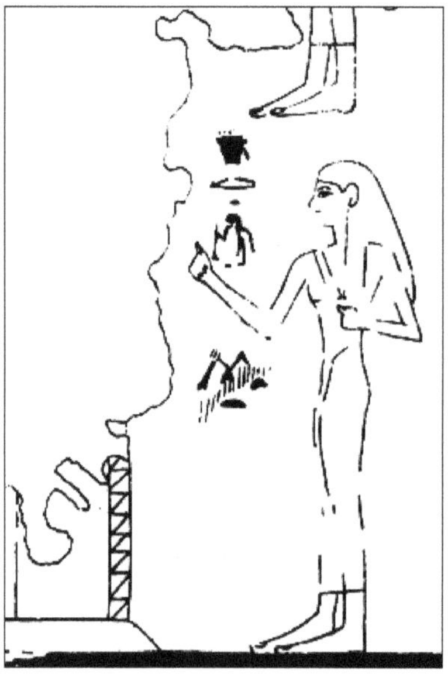

Figure 20: Scene depicting a woman with the label *ḏr(y)t wrt dmḏ(y)t* from TT 82 (Gardiner 1915: plate XIII).

Figure 21: Scene depicting two women labeled *dmḏ(y)t* in TT 20 (Davies 1913, plate XIV).

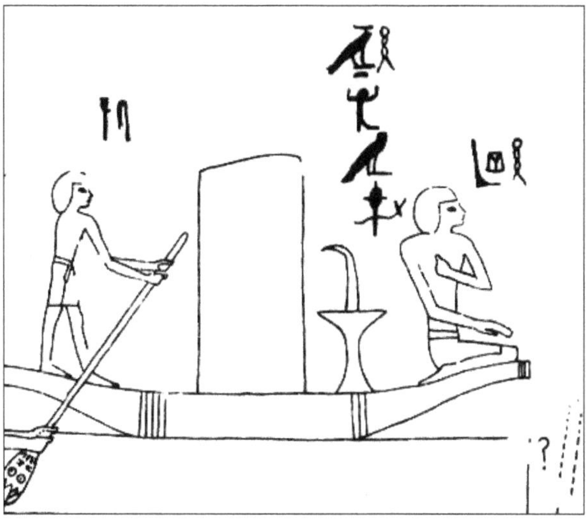

Figure 22: Scene depicting the skiff in the tomb of Amenemhet, TT 82 (Davies and Gardiner 1915, plate IX).

Figure 23: Scene depicting the skiff in the tomb of Paheri (Tylor and Griffith 1894: plate V).

Figure 24: The pr-nfr from TT C4 (Wilkinson, Manners & Customs*, ed. Birch, No. 134).*

Figure 25: Gardiner's A 28 sign.

*Figure 26: Tomb of Iy-Mery at Giza (*LD *II 52).*

Figure 27: Tomb of Khety at Beni Hasan (Newberry 1893, 2: plate XIII).

Figure 28: Tomb of Khety at Beni Hasan (Newberry 1893, 2: plate XIII).

Figure 29: Tomb of Ahanakht at el-Bersheh (Griffith and Newberry 1894, 2: plate XIV).

Figure: 30: PT §550.

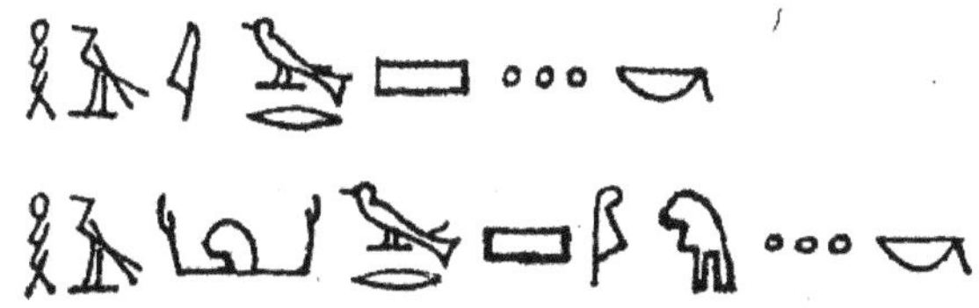

Figure 31: PT §744.

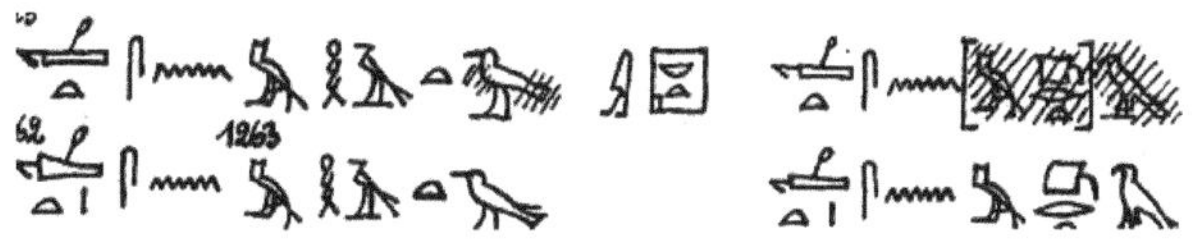

Figure 32: PT §1255.

Figure 33: PT §1280.

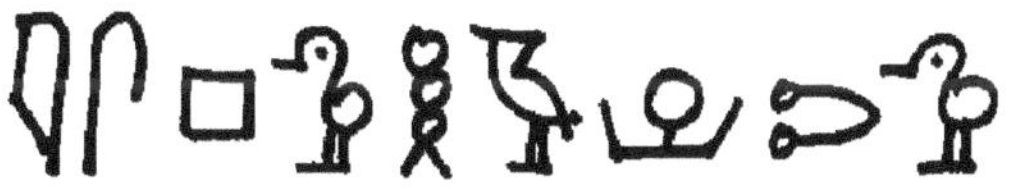

Figure 34: PT §1585 (Hand copy by author).

Figure 35: PT §1585 (Sethe 1908).

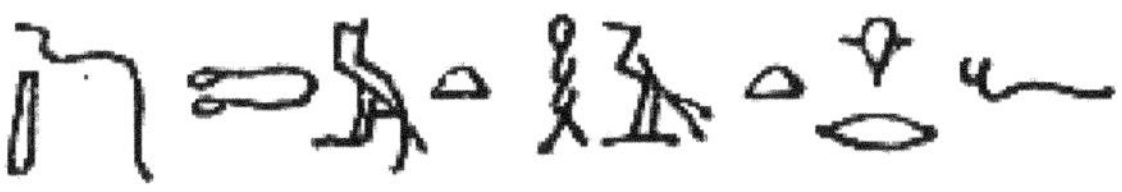

Figure 36: PT §1791.

Figure 37: PT §2112.

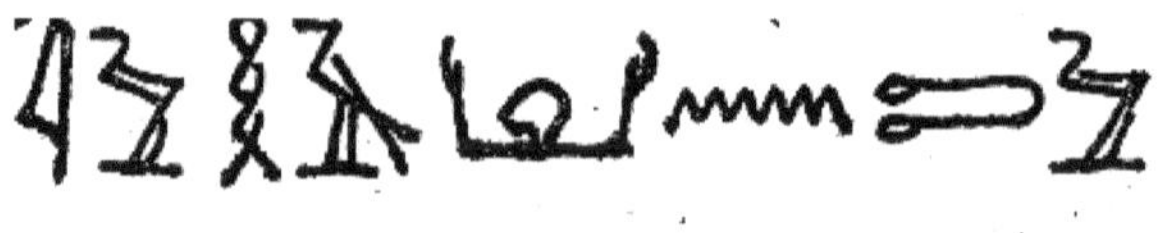

Figure 38: PT §2117-2118.

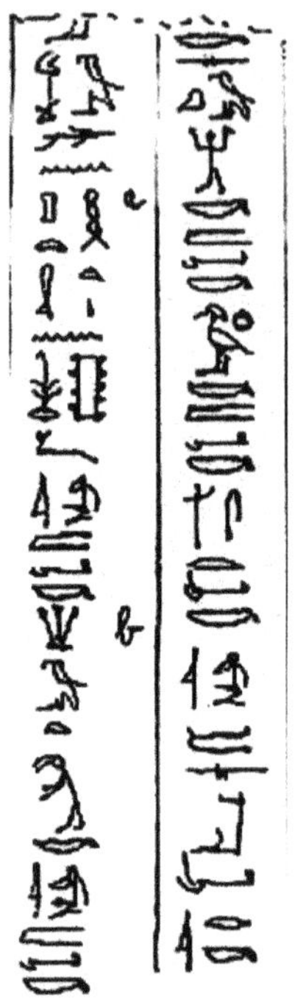

Figure 39: Flor 1594. Hand copy by Gloria Rosati.

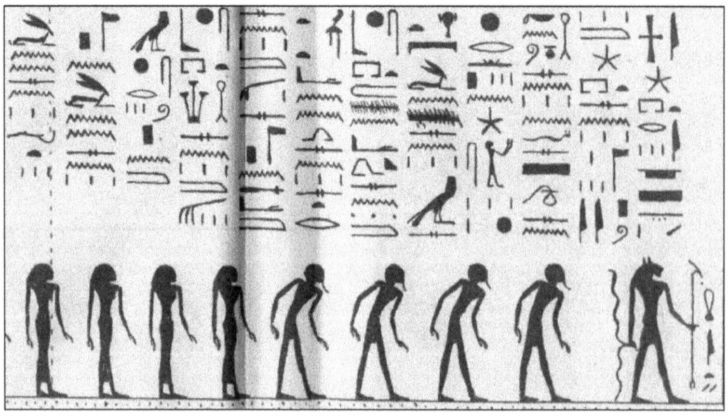

Figure 40: Book of Gates, Twelfth Hour (Bonomi and Sharpe 1864, plate 9).

Figure 41: Book of the Amduat, Third Hour, from tomb of Seti I (Budge 1906, 53).

Figure 42: Ptolemaic coffin of Khaif (Daressy 1917, 11).

Figure 43: Ptolemaic coffin of Khaif (Daressy 1917, 17).

Figure 44: Ptolemaic coffin of Khaif (Daressy 1917, 18).

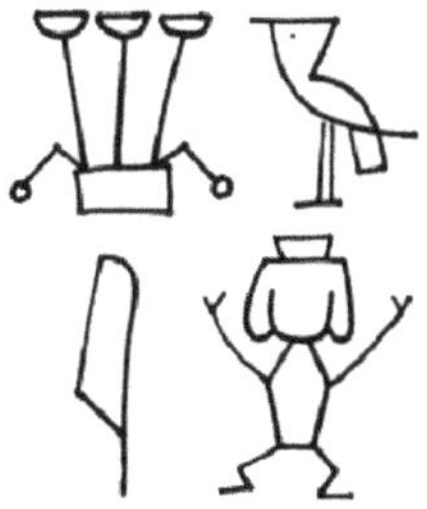

Figure 45: Example of ḥꜣi from Chamber T (XV) (Hand drawing by author).

Bibliography

Abbreviations

ASAE	*Annales du service des antiquités de l'Égypte*
ASE	*Archaeological Survey of Egypt*
AV	*Archäologische Veröffentlichungen.*
BAR	*British Archaeological Reports*
BdE	*Bibliothèque d'Études, IFAO*
BIFAO	*Bulletin del'IFAO, Cairo.*
IFAO	*Institut français d'archéologie orientale*
JARCE	*Journal of the American research Center in Egypt*
JEA	*Journal of Egyptian Archaeology*
JNES	*Journal of Near Eastern Studies*
JSSEA	*Journal of the Society for the Study of Egyptian Antiquities*
LÄ	*Lexikon der Ägyptologie,* ed. Wolfgang Helck and Eberhard Otto. Wiesbaden: Otto Harrassowitz.
LD	Lepsius 1849-1859. *Denkmäler aus Ägypten und Äthiopien.* Berlin: Nicolaische Buchhandlung.
MÄS	*Münchner Ägyptologische Studien*
MDAIK/MDIAAK	*Mitteilungen des Deutschen Archäologischen Instituts.*
MIFAO	*Mémoires publié par les membres de l'Institut Français d'Archéologie Orientale, Cairo.*
MMAF	*Mémoires publiés par les membres de la mission archéologique français au Caire.*
OLA	*Orientalia Lovaniensia Analecta*
P. Ch. Beatty III	Gardiner, A. H. 1935
P. Sallier IV	Gardiner, A. H. 1937
PM	Porter, Bertha and Moss L. B. Moss. 1960-. *Topographical Bibliography of Ancient Egyptian Hieroglyphic Texts, reliefs, and paintings.* 2nd edition revised. Oxford: Claredon Press.
SAK	*Studien zur Altägyptischen Kultur*
SAOC	*Studies in Ancient Oriental Civilization*
SASAE	*Supplément au Annales du service des antiquités de l'Égypte*
Urk.	Sethe, K. et al. 1906-. *Urkunden des ägyptischen Altertums.* Leipzig.

References

Abou Ghazi, Dia'
1968 Bewailing the King in the Pyramid Texts. *BIFAO* 66:157-164.

Aldred, Cyril
1965 *Egypt to the End of the Old Kingdom*. London: Thames and Hudson.

Allen, James
1984 *The Inflection of the Verb in the Pyramid Texts*. Malibu: Undena Publications.

1988 Funerary Texts and their Meaning. In *Mummies and Magic: The Funerary Arts of Ancient Egypt*, ed. D'Auria, Sue, Peter Lacovara, and Catharine H. Roehrig, 38-49. Dallas: Dallas Museum of Art. (1992. 2d ed.)

2005 *The Ancient Egyptian Pyramid Texts*. Writings From the Ancient World 23, ed. Peter Der Manuelian. Atlanta: Society of Biblical Literature.

Allen, Thomas George
1974 *The Book of the Dead or Going Forth by Day*. SAOC 37. Chicago: University of Chicago Press.

Alster, B
1983 The Mythology of Mourning. *Acta Sumerologica* 5:1-16.

Ältenmüller, Hartwig
1975 Zur Bedeutung der Harfnerlieder des Alten Reiches. In *SAK* 6:1-24.

Anderson, Gary A
1991 *A Time to Mourn, a Time to Dance: The Expression of Grief and Joy in the Israelite Religion*. University Park: Pennsylvania State University Press.

Anthes, Rudolf
1928 *Die Felseninschriften von Hatnub*. Leipzig: J.C. Hinrichs'sche Buchhandlung.

1959 Egyptian Theology in the Third Millennium B.C. *JNES* 18:169-212.

Artzi, P
1980 Mourning in International Relations. In *Death in Mesopotamia*, ed. B. Alster, 161-70. Copenhagen: Akademisk Forlag.

Assmann, J
1990 Egyptian Mortuary Liturgies. In *Studies in Egyptology Presented to Miriam Lichtheim*, ed. Sarah Israelit-Groll, 1-45. Jerusalem: Hebrew University.

1999 *Ägyptische Hymnen und Gebete*. Freiburg: Universitätsverlag. (Orig. pub.1975.)

2005 *Death and Salvation in Ancient Egypt*. Ithaca and London: Cornell University Press.

Badawy, Alexander
1978 *The Tomb of Nyhetep-Ptah at Giza and the Tomb of Ankhm'ahor at Saqqara*. Los Angeles: University of California Press.

Baines, John.
1990 Restricted Knowledge, Hierarchy, and Decorum: Modern Perceptions and Ancient Institutions. *JARCE* 27: 1-23.

1991 Egyptian Myth and Discourse: Myth, Gods, and the Early Written and Iconographic Record. *JNES* 50: 81-105.

Baines, John and Jaromír Málek
1994 *Atlas of Ancient Egypt*. New York: Facts on File. (Orig. pub. 1980.)

Bard, Kathryn
2008 *An Introduction to the Archaeology of Ancient Egypt*. Malden, Oxford: Blackwell Publishing.

Barré, Michael
2001 Wandering About as a *Topos* of Depression in Ancient Near Eastern Literature and in the Bible. *JNES* 60: 177-187.

Baum Nathalie
1988 *Arbres et arbustes de l'Égypte ancienne: La liste de la tombe thébaine d'Inéni (nº 81)*. Orientalia Lovaniensia Analecta 31. Leuven: Peeters.

Beinlich-Seeber, Christine
1976 *Untersuchungen zur Darstellung des Totengerichts im Alten Ägypten*. MÄS 35. Munich: Deutscher Kunstverlag.

1978 Klagefrau. *LÄ* 3:444-447.

Baum Nathalie and Abdel Ghaffer Shedid
1987 *Das Grab des Userhat*. AV (Deutsches Archäologisches Institut, Abteilung Kairo), no. 50. Mainz: Zabern.

Bell, Lanny
1985 Luxor Temple and the Cult of the Royal *Ka*. *JNES* 44:251-294.

Bellion, Madeleine
1987 *Egypt ancienne: Catalogue des manuscrits hiéroglyphiques et hiératiques et des dessins, sur papyrus, cuir ou tissu, publiés ou signalés.* Paris: Epsilon Reproduction.

Bierbrier, Morris
1989 *The Tomb-Builders of the Pharaohs*. Cairo: The American University in Cairo Press.

Bietak, Manfred
1978 *Das Grab des 'Anch-Hor*. Vol. I. Vienna: Verlag der Österreichischen Akademie der Wissenschaften.

Blackman, Aylward, M
1914 *The Rock Tombs of Meir*. Vol. 1. ASE 22. London: Egyptian Exploration Fund.

1915 *The Rock Tombs of Meir*. Vol. 2. ASE 23. London: Egyptian Exploration Fund.

1921 On the Position of Women in the Ancient Egyptian Hierarchy. *JEA* 7: 8-30.

1932 *The Story of Sinuhe*. Bibliotheca Aegyptiaca, no. 2. Bruxelles: Fondation Egyptogique Reine Elisabeth.

1933 Myth and Ritual in Ancient Egypt. In *Myth and Ritual: Essays on the Myth and Ritual of the Hebrews in Relation to the Culture Pattern of the Ancient East* ed. S. H. Hooke, 15-39. London: Oxford University Press.

1953 *The Rock Tombs of Meir*. Vol. 5. ASE 28. London: Egyptian Exploration Fund.

Bleeker, Claas J.
1963 Isis and Nephthys as Wailing Women. *The Sacred Bridge: Researches into the Nature and Structure of Religion.* In Studies in the History of Religions (Supplements to *Numan*) 7, ed. 190-205. Leiden: Brill.

Bloch-Smith, Elizabeth
1992 *Judahite Burial Practices and Beliefs about the Dead.* JSOT/ASOR Monograph Series 7. Sheffield: Sheffield Academic Press.

Boeser, P. A. A.
1905-32 *Beschreibung der Aegyptischen Sammlung des Niederländishen Rijksmuseum der Altertümer in Leiden*. Haag: M. Nijhoff.

Bolshakov, Andrey
1991 The Old Kingdom Representations of Funeral Procession. *Göttinger Miszellen* 121: 31-54.

Bonnet, Hans
1971 *Reallexikon der ägyptischen Religions-geschichte*. Berlin: Walter de Gruyter.

Bonomi, J. and S. Sharpe
1864 *The Alabaster Scarcophagus of Oimenepthah I, King of Egypt*. London: Longman, Roberts, and Green.

Borghouts, J. F.
1982 Divine Intervention in Ancient Egypt and its Manifestation (bAw). In *Gleanings from Deir el -Medîna*, eds. R. J. Demarée and Jac. J. Janssen, 1-70. Leiden: Nederlands Instituut Voor Het Nabije Oosten.

Bosticco, Sergio
1959 *Museo Archeologico di Firenze*. Rome: Instituto Poligrafico dello Stato.

Brack, Annelies, and Artur Brack
1980 *Das Grab des Haremheb. Theben Nr. 78*. AV (Deutsches Archäologisches Institut. Abteilung, Kairo) 50. Mainz: Zabern.

Breasted, James H
1912 *Development of Religion and Thought in Ancient Egypt*. Philadelphia: University of Pennsylvania Press.

2001 *Ancient Records of Egypt: The First through the Seventeenth Dynasties*. Vol. 1. Urbana: University of Illinois Press. (Orig. pub. 1906.)

Brovarski, Edward
1977 The Doors of Heaven. *Orientalia* 46:107-115.

Brugsch, Heinrich
1879 *Dictionnaire géographique de l'ancienne Égypte*. Leipzig: J. C. Hinrichs.

1970 *Geographische Inschriften altägyptischer Denkmäler*. Amsterdam: Verlag Hamer.

Brunner-Traut, Emma
1992 *Der Tanz im Alten Ägypten: nach bildlichen und inschriftlichen Zeugnissen.* Ägyptologische Forschungen 6. Glückstadt: J. J. Augustin. (Orig. pub. 1937.)

Bryan, Betsy M
1982 The Etymology of xnr "Group of Musical Performers." *Bulletin of the Egyptological Seminar* 4:35-53.

de Buck, Adriaan
1935-61 *The Egyptian Coffin Texts*. 8 vols. Chicago: University of Chicago Press.

1948 *Egyptian Readingbook.* Vol. 1. Leyden: Brill.

Budge, E. A. W.

1898 *The Book of the Dead.* Vol. 1. London: K. Paul, Trench, Trübner, Ltd.

1909 *A Guide to the Egyptian Galleries.* London: British Museum.

1910 *Hieratic Papyri in the British Museum, with Descriptions.* London: British Museum.

1923 *Egyptian Hieratic Papyri in the British Museum.* 2nd Series. London: British Museum.

1977 *An Egyptian Reading Book for Beginners.* London: Kegan Paul, Trench, Trübner & Co., Ltd. (Orig. pub. 1896).

Bull, Ludlow

1932 "A Group of Egyptian Antiquities." *BMMA* 27, no. 5 (May):130-134.

Buurman, Jan, Nicolas Grimal, Michael Hainsworth, Jochen Hallof and Dirk van der Plas

1988 *Inventaire des signes hiéroglyphiques en vues de leur saisie informatique 2.* 3rd ed. Paris: Institut de France.

Caminos, Ricardo A

1956 *Literary Fragments in the Hieratic Script.* Oxford: Griffith Institute.

1977 *A Tale of Woe: From A Hieratic Papyrus in the A. S. Pushkin Museum of Fine Arts in Moscow.* Oxford: Griffith Institute, Ashmolean Museum.

Carnarvon, George Herbert, and Howard Carter

1912 *Five Years' Explorations at Thebes.* New York: H. Frowde.

Cauville, Sylvie

1984 *Edfou.* Cairo: IFAO.

1997a *Le temple de Dendara, Les chapelles osirienne. Dendara* 10 (1/2). Cairo: IFAO.

1997b *Le temple de Dendara, Les chapelles osiriennes.* BdE 117-118. Cairo: IFAO.

1998 *Dendara: traduction.* 5 vols. Leuven: Peeters.

Cerný, Jaroslav

1939 *Late Ramesside Letters.* Bibliotheca Aegyptiaca, no. 9. Bruxelles: Fondation Egyptologique Reine Elisabeth.

1952 *Ancient Egyptian Religion.* London: Hutchinson's University Library.

Cerný, Jaroslav, and Alan H. Gardiner

1957 *Hieratic Ostraca.* Oxford: Oxford University Press.

Chabas, François

1857 Un hymne à Osiris. *Revue archéologique* 14:65-81; 193-212.

1899 Un hymne à Osiris. In *Œuvres diverses* 1, 95-139. Paris: Ernest Leroux.

Chassinat, Émile

1892-1934 *Le temple d'Edfou.* Mémoires publiés par les membres de la mission archéologique français 10-11. Paris: Leroux.

Clère, J. J. and J. Vandier

1948 *Textes de première période intermédiaire et de XIème dynastie.* Bibliotheca Aegyptiaca 10. Bruxelles: Foundation Égyptologique Reine Élisabeth.

Culshaw, W. J.

1949 *Tribal Heritage.* London: Lutterworth Press.

Daressy, M. G.

1917 Fragments de deux cercuils de Saqqarah. *ASAE* 17: 1-20.

Davies, Nina

1933 *The Tombs of Menkheperrasonb, Amenmose, and Another (Nos. 86, 112, 42, 226).* The Theban Tombs Series 5. London: Egyptian Exploration Society.

1963 *Scenes from Some Theban Tombs (Nos. 38, 66, 162, with excerpts from 81).* Private Tombs at Thebes, no. 4. Oxford: Oxford University Press.

Davies, Nina and A. H. Gardiner

1915 *The Tomb of Amenemhet (No. 82).* The Theban Tombs Series 1. London: Egyptian Exploration Fund.

Davies, Norman de Garis

1902 *The Rock Tombs of Deir el Gebrâwi.* Vol. 2. Archaeological Survey of Egypt, Memoir 12. London: Egyptian Exploration Fund.

1913 *Five Theban Tombs.* Archaeological Survey of Egypt, Memoir 21. London: Egypt Exploration Fund.

1920 *The Tomb of Antefoker, Vizier of Sesostris I, and his Wife, Senet (No. 60). (With a Chapter by*

Gardiner). The Theban Tombs Series 2. London: G. Allen & Unwin.

1923 *The Tombs of Two Officials of Tuthmosis the Fourth (Nos. 75 and 90)*. The Theban Tombs Series 3. London: Egypt Exploration Fund.

1941 *The Tomb of the Vizier Ramose*. London: Egyptian Exploration Society.

1943 *Tomb of Rekh-mi-re at Thebes*. Metropolitan Museum of Art. Egyptian Expedition Publications, Reprint Edition 11. New York: Arno Press.

1973a *The Rock Tombs of El Amarna* III, 2nd ed. Archaeological Survey of Egypt, Memoir 15. Oxford: University Press.

1973b *The Tomb of Nefer-hotep at Thebes*. Metropolitan Museum of Art. Egyptian Expedition Publications, Reprint Edition, no. 9. New York: Arno Press. (Orig. pub. 1933.)

Dawson, Warren R
1927 Making a Mummy. *JEA*13: 40-49.

Diamond, Kelly-Anne
2007 Ancient Egyptian Funerary Ritual: The Term *ḥ3i*. PhD diss., Brown University.

2008a *dmḏ(y)t*: The Bone Collector. *GM* 218: 17-32.

2008b A Re-evaluation of the Ancient Egyptian Term *ḥ3i*. *JSSEA* 35:163-180.

2009 An Investigation into the Sacred District as Depicted in New Kingdom Private Tombs. *ARCE Bulletin* 195:23-27.

Dodson, Aidan and Salima Ikram
2008 *The Tomb in Ancient Egypt*. Cairo: The American University in Cairo Press.

Dominicus, Brigitte
1994 *Gesten und Gebärden in Darstellungen des Alten und Mittleren Reiches*. Heidelberger: Orientverlag.

Donadoni Roveri, A. M.
1990 Gebelein. In G. Robins (ed.), *Beyond the Pyramids: Egyptian Regional Art from the Museo Egizio*, 23-29. Exhibition catalogue. Atlanta: Emery Museum of Art and Archaeology and Museo Egizio di Torino.

Donohue, V. A.
1978 Pr-nfr. *JEA* 64: 143-148.

1992 A Gesture of Submission. In *Studies in Pharaonic Religion and Society in Honour of J. Gwyn Griffiths*, ed. Alan B. Lloyd, 226-235. London: EES.

Eaton-Krauss, Marianne
1984 *The Representations of Statuary in Private Tombs of the Old Kingdom*. Ägyptologische Abhandlungen 39. Wiesbaden: Otto Harrassowitz.

1987 The Earliest Representation of Osiris? *Varia Aegyptiaca* 3:233-236.

Edel, Elmar
1955-1964 *Altägyptische Grammatik*. Analecta Orientalia 34, 89. Roma: Pontificium Institutum Biblicum.

1961-1963 *Die Jahreszeitenreliefs aus dem Sonnenheiligtum des Konigs Ne-user-re*. Göttingen: Vandenhoeck & Ruprecht.

1969 *Beiträge zum ägyptischen Lexikon V*. *ZÄS* 96:4-14.

1970 *Das Akazienhaus und seine Rolle in den Begräbnisriten des alten Ägyptens*. MÄS 24. Berlin: Bruno Hessling.

Eliade, Mircea
1961 *Images and Symbols: Studies in Religious Symbolism*. New York: Sheed &Ward.

1971 *The Myth of the Eternal Return*. Princeton: Princeton University Press.

El-Sayed, Ramadan
1982 *La déesse Neith de Saïs*. Vol 1 of Importance et rayonnement de son culte. BdE 86/1. Cairo: IFAO.

Faulkner, R. O.
1933 *The Papyrus Bremner-Rhind*. Bibliotheca Aegyptiaca 3. Bruxelles: Fondation Egyptologique Reine Elisabeth.

1934 The Lamentations of Isis and Nephthys. In *Mélanges Maspero* I: *orient ancien*, 337-348. MIFAO 66. Caire: IFAO.

1936 The Bremner-Rhind Papyrus — I. *JEA* 22:121-140.

1956 The Man Who was Tired of Life. *JEA* 42:21-40.

1991 A Concise Dictionary of Middle Egyptian. 2nd ed. Oxford: Griffith Institute. (Orig. pub. 1972.)

1994 *The Egyptian Book of the Dead: The Book of Going Forth by Day*. San Francisco: Chronicle Books.

1998 *The Ancient Egyptian Pyramid Texts*. Oxford: Clarendon Press. (Orig. pub. 1969)

2004 *The Ancient Egyptian Coffin Texts*. Oxford: Aris & Phillips. (Orig. pub. 1973-1978.)

Feldman, Emanuel
1977 *Biblical and Post-Biblical Defilement and Mourning: Law as Theology*. New York: Yeshiva University Press.

Feucht, Erika
1984 Ein Motiv der Trauer. In *Studien zu Sprache und Religion Ägyptens: Zu ehren von Wolfhart Westendorf*, 1103-1111. Göttingen.

Fischer, Henry George
1960 The Butcher *pḥ-r-nfr*. *Orientalia* 29:168-190.

1962 The Cult and Nome of the Goddess Bat. *JARCE* 1: 7-23.

1976 Representations of *ḏryt*-mourners in the Old Kingdom. In *Varia*, 39-50. Egyptian Studies 1. New York: Metropolitan Museum of Art.

1989 Women in the Old Kingdom and the Heracleopolitan Period. In *Women's Earliest Records: From Ancient Egypt and Western Asia*, ed. B. Lesko, 5-24. Atlanta: Scholars Press.

Fletcher, Joann and Dominic Montserrat
1995 The Human Hair in the Tomb of Tutankhamun: a Re-evaluation. Abstract. *Abstracts of Papers (Seventh International Congress of Egyptologists, Cambridge, 3-9 September 1995)*, ed. C. Eyre: 59-60. Oxford: Oxbow Books.

Foster, John L and Susan Tower Hollis (ed.)
1995 *Hymns, Prayers and Songs: An Anthology of Ancient Egyptian Lyric Poetry*. Atlanta: Scholars Press.

Foucart, George
1932 Le Tombeau d'Amonmos. *MIFAO* 57.3. Cairo: IFAO.

Fox, Michael V.
1985 *The Song of Songs and the Ancient Egyptian Love Songs*. Madison: University of Wisconsin Press.

Frandsen, Paul John
1992 On the Root *nfr* and a 'Clever' Remark on Embalming. In *The Heritage of Ancient Egypt: Studies in Honour of Erik Iversen*, eds. Jürgen Osing and Erland Kolding Nielsen, 49-62. Copenhagen: Museum Tusculanum Press.

Frankfort, Henri
1948 *Kingship and the Gods: A Study of Ancient Near Eastern Religion as the Integration of Society and Nature*. Chicago: University of Chicago Press.

Frankfort, Henri and H. A. Frankfort
1977 *The Intellectual Adventure of Ancient Man: An Essay on Speculative Thought in the Ancient Near East*. Chicago: The University of Chicago Press. Orig. pub. 1946.

Frazer, J. G.
1890 *The Golden Bough*, 2 vols. London: Macmillan.

Gaballa, G. A.
1977 *The Memphite Tomb-Chapel of Mose*. Warminster: Aris & Phillips.

Galvin, Marianne
1981 The Priestesses of Hathor in the Old Kingdom and the 1st Intermediate Period. PhD diss., Brandeis University.

Gardiner, Alan Henderson
1910 The Colour of Mourning. *ZÄS* 47: 161-162.

1916 *Notes on the Story of Sinuhe*. Paris: Librairie Honoré Champion.

1931 *The Chester Beatty Papyrus No. 1: The Library of A. Chester Beatty*. London: J. Johnson at the Oxford University Press & E. Walker.

1932 *Late-Egyptian Stories*. Bibliotheca Aegyptiaca 1. Bruxelles: Fondation Egyptologique Reine Elisabeth.

1935a *The Attitude of the Ancient Egyptians to Death and the Dead*. Cambridge: The University Press.

1935b *Hieratic Papyri in the British Museum*. 3rd Series. Vol. 1. London: British Museum.

1937 *Late Egyptian Miscellanies*. Bibliotheca Aegyptiaca 7. Bruxelles: Fondation Égyptologique Reine Elisabeth.

1947 *Ancient Egyptian Onomastica*. 2 vols. London: Oxford University Press.

1950 The Baptism of Pharaoh. *JEA* 36:3-12.

1955 A Unique Funerary Liturgy. *JEA* 41: 9-17.

1969 *The Admonitions of an Egyptian Sage from a Hieratic Papyrus in Leiden (Pap. Leiden 344 recto).* Hildesheim: G. Olms Verlag. (Orig. pub. 1909.)

1994 *Egyptian Grammar.* Oxford: Griffith Institute. (3rd ed. Orig. pub. 1957.)

Gastor, Theodore H

1954 Myth and Story. *Numen* 1, fasc. 3: 184-212.

Gauthier, M. Henri

1920 Les statues thébaines de la déesse Sakhmet. *ASAE* 19:183-207.

Gayet, Albert Jean

1889 *Musée du Louvre. Stèles de la XIIe dynastie.* Paris: F. Vieweg.

Gee, John Laurence

1998 The Requirements of Ritual Purity in Ancient Egypt. PhD diss., Yale University.

Gennep, Arnold van

1960 *The Rites of Passage.* Chicago: University of Chicago Press.

Germond, Philippe

1981 *Sekhmet et la protection du monde.* Aegyptiaca Helvetica 9. Geneva: Ägyptologisches Seminar der Universität Basel et Faculté des Lettres de l'Université de Genève.

Goedicke, Hans

1988 *Old Hieratic Paleography.* Baltimore: Halgo, Inc.

Goelet, Ogden

1993 Nudity in Ancient Egypt. *Notes in the History of Art,* no. 2, vol. 12: 20-31.

1994 A Commentary on the corpus of Literature and Tradition Which Constitutes The Book of Going Forth by Day. In *The Egyptian Book of the Dead: The Book of Going Forth by Day,* ed. Eva von Dassow, 139-170. San Francisco: Chronicle Books.

Goodman, Steven M and Peter L. Meininger

1989 *The Birds of Egypt.* Oxford: Oxford University Press.

Goody, J.

1962 *Death, Property and the Ancestors: A Study of the Mortuary Customs of the LoDagaa of West Africa.* Stanford: Stanford University Press.

Graff, Gwenola

2008 A propos d'une brasseuse de biere prédynastique. *JSSEA* 35: 133-151.

Grapow, H.

1915-1917 *Religiöse Urkunden.* Leipzig: J. C. Hinrichs.

Grayson, A. K. and Donald Redford, eds.

1973 *Papyrus and Tablet.* Englewood, NJ: Prentice-Hall Inc.

Grdseloff, Bernhard

1941 *Das ägyptische Reinigungszelt: Archäologische Untersuchung.* Cairo: IFAO.

1951 "Nouvelles données concernant la tente de purification." *ASAE* 51:129-140.

Green, Lyn

2001 "Hairstyles" *The Oxford Encyclopedia of Ancient Egypt,* ed. Donald B. Redford. Copyright ©2001, 2005 by Oxford University Press. The Oxford Encyclopedia of Ancient Egypt: (e-reference edition). Oxford University Press.

Griffith, Francis Llewellyn

1909 *Catalogue of the Demotic Papyri in the John Rylands Library.* Manchester: University Press; London: B. Quaritch.

Griffith, Francis Llewellyn and W. M. F. Petrie

1889 *Two Hieroglyphic Papyri from Tanis.* Memoirs 9. London: EEF.

Griffiths, J. Gwyn

1958 The Tekenu, the Nubians and the Butic Burial. *Kush* 6:106-120.

1980 *The Origins of Osiris and His Cult.* Leiden: Brill.

Gunn, Battiscombe

1930 Rev. of *Egyptian Letters to the Dead, mainly from the Old and Middle Kingdoms,* by Alan H. Gardiner and Kurt Sethe. *JEA* 16: 147-155.

Hannig, Rainer

1995 *Die Sprache der Pharaonen. Großes Handwörterbuch: Ägyptisch-Deutsch.* Mainz: Zabern.

2000 *Die Sprache der Pharaonen. Großes Handwörterbuch: Deutsch-Ägyptisch*. Mainz: Zabern.

2003 *Ägyptisches Wörterbuch I: Altes Reich und Erste Zwischenzeit*. Mainz: Zabern.

Hannig, Rainer, and Petra Vomberg
1999 Wortschatz der Pharaonen in Sachgruppen. Mainz: Zabern.

Harpur, Yvonne
1987 Decoration in Egyptian Tombs of the Old Kingdom: Studies in Orientation and Scene Content. London: Kegan Paul International.

Harrison, Jane Ellen
1912 *Themis: A Study of the Social Origins of Greek Religion*. Cambridge: Cambridge University Press.

1951. *Ancient Art and Ritual*. New York: Greenwood Press.

Hassan, Fekri A.
1992. Primeval Goddess to Divine King: The Mythogenesis of Power in the Early Egyptian State. In *The Followers of Horus*, ed. Renée Friedman and Barbara Adams, 307-322. Egyptian Studies Association 2. Oxford: Oxbow Books.

Hassan, Selim
1928 *Hymnes religieux du Moyen Empire*. Cairo: IFAO

1943 *Excavations at Giza 1932-1933*. Vol. IV. Cairo: Government Press.

1975. *The Mastaba of Neb-Kaw-Her*, ed. Zaky Iskander. Cairo: General Organisation for Government Printing Offices.

Hendrickx, Stan
2002 Bovines in Egyptian Predynastic and Early Dynastic Iconography. In *Droughts, Food and Culture: Ecological Change and Food Security in Africa's Later Prehistory*, Ed. F. A. Hassan, 275-318. New York and London: Kluwer Academic/Plenum.

Hendrickx, Stan, Dirk Huyge, and Willeke Wendrich
2010 Worship without Writing. In *Egyptian Archaeology*, ed. Willeke Wendrich, 15-35. *Malden:* Wiley-Blackwell.

Hermann, Alfred
1963 Jubel bei der Audienz. *ZÄS* 90:49-66.

Hocart, A. M.
1933 *The Progress of Man*. London: Methuen & Co. Ltd.

1952 *The Life-Giving Myth and other essays*. London: Methuen.

1954 *Social Origins*. London: Watts & Co.

Hodel-Hoenes, Sigrid
2000 *Life and Death in Ancient Egypt*. Ithaca: Cornell University Press.

Hoffmeier, James K.
1981 The Possible Origins of the Tent of Purification in the Egyptian Funerary Cult. *Studien zur Altägyptischen Kultur* 9:167-177.

1985 *Sacred* in the Vocabulary of Ancient Egypt: The Term *ḏsr*, with special Reference to Dynasties I-XX. Fribourg: Universitätsverlag Freiburg Schweiz Vandenhoeck & Ruprecht Göttingen.

Hollis, Susan
1990 *The Ancient Egyptian "Tale of Two Brothers."* University of Oklahoma Press: Norman and London.

Hooke, S. H.
1933. The Myth and Ritual pattern of the Ancient East. In *Myth and Ritual*, ed. Hooke, 1-14. London: Oxford University Press.

Hornblower, G. D.
1929 Predynastic Figures of Women and their Successors. *JEA* 15:29-47.

Hornung, Erik
1979a *Das Totenbuch der Ägypter*. Zurich: Artemis Verlag.

1979b *Das Buch von den Pforten des Jenseits*. Vol. 1. Aegyptiaca Helvetica 7 Basel: Ägyptologisches Seminar der Universität Basel.

1980 *Das Buch von den Pforten des Jenseits*. Vol. 2. Aegyptiaca Helvetica 8. Basel: Ägyptologisches Seminar der Universität Basel.

1982 *Conceptions of God in Ancient Egypt: The One and the Many*. Ithaca: Cornell University Press.

1984 *Ägyptische Unterweltsbücher*. Zürich: Artemis Verlag. (Orig. pub. 1972.)

1987 *Texte zum Amduat*. Vol. 1. Aegyptiaca Helvetica 13. Basel: Ägyptologisches Seminar der Universität Basel.

1992 *Idea into Image: Essays on Ancient Egyptian Thought.* Trans. Elizabeth Bredeck. New York: Timken Publishers.

1999 *The Ancient Egyptian books of the Afterlife.* Trans. David Lorton. Ithaca: Cornell University Press.

Houlihan, Patrick F.
1996 *The Animal World of the Pharaohs.* London: Thames and Hudson.

Houlihan, Patrick F. and Steven M. Goodman
1986 *The Birds of Ancient Egypt.* The Natural History of Egypt 1. Warminster: Aris & Phillips.

Ikram, Salima and Aidan Dodson
1998 *The Mummy in Ancient Egypt: Equipping the Dead for Eternity.* London: Thames and Hudson.

James, E. O.
1948 *The Beginnings of Religion.* London: Hutchinson.

Jones, Dilwyn
2000 *An Index of Ancient Egyptian Titles, Epithets and Phrases of the Old Kingdom.* Vols 1-2. Oxford: BAR International Series 866 (I-II).

Junker, Hermann
1910 *Die Stundenwachen in den Osirismysterien nach den Inschriften von Dendera, Edfu und Philae.* Denkschriften der Kaiserlichen Akademie der Wissenschaften, Philosophisch-Historische Klasse. Wien: Aus der Kaiserlich-Königlichen Hof-und Staatsdruckerei.

1940 Der Tanz der Mww und das Butische Begräbnis im Alten Reich. *MDAIK* 9:1-39.

1972 *Grammatik der Denderatexte.* Leipzig: Zentralantiquariat der Deutschen Demokratischen Republik. (Orig. pub. 1906.)

Kanawati, Naguib
2001 *The Tomb and Beyond: Burial Customs of Egyptian Officials.* Warminster: Aris & Phillips.

Kanawati, Naguib and A. Hassan
1996 *The Teti Cemetery at Saqqara.* Vol. 2. Warminster: Aris & Phillips.

Kloth, N.
2002 Die (auto-) biographischen Inschriften des agyptischen Alten Reiches: Untersuchungen zu Phraseologie und Entwicklung, *SAK* 8. Hamburg: Buske.

Koemoth, Pierre
1994 *Osiris et les arbres: Contribution à l'étude des arbres sacrés de l'Égypte ancienne.* Aegyptiaca Leodiensia 3. Liège: Centre Informatique de Philosophie et Letters.

Lacau, P.
1904-1906 *Sarcophages antérieurs au Nouvel Empire.* 2 volumes. Catalogue général des antiquités égyptiennes du Musée du Cairo. Cairo: IFAO.

Lacovara, Peter
1988 Funerary Architecture. In *Mummies and Magic: The Funerary Arts of Ancient Egypt,* ed. Sue D'Auria, Peter Lacovara, and Catharine H. Roehrig, 20-26. Dallas: Dallas Museum of Art. (1992. 2d ed.)

Laneri, Nicola
2007 An Archaeology of Funerary Rituals. In *Performing Death: Social Analyses of Funerary Traditions in the Ancient Near East and Mediterranean,* ed. Nicola Laneri, 1-14. Chicago: University of Chicago.

Leahy, Anthony
1984 Death by Fire in Ancient Egypt. *Journal of the Economic and Social History of the Orient.* Vol. 27, No. 2: 199-206.

1989 A Protective Measure at Abydos in the Thirteenth Dynasty. *JEA* 75: 41-60.

Leclant, Jean
1951 Le rôle du lait et de l'allaitement d'après les textes des pyramides. *JNES* 10:123-127.

1957 Une coupe hathorique au nom de Montouemhat. *Wiener Zeitschrift für die Kunde des Morgenlandes: Festschrift Hermann Junker* 54. Wien: Orientalischen Institutes.

Lehner, Mark
1997 *The Complete Pyramids.* London: Thames and Hudson.

Lesko, Barbara S.
1999 *The Great Goddesses of Egypt.* Norman: University of Oklahoma Press.

Lesko, Leonard
2007 A Note on Book of the Dead 172. *Etudes et Travaux* 21: 79-82.

Lepsius, Richard
1849-1859 *Denkmäler aus Ägypten und Äthiopien.* Berlin: Nicolaische Buchhandlung.

Levai, Jessica
2007 Aspects of the Goddess Nephthys, Especially during the Graeco-Roman Period in Egypt. PhD. diss., Brown University.

Lewis, Theodore J.
1989 *Cults of the Dead in Ancient Israel and Ugarit*, ed. Frank Moore Cross. Harvard Semitic Monographs 39. Atlanta: Scholars Press.

2002 How Far Can Texts Take Us? In *Sacred Time, Sacred Place Archaeology and the Religion of Israel*, ed. Barry Gittlen, 169-218. Winona Lake: Eisenbrauns.

Lexová Irena
2000 *Ancient Egyptian Dances.* Prague: Oriental Institute. (Orig. pub. 1935.)

Lichtheim, Miriam
1973-1980 *Ancient Egyptian Literature*. 3 vols. Los Angeles: University of California Press.

Lloyd, Alan B.
1989 Psychology and Society in the Ancient Egyptian cult of the Dead. In *Religion and Philosophy in Ancient Egypt*, ed. James P. Allen, et al., 117-133. Yale Egyptological Studies 3. New Haven: Yale Egyptological Seminar, Department of Near Eastern Languages and Civilizations, The Graduate School, Yale University.

Lucas, A. and J. R. Harris
1999 *Ancient Egyptian Material and Industries.* Mineola, New York: Dover. (Orig. pub. 1962.)

Lüddeckens, Erich
1943 Untersuchungen über religiösen Gehalt, Sprache und Form der ägyptischen Totenklagen. *MDAIK* 11: 1-188.

Lurker, Manfred
1995 *An Illustrated Dictionary of the Gods and Symbols of Ancient Egypt.* London: Thames and Hudson.

Malinowski, Bronislaw
1926 *Myth in Primitive Psychology*. Westport: Negro Universities Press.

Manniche, Lise
1987a *City of the Dead: Thebes in Egypt*. London: British Museum.

1987b *Sexual Life in Ancient Egypt*. London: Kegan Paul International.

1988 *Lost Tombs: A Study of Certain Eighteenth Dynasty Monuments in the Theban Necropolis.* London: Kegan Paul International.

Mariette, Auguste
1870-1875 *Dendérah*: *Déscription général du grand temple de cette ville.* 6 vols. Paris: A. Franck.

1889 *Les mastabas de l'Ancien Empire: Fragment du dernier ouvrage de A. Mariette*. Paris: F. Vieweg.

Martin, Geoffrey T.
1974 *The Royal Tomb at El-'Amarna*. ASE 35. London: Egyptian Exploration Society.

1993 *The Hidden Tombs of Memphis: New Discoveries from the Time of Tutankhamun and Ramesses the Great.* 3d ed. London: Thames and Hudson.

Meeks, Dimitri
1998 *Année lexicographique Égypte ancienne*, 2nd ed. Paris: Cybele.

Mercer, Samuel A. B.
1952 *The Pyramid Texts in Translation and Commentary.* 4 vols. New York: Longmans, Green and Co.

Metcalf, P., and R. Huntington
1991 *Celebrations of Death: The Anthropology of Mortuary Ritual.* 2d ed. Cambridge: Cambridge University Press.

De Meulenaere, H.
1959 Prosopographica Ptolemaica. *Chronique d'Égypte* 34, no. 68:244-249.

Moens, M. I.
1984 The Ancient Garden in the New Kingdom. A Study of Representations. *Orientalia Lovaniensia periodica* 15: 11-53.

Mohr, Herta Therese
1943 *The Mastaba of Hetep-her-akhti: Study on an Egyptian Tomb Chapel in the Museum of Antiquities, Leiden.* Mededeelingen en Verhandelingen 5. Leiden: Brill.

Möller, Georg
1913. *Die beiden Totenpapyrus Rhind des Museums zu Edinburg*. Leipzig: J. C. Hinrichs.

1961 *Hieratic Lesestücke für dem Akademischen Gebrauch*. Berlin: Akademie-Verlag. (Orig. pub. 1927.)

1965 *Hieratische Paläographie*. Osnabrück: Otto Zeller. (Orig. pub. 1927.)

Moret, Alexandre
1931 La légende d'Osiris à l'époque théban d'après l'hymne à Osiris du Louvre. *BIFAO* 30:725-750.

Morris, Ian
1992 Death Ritual and Social Structure in Classical Antiquity. New York: Cambridge University Press.

Moussa, A and Hartwig Altenmüller
1977 *Das Grab des Nianchchnum und Chnumhotep*. AV (Deutsches Archäologisches Institut. Abteilung Kairo) 21. Mainz: Zabern.

Muhammed, M. Abdul-Qader
1966 *The Development of the Funerary Beliefs and Practices Displayed in the Private Tombs of the New Kingdom at Thebes*. Cairo: General Organisation for Government Printing Offices.

Münster, Maria
1968 *Untersuchungen zur Göttin Isis, vom Alten Reich biz zum Ende des Neuen Reiches*. Berlin: B. Hessling.

Murray, M. A.
1956 Burial Customs and Beliefs in the Hereafter in Predynastic Egypt. *JEA* 42:86-96.

Naville, Édouard
1971 *Das aegyptische Todtenbuch der XVIII. bis XX. Dynastie*. Berlin: A. Asher & Co. (Orig. pub. 1886.)

Needler, Winifred
1984 *Predynastic and Archaic Egypt in The Brooklyn Museum*. New York: Brooklyn Museum.

Newberry, Percy Edward
1893-94 *El Bersheh*. 2 vols. ASAE 3-4. London: Egyptian Exploration Fund.

1893-1900 *Beni Hasan*. 4 vols. ASE 1, 2, 5, 7. London: Egyptian Exploration Fund.

Nord, Del
1981 The Term xnr: 'Harem' or 'Musical Performers'? In *Studies in Ancient Egypt, the Aegean, and the Sudan: Essays in Honor of Dows Dunham on the Occasion of his 90th Birthday, June 1, 1980*, eds. W. K. Simpson and W. M. Davis, 137-145. Boston: Department of Egyptian and Ancient Near Eastern Art, Museum of Fine Arts.

Olyan, Saul
2000 The Biblical Prohibition of the Mourning Rites of Shaving and Laceration: Several Proposals. In *"A Wise and Discerning Mind": Essays in Honor of Burke O. Long*, ed. Saul M. Olyan and C. Culley, 181-190. Providence: Brown Judaic Studies, 2000.

Parker, Richard A.
1965 Hathor, Lady of the Acacia. *JARCE* 4:151.

Parker, Richard A., J. Leclant and J. C. Goyon
1979 *The Edifice of Taharqa by the Sacred Lake of Karnak*. Providence: Brown University Press.

Parkinson, R. B.
1991 *Voices from Ancient Egypt: An Anthology of Middle Kingdom Writings*. London: British Museum Press.

Parkinson, R. B. and Stephen Quirke
1992 The Coffin of Prince Herunefer and the Early History of the *Book of the Dead*. In *Studies in Pharaonic Religion and Society in Honour of J. Gwyn Griffiths*, ed. Alan B. Lloyd, 37-51. London: EES.

Pinch, Geraldine
1994 *Magic in Ancient Egypt*. Austin: University of Texas Press.

2002 *Egyptian Mythology: A Guide to the Gods,* Goddesses, *and Traditions of Ancient Egypt*. Oxford: Oxford University Press.

Polz, Daniel
1997 *Das Grab des Hui und des Kel, Theben Nr. 54*. Mainz: Verlag Philipp von Zabern.

Pritchard, James B.
1958 *The Ancient Near East: An Anthology of Texts and Pictures, Vol. 1*. Princeton: Princeton University Press.

Radwan, Ali
1974 Der Trauergestus als Datierungsmittel. *MDAIK* 30: 115-129.

Raglan, Lord
1949 *The Origins of Religion*. London: Watts & Co.

1955 Myth and Ritual. *The Journal of American Folklore* 68, no. 270: 454-461.

Redford, Donald B. (ed.)
2001. *The Oxford Encyclopedia of Ancient Egypt.* Oxford: Oxford University Press.

Reeder, Greg
1995 The Mysterious Muu and the Dance They Do. *KMT* 6, no. 3: 68-77, 83.

Richards, J.
2010. Kingship and Legitimation. In *Egyptian Archaeology*, ed. Willeke Wendrich, 55-84. Boston: Wiley-Blackwell.

Ritner, Robert Kriech
1993 *The Mechanics of Ancient Egyptian Magical Practice.* SAOC 54. Chicago: Oriental Institute of the University of Chicago.

Roberts, Alison
1984 *Cult Objects of Hathor: an Iconographic Study*. 2 vols. PhD diss., University of Oxford.

Robins, Gay
1993 *Women in Ancient Egypt*. Cambridge: Harvard University Press.

1996 Dress, Undress, and the Representation of Fertility and Potency in New Kingdom Egyptian Art. In *Sexuality in Ancient Art*, ed. Natalie Boymel Kampen, 27-40.Cambridge Studies in New Art History and Criticism. Cambridge: Cambridge University Press.

1997 *The Art of Ancient Egypt*. Cambridge: Harvard University Press.

1999 Hair and the Construction of Identity in Ancient Egypt, c. 1480-1350 B.C. *JARCE* 36:55-69.

Roccati, Alessandro
1982 *La littérature historique sous l'Ancien Empire égyptien*. Paris: Les Éditions du Cerf.

Rössler-Köhler, Ursula
1985 Totenklage. *LÄ*. 6:657-658.

Roth, Ann Macy
2001 Funerary Ritual. In *The Oxford Encyclopedia of Ancient Egypt,* ed. Donald B. Redford vol. I, 575-580. Oxford: Oxford University Press.

Saad, Zaki
1947 Preliminary Report on the Royal Excavations at Helwan (1943-1944). *SASAE* 3:105-160.

Sadek, Ashraf I.
1979 Glimpses of Popular Religion in New Kingdom Egypt I. Mourning for Amenophis I at Deir el Medina. *GM* 36: 51-56.

Sauneron, Serge
1952 *Rituel de l'embaumement, Pap. Boulaq III, Pap Louvre 5.158*. Cairo: Imprimerie Nationale.

Säve-Söderbergh, Torgny
1957 *Four Eighteenth Dynasty Tombs.* Private Tombs at Thebes 1. Oxford: Oxford University Press.

Scamuzzi, E.
1965 *Egyptian Art in the Egyptian Museum of Turin.* New York: Harry N. Abrams.

Schäfer, H. (ed.)
1905-1908 *Urkunden der älteren Äthiopenkönige Urk.* 3.

Schiaparelli, E.
1887 *Museo Archeologico di Firenze: antichità egizie*. Rome: Salviucci.

Schott, Siegfried
1929-1939 *Urkunden mythologischen Inhalts*. *Urk*. 6.

Segal, Robert A.
1998 *The Myth and Ritual Theory*. Malden: Blackwell Publishers.

Sethe, Kurt
1903 *Urkunden des Alten Reiches*. *Urk*. 1.

1908 *Die altägyptischen Pyramidentexte nach den Papierabdrücken und Photographien des Berliner Museums*. Vol. 2. Hildesheim: G. Olms.

Settgast, Jürgen
1963 *Untersuchung zu altägyptischen Bestättungsdarstellungen*. Glückstadt: J.J. Augustin.

Shaw, Ian and Paul Nicholson
1995 *The Dictionary of Ancient Egypt*. London: Harry N. Abrams, Inc.

Shore, A. F.
1992 Human and Divine Mummification. In *Studies in Pharaonic Religion and Society in Honour of J. Gwyn Griffiths*, ed. Alan B. Lloyd, 226-235. London: EES.

Simpson, William Kelly, (ed.)
2003 *The Literature of Ancient Egypt: An Anthology of Stories, Instructions, and Poetry*. New Haven: Yale University Press. (Orig. pub. 1973.)

1976 *The Mastabas of Qar and Idu*. Giza Mastabas 2. Boston: Department of Egyptian and Ancient Near Eastern Art, Museum of Fine Arts.

Smith, William Robertson
1889 *Lectures on the Religion of the Semites*. Edinburgh: Black.

Smith, Stewart Tyson
1991 They Did Take it with Them. *KMT* Vol. 2, no. 3 fall: 28-45.

Smith, G. E. and W. R. Dawson
2002 *Egyptian Mummies*. London: Kegan Paul. (Orig. pub. 1924.)

Spencer, Patricia
2003 Dance in Ancient Egypt. *Near Eastern Archaeology* 66, no. 3:111-121.

Strudwick, Nigel
1996 *The Tombs of Amenhotep, Khnummose, and Amenmose at Thebes: (nos. 294, 253, and 254)*. 2 vols. Oxford: Griffith Institute.

2005 *Texts from the Pyramid Age*. Writings from the Ancient World 16, ed. Ronald J. Leprohon. Atlanta: Society of Biblical Literature.

Taylor, John H.
2001 *Death and the Afterlife in Ancient Egypt*. Chicago: University of Chicago Press.

Te Velde, Herman
1988 Funerary Mythology. In *Mummies and Magic: The Funerary Arts of Ancient Egypt,* ed. D'Auria, Sue, Peter Lacovara, and Catharine H. Roehrig, 27-37. Dallas: Dallas Museum of Art. (1992. 2d ed.)

Trigger, Bruce G.
2003 *Understanding Early Civilizations*. Cambridge: Cambridge University Press.

Tylor, Edward B.
1871 *Primitive Culture*. London: Murray.

Tylor, J. J.
1900 *Tomb of Renni*. Wall Drawing and Monuments of El Kab 4. London: Egypt Exploration Fund.

Tylor, J. J. and F. Ll. Griffith
1894 *The Tomb of Paheri at El Kab*. Excavation Memoir 11. London: Egypt Exploration Fund.

Ucko, P. J.
1968 *Anthropomorphic Figurines of Predynastic Egypt and Neolithic Crete with Comparative Material from the Prehistoric Near East and Mainland Greece*. Occasional Papers of the RAI 24. London: Andrew Szmidla.

Van der Molen, Rami
2000 *A Hieroglyphic Dictionary of Egyptian Coffin Texts*. Leiden: Brill.

Van Dijk, Jacobus
1995 Myth and Mythmaking in Ancient Egypt. In *Civilizations of the Ancient Near East* 3, ed. J. Sasson, 1697-1709. New York: Charles Scribner's Sons.

Van Lepp, Jonathan
1987 The Dance Scene of Wa'tetkhethor: An Art Historical Approach to the Role of Dance in Old Kingdom Funerary Ritual. Master's thesis, University of California.

Virey, Philippe
1891 *Le tombeau de Amenemhet. Sept tombeax thébains de la XVIIIe,* 224-285. MMAS 5, 2.

Vittmann, Günter
1998 *Der demotische Papyrus Rylands 9*. 2 vols. Ägypten und Altes Testament 38. Wiesbaden: Harrassowitz Verlag.

Vos, R. L.
1993 *The Apis Embalming Ritual: P. Vindob. 3873*. OLA 50. Leuven: Peeters.

Ward, William A.
1986 *Essays on Feminine Titles of the Middle Kingdom and Related Subjects*. Beirut: American University of Beirut.

Watterson, Barbara
1998 *The House of Horus at Edfu: Ritual in an Ancient Egyptian Temple*. Stroud, Gloucestershire: Tempus.

Weeks, Kent R.
1994 *Mastabas of Cemetery G 6000, Including G 6010 (Neferbauptah); G 6020 (Iymery); G 6030 (Ity); G 6040 (Shepseskafankh)*. Giza Mastabas 5. Boston: Department of Ancient Egyptian, Nubian, and Near Eastern Art, Museum of Fine Arts.

Weisinger, Herbert
1965 Before Myth. *Journal of the Folklore Institute* 2, no. 2: 120-131.

Wengrow, David
2006 *The Archaeology of Early Egypt: Social Transformations in North-East Africa, 10,000 to 2650 BC.* Cambridge: Cambridge University Press.

Wente, Edward
1969 Hathor at the Jubilee. In *Studies in Honor of John A. Wilson, September 12, 1969*, ed. E. B. Hauser, 83-91. SAOC 35. Chicago: University of Chicago Press.

Werbrouck, Marcelle
1938 *Les pleureuses dans l'Égypte ancienne.* Bruxelles: Fondation Égyptologique Reine Élisabeth.

Westendorf, Wolfhart
1985 Trauer. *LÄ* 6:744-745.

Widengren, Geo
1951 *The King and the Tree of Life in Ancient Near Eastern Religion.* In Acta Universitatis Upsaliensis. Uppsala: Otto Harrassowitz.

Wild, H.
1954 Statue de Hor.néfer au Musée des Beaux-Arts de Lausanne. *BIFAO* 54:173-219.

Wilkinson, Alix
1994a Symbolism and Design in Ancient Egyptian Gardens. *Garden History*, vol. 22, No. 1 (Summer): 1-17.

1994b Landscapes for Funeral Rituals in Dynastic Times. In *The Unbroken Reed; Studies in the Culture and Heritage of Ancient Egypt; in Honour of A. F. Shore*, ed. C. J. Eyre, *et al.*, 391-401. London: EES.

1998 *The Garden in Ancient Egypt.* London: The Rubicon Press.

Wilkinson, Richard H.
1992 *Reading Egyptian Art: A Hieroglyphic Guide to Ancient Egyptian Painting and Sculpture.* London: Thames and Hudson.

1999 *Symbol and Magic in Egyptian Art.* London: Thames and Hudson. (Orig. pub. 1994.)

2003 *The Complete Gods and Goddesses of Ancient Egypt.* London: Thames and Hudson.

Willems, Harco
1990 Crime, Cult and Capital Punishment (Mo'alla Inscription 8). *JEA* 76: 27-54.

Wilson, John
1944 Funeral Services of the Egyptian Old Kingdom. *JNES* 3:201-218.

1955 Buto and Hierakonpolis in the Geography of Egypt. *JNES* 14:209-336.

Wilson, Penelope
1997 *A Ptolemaic Lexikon: A Lexicographical Study of the Texts in the Temple of Edfu.* OLA 78. Leuven: Peeters.

Wylie, Turrell V.
1965 Mortuary Customs at Sa-Skya, Tibet. *Harvard Journal of Asiatic Studies* 25: 229-242.

Yoyotte, Jean
1961 Études géographiques. I. "La Cite des Acacias" (Kafr Ammar). *Revue d'Égyptologie* 13:71-105.

Žabkar, Louis V.
1968 *A Study of the Ba Concept in Ancient Egyptian Texts.* SAOC 34. Chicago: University of Chicago Press.

Zandee, Jan
1960 *Death as an Enemy according to Ancient Egyptian Conceptions.* Studies in the History of Religions (Supplements to *Numen*) 5. Leiden: Brill.

www.ingramcontent.com/pod-product-compliance
Lightning Source LLC
Chambersburg PA
CBHW061003030426
42334CB00033B/3340